EXAMCRAM

CompTIA® A+
Practice Questions Core 1 (220-1101) and Core 2 (220-1102)

David L. Prowse

CompTIA® A+ Practice Questions Exam Cram Core 1 (220-1101) and Core 2 (220-1102)

David L. Prowse

Copyright © 2023 Pearson Education, Inc.

Published by:

Pearson Education

221 River St.

Hoboken, NJ 07030 USA

Library of Congress Control Number: 2022912390

ISBN-13: 978-0-13-765818-3

ISBN-10: 0-13-765818-4

Warning and Disclaimer

This book is designed to provide information about the CompTIA A+ Core 1 (220-1101) and Core 2 (220-1102) exams for the CompTIA A+ certification. Every effort has been made to make this book as complete and as accurate as possible, but no warranty or fitness is implied.

The information is provided on an "as is" basis. The author and publisher shall have neither liability nor responsibility to any person or entity with respect to any loss or damages arising from the information contained in this book or from the use of the discs or programs that may accompany it.

The opinions expressed in this book belong to the author.

Microsoft and/or its respective suppliers make no representations about the suitability of the information contained in the documents and related graphics published as part of the services for any purpose all such documents and related graphics are provided "as is" without warranty of any kind. Microsoft and/or its respective suppliers hereby disclaim all warranties and conditions with regard to this information, including all warranties and conditions of merchantability, whether express, implied or statutory, fitness for a particular purpose, title and non-infringement. In no event shall Microsoft and/or its respective suppliers be liable for any special, indirect or consequential damages or any damages whatsoever resulting from loss of use, data or profits, whether in an action of contract, negligence or other tortious action, arising out of or in connection with the use or performance of information available from the services.

The documents and related graphics contained herein could include technical inaccuracies or typographical errors. Changes are periodically added to the information herein. Microsoft and/or its respective suppliers may make improvements and/or changes in the product(s) and/or the program(s) described herein at any time. Partial screen shots may be viewed in full within the software version specified.

Trademark Acknowledgments

All terms mentioned in this book that are known to be trademarks or service marks have been appropriately capitalized. Pearson IT Certification cannot attest to the accuracy of this information. Use of a term in this book should not be regarded as affecting the validity of any trademark or service mark.

Microsoft® Windows®, and Microsoft Office® are registered trademarks of the Microsoft Corporation in the U.S.A. and other countries. This book is not sponsored or endorsed by or affiliated with the Microsoft Corporation.

Special Sales

For information about buying this title in bulk quantities, or for special sales opportunities (which may include electronic versions; custom cover designs; and content particular to your business, training goals, marketing focus, or branding interests), please contact our corporate sales department at corpsales@pearsoned.com or (800) 382-3419.

For government sales inquiries, please contact governmentsales@pearsoned.com.

For questions about sales outside the U.S., please contact intlcs@pearson.com.

Editor-in-Chief
Mark Taub

Director, ITP Product Management
Brett Bartow

Executive Editor
Nancy Davis

Managing Editor
Sandra Schroeder

Development Editor
Christopher A. Cleveland

Project Editor
Mandie Frank

Copy Editor
Kitty Wilson

Technical Editor
Chris Crayton

Editorial Assistant
Cindy Teeters

Designer
Chuti Prasertsith

Composition
codeMantra

Proofreader
Donna E. Mulder

1 2022[ ]   [ ]   nt[ ]?Code   e

Pearson's Commitment to Diversity, Equity, and Inclusion

Pearson is dedicated to creating bias-free content that reflects the diversity of all learners. We embrace the many dimensions of diversity, including but not limited to race, ethnicity, gender, socioeconomic status, ability, age, sexual orientation, and religious or political beliefs.

Education is a powerful force for equity and change in our world. It has the potential to deliver opportunities that improve lives and enable economic mobility. As we work with authors to create content for every product and service, we acknowledge our responsibility to demonstrate inclusivity and incorporate diverse scholarship so that everyone can achieve their potential through learning. As the world's leading learning company, we have a duty to help drive change and live up to our purpose to help more people create a better life for themselves and to create a better world.

Our ambition is to purposefully contribute to a world where

- ▶ Everyone has an equitable and lifelong opportunity to succeed through learning

- ▶ Our educational products and services are inclusive and represent the rich diversity of learners

- ▶ Our educational content accurately reflects the histories and experiences of the learners we serve

- ▶ Our educational content prompts deeper discussions with learners and motivates them to expand their own learning (and worldview)

While we work hard to present unbiased content, we want to hear from you about any concerns or needs with this Pearson product so that we can investigate and address them.

Please contact us with concerns about any potential bias at https://www.pearson.com/report-bias.html.

Contents at a Glance

Table of Contents

About the Author

David L. Prowse is the author of more than a dozen computer training books and video products. He has worked in the computer field for over 20 years and loves to share his experience through teaching and writing.

He runs the website https://dprocomputer.com, where he gladly answers questions from readers and students.

About the Technical Reviewer

Chris Crayton (MCSE) is an author, technical consultant, and trainer. He has worked as a computer technology and networking instructor, information security director, network administrator, network engineer, and PC specialist. Chris has authored several print and online books on PC repair, CompTIA A+, CompTIA Security+, and Microsoft Windows. He has also served as technical editor and content contributor on numerous technical titles for several of the leading publishing companies. He holds numerous industry certifications, has been recognized with many professional teaching awards, and has served as a state-level SkillsUSA competition judge.

Acknowledgments

Thanks to Nancy Davis, Chris Cleveland, and Chris Crayton. Also, my thanks to everyone at Pearson for your expertise and help throughout this project.

We Want to Hear from You!

As the reader of this book, *you* are our most important critic and commentator. We value your opinion and want to know what we're doing right, what we could do better, what areas you'd like to see us publish in, and any other words of wisdom you're willing to pass our way.

We welcome your comments. You can email or write to let us know what you did or didn't like about this book—as well as what we can do to make our books better.

Please note that we cannot help you with technical problems related to the topic of this book.

When you write, please be sure to include this book's title and author as well as your name and email address. We will carefully review your comments and share them with the author and editors who worked on the book.

Email: community@pearsonITcertification.com

Reader Services

Register your copy of *CompTIA A+ Practice Questions Exam Cram Core 1 (220-1101) and Core 2 (220-1102)* at www.pearsonitcertification.com for convenient access to downloads, updates, and corrections as they become available. To start the registration process, go to www.pearsonitcertification.com/register and log in or create an account.* Enter the product ISBN **9780137658183** and click **Submit**. When the process is complete, you will find any available bonus content under Registered Products.

*Be sure to check the box indicating that you would like to hear from us to receive exclusive discounts on future editions of this product.

Introduction

Welcome to *CompTIA A+ Practice Questions Core 1 (220-1101) and Core 2 (220-1102) Exam Cram*. The purpose of this book is to provide you with practice questions that are complete with answers and explanations to help you learn, drill, and review for the CompTIA A+ certification exams. The book offers 480 questions that help you practice each exam domain and help you assess your knowledge before you take the real exams. The detailed answers to every question aid in reinforcing your knowledge about the concepts associated with the CompTIA A+ exams.

Who This Book Is For

The CompTIA A+ exams are designed for individuals with at least 12 months of hands-on experience in a lab or in the field. If you have that experience, this book will be an excellent late-stage study tool. However, if you have not acquired that experience, I recommend that you register for a hands-on A+ course or, at the very least, purchase an A+ study guide such as the *CompTIA A+ Core 1 220-1101 and Core 2 220-1102 Exam Cram* textbook or consider my *CompTIA A+ 220-1101 Complete Video Course* and *CompTIA A+ 220-1102 Complete Video Course*. After you take the course and/or read the study guide, return to this book as your late-stage test preparation to be used just before taking the real exams.

What You Will Find in This Book

In every chapter devoted to practice exams, you will find the following three elements:

- ▶ **Practice Questions:** Each chapter includes 80 questions that help you learn, drill, and review for the exams.

- ▶ **Quick-Check Answer Key:** After you finish answering the questions, you can quickly grade your exam from this section. Only correct answers are given in this section. No explanations are offered yet. Even if you answered a question incorrectly, do not be discouraged. Keep in mind that this is not the real exam. You can always review the topic and revisit the questions again.

▶ **Answers and Explanations:** This section provides you with correct answers as well as explanations about the content posed in that question. Use this information to learn why an answer is correct and to reinforce the content in your mind for exam day.

The book also comes with a companion website. It contains a simulated testing environment where you can take all the exams on a computer in study mode or in full practice test mode. It also includes two bonus exams. Create an account and register this book at http://www.pearsonitcertification.com to get access to the bonus content. For those who purchased a Kindle edition from Amazon, the access code will be supplied directly by Amazon.

Hints for Using This Book

Complete your exams on a separate piece of paper so that you can reuse the practice questions if necessary. Also, plan to score 90% or higher on each exam before moving on to the next one. The higher you score on these practice questions, the better your chances for passing the real exams.

I am available for questions at my website: https://dprocomputer.com.

Companion Website

Register this book to get access to the Pearson IT Certification test engine and other study materials plus additional bonus content. Check this site regularly for new and updated postings written by the author that provide further insight into the most troublesome topics on the exam. Be sure to check the box indicating that you would like to hear from us to receive updates and exclusive discounts on future editions of this product or related products.

To access the companion website, follow these steps:

1. Go to **www.pearsonitcertification.com/register** and log in or create a new account.

2. Enter the ISBN: **9780137658183**.

3. Answer the challenge question as proof of purchase.

4. Click the **Access Bonus Content** link in the Registered Products section of your account page to be taken to the page where your downloadable content is available.

Please note that many of our companion content files (especially image and video files) are very large.

If you are unable to locate the files for this title by following these steps, please visit www.pearsonITcertification.com/contact and select the **Site Problems/ Comments** option. Our customer service representatives will assist you.

Pearson Test Prep Practice Test Software

As noted previously, this book comes complete with the Pearson Test Prep practice test software, all the exams from the book. These practice tests are available to you either online or as an offline Windows application. To access the practice exams that were developed with this book, please see the instructions in the card inserted in the sleeve in the back of the book. This card includes a unique access code that enables you to activate your exams in the Pearson Test Prep software.

Accessing the Pearson Test Prep Software Online

The online version of this software can be used on any device with a browser and connectivity to the Internet, including desktop machines, tablets, and smartphones. To start using your practice exams online, simply follow these steps:

Step 1. Go to **https://www.PearsonTestPrep.com**.

Step 2. Select **Pearson IT Certification** as your product group.

Step 3. Enter your email/password for your account. If you don't have an account on PearsonITCertification.com, you need to establish one by going to **PearsonITCertification.com/join**.

Step 4. In the **My Products** tab, click the **Activate New Product** button.

Step 5. Enter the access code printed on the insert card in the back of your book to activate your product. The product will now be listed in your My Products page.

Step 6. Click the **Exams** button to launch the exam settings screen and start your exam.

Accessing the Pearson Test Prep Software Offline

If you wish to study offline, you can download and install the Windows version of the Pearson Test Prep software. There is a download link for this software on the book's companion website, or you can just enter this link in your browser: http://www.pearsonitcertification.com/content/downloads/pcpt/engine.zip.

To access the book's companion website and the software, simply follow these steps:

Step 1. Register your book by going to **PearsonITCertification.com/ register** and entering the ISBN: **9780137658183**.

Step 2. Answer the challenge questions.

Step 3 Go to your account page and click the **Registered Products** tab.

Step 4. Click the **Access Bonus Content** link under the product listing.

Step 5. Click the **Install Pearson Test Prep Desktop Version** link under the Practice Exams section of the page to download the software.

Step 6. After the software finishes downloading, unzip all the files on your computer.

Step 7. Double-click the application file to start the installation and follow the onscreen instructions to complete the registration.

Step 8. After the installation is complete, launch the application and click the **Activate Exam** button on the My Products tab.

Step 9. Click the **Activate a Product** button in the Activate Product Wizard.

Step 10. Enter the unique access code found on the card in the sleeve in the back of your book and click the **Activate** button.

Step 11. Click **Next** and then click **Finish** to download the exam data to your application.

Step 12. Start using the practice exams by selecting the product and clicking the **Open Exam** button to open the exam settings screen.

Note that the offline and online versions will sync together, so saved exams and grade results recorded on one version will be available to you on the other as well.

Customizing Your Exams

Once you are in the exam settings screen, you can choose to take exams in one of three modes:

- ▶ **Study mode:** This mode allows you to fully customize your exams and review answers as you are taking an exam. This is typically the mode you would use first to assess your knowledge and identify information gaps.

- ▶ **Practice Exam mode:** This mode locks certain customization options in order to present a realistic exam experience. Use this mode when you are preparing to test your exam readiness.

- ▶ **Flash Card mode:** This mode strips out the answers and presents you with only the question stem. This mode is great for late-stage preparation, when you really want to challenge yourself to provide answers without the benefit of seeing multiple-choice options. This mode does not provide the detailed score reports that the other two modes provide, so it is not the best mode for helping you identify knowledge gaps.

In addition to these three modes, you will be able to select the source of your questions. You can choose to take exams that cover all of the chapters, or you can narrow your selection to just a single chapter or the chapters that make up specific parts in the book. All chapters are selected by default. If you want to narrow your focus to individual chapters, simply deselect all the chapters and then select only those on which you wish to focus in the Objectives area.

You can also select the exam banks on which to focus. Each exam bank comes complete with a full exam of questions that cover topics in every chapter. The exams printed in the book are available to you, as are two additional exams of unique questions. You can have the test engine serve up exams from all banks or just from one individual bank by selecting the desired banks in the exam bank area.

There are several other customizations you can make to your exam from the exam settings screen, such as the time allowed for taking the exam, the number of questions served up, whether to randomize questions and answers, whether to show the number of correct answers for multiple-answer questions, and whether to serve up only specific types of questions. You can also create custom test banks by selecting only questions that you have marked or questions on which you have added notes.

Updating Your Exams

If you are using the online version of the Pearson Test Prep software, you should always have access to the latest version of the software as well as the exam data. If you are using the Windows desktop version, every time you launch the software, it will check to see if there are any updates to your exam data and automatically download any changes made since the last time you used the software. This requires that you be connected to the Internet at the time you launch the software.

Sometimes, due to a number of factors, the exam data might not fully download when you activate your exam. If you find that figures or exhibits are missing, you might need to manually update your exams. To update a particular exam you have already activated and downloaded, simply select the Tools tab and click the Update Products button. Again, this is only an issue with the desktop Windows application.

If you wish to check for updates to the Windows desktop version of the Pearson Test Prep exam engine software, simply select the Tools tab and click the Update Application button. Doing so allows you to ensure that you are running the latest version of the software engine.

Need Further Study?

Consider taking a hands-on A+ course and be sure to see the following companion products to this book:

CompTIA A+ Core 1 220-1101 and Core 2 220-1102 Exam Cram by David L. Prowse (ISBN: 978-0-1376-3754-6)

CompTIA A+ Core 1 220-1101 Complete Video Course by David L. Prowse (ISBN: 978-0-13-790378-8)

CompTIA A+ Core 2 220-1102 Complete Video Course by David L. Prowse

Figure Credit

Figure 9.1   Microsoft Corporation

1

CHAPTER ONE

Introduction to the 220-1101 Exam

The CompTIA A+ Core 1 (220-1101) exam is all about mobile devices, PC hardware, computer networking, and troubleshooting of those technologies. It also contains a small percentage of questions on cloud computing and virtualization.

In this chapter, I briefly discuss how the exam is categorized, give you some test-taking tips, and prepare you to take the three 220-1101 practice exams that follow this chapter.

Exam Breakdown

The CompTIA A+ Core 1 (220-1101) exam objectives are divided by domain. Each domain makes up a certain percentage of the test. The five domains of the A+ 220-1101 exam and their respective percentages are listed in Table 1.1.

TABLE 1.1   220-1101 Domains

Domain	Percentage of Exam
1.0 Mobile Devices	15%
2.0 Networking	20%
3.0 Hardware	25%
4.0 Virtualization and Cloud Computing	11%
5.0 Hardware and Network Troubleshooting	29%
Total	100%

Chances are that when you take the real CompTIA exam, the questions will be based on these percentages, but you never know. The questions are chosen at random, so you have to be prepared for anything and study all of the objectives.

Each domain has several objectives. There are far too many to list in this book, but I recommend that you download a copy of the objectives for yourself. You can get them from CompTIA's A+ web page (https://www.comptia.org/certifications/a), and I link to them at my website (https://dprocomputer.com) as well.

Let's talk about each domain briefly.

Domain 1.0: Mobile Devices (15%)

CompTIA refers to any portable computers as mobile devices, including laptops, tablets, smartphones, and hybrid versions of those devices. This domain comprises only 15% of the exam, but remember that every domain is important. You should be able to demonstrate the ability to install and configure laptop hardware and software. You also should know how to operate laptops' special functions, such as dual displays, wireless, and Bluetooth. Finally, because of the explosion of mobile devices in the tech world and the increased adoption of bring your own device (BYOD) policies by companies, you need to understand the hardware side of smartphones and tablets for the 220-1101 exam.

Domain 2.0: Networking (20%)

The Networking domain covers network standards, cabling, connectors, and tools. TCP/IP is also a big topic in this domain; you will undoubtedly see questions on IP addresses, ports, and protocols. You should be able to install and configure a basic wired or wireless SOHO network and use the appropriate networking tools. Plus, you should be able to describe the various types of servers and networking hardware available.

Domain 3.0: Hardware (25%)

The Hardware domain concerns building, upgrading, and maintaining a computer. The motherboard, CPU, and RAM are the guts of a desktop computer, so to speak. They are installed inside a computer case.

You are required to understand motherboard form factors and compatibility concerns as well as the ports, connectors, and expansion slots of a motherboard. You should also know how to access, configure, and update the BIOS/UEFI and understand the relationship between the BIOS/UEFI, CMOS, and lithium battery.

> **NOTE**
>
> The BIOS/UEFI is also known as UEFI/BIOS, or just BIOS or UEFI. You might see any of these terms on the A+ exams or in the IT field. Remember that the UEFI is a newer technology that augments the BIOS and allows for more security and better communication with the operating system.

Then there's everything that connects to the motherboard: CPU and fan, RAM, expansion cards, and storage drives. Plus, there are all of the ports on a computer, such as USB, video, and audio ports. Finally, you should know peripherals such as monitors, printers, USB flash drives, and other devices that interact with the computer.

Domain 4.0: Virtualization and Cloud Computing (11%)

The Virtualization and Cloud Computing domain is new to the A+ Core 1 (220-1101) exam. Coming in at 11% of the exam—but still quite important—this domain summarizes cloud-computing concepts such as common cloud models, cloud characteristics, and desktop virtualization. It also covers the purpose of virtual machines (VMs) and resource and security requirements. If you are not using VMs now, you will be. And chances are that you already make use of some type of cloud-based services. This domain is considered to be an introduction to the cloud, but you should study it carefully because you will be dealing with the cloud and VMs often.

Domain 5.0: Hardware and Network Troubleshooting (29%)

Troubleshooting is key; it is the most vital ability a technician should possess. You need to understand how to troubleshoot hardware failures, bootup issues, no-display obstacles, network connectivity difficulties, and, of course, printing problems. This is the crux of the exam (both A+ exams, to be accurate), and you need to study and practice accordingly.

Expect one question out of four (or more) to be based on a troubleshooting scenario. Practice the questions in this book, understand the concepts, and—importantly—practice the topics on real computers in a hands-on way whenever possible. Hands-on experience plays a big role in troubleshooting, and CompTIA recommends that a test-taker have 12 months of hands-on experience in the lab or field.

Remember this: Troubleshooting is a huge portion of what you do as a computer technician. To increase your job security, you need to be a good troubleshooter. Today's CompTIA A+ exams reflect this concept by incorporating many paragraph-based, scenario-oriented troubleshooting questions. You need to imagine yourself in the situation and think carefully about how to fix the problem. One thing that can aid you in this process is the CompTIA A+ six-step troubleshooting process. Memorize it!

Step 1. **Identify the problem.**

> ▶ Gather information from the user, identify user changes, and, if applicable, perform backups before making changes.

> ▶ Inquire regarding environmental or infrastructure changes.

Step 2. **Establish a theory of probable cause. (Question the obvious.)**

> ▶ If necessary, conduct external or internal research based on symptoms.

Step 3. **Test the theory to determine the cause.**

> ▶ Once the theory is confirmed, determine the next steps to resolve the problem.

> ▶ If the theory is not confirmed, establish a new theory or escalate.

Step 4. **Establish a plan of action to resolve the problem and implement the solution.**

> ▶ Refer to the vendor's instructions for guidance.

Step 5. **Verify full system functionality and, if applicable, implement preventative measures.**

Step 6. **Document the findings, actions, and outcomes.**

NOTE

Always consider corporate policies, procedures, and impacts before implementing changes.

I really can't stress enough the importance of this domain. Practice on real systems and be ready to troubleshoot!

Test-Taking Tips

My first recommendation is to take the exams slowly. Don't rush through, especially on the first exam. Carefully read each question. Some questions are tricky by design. Others may seem tricky if you lack knowledge in certain areas. Still other questions are somewhat vague, and that is intentional as well. You need to place yourself in the scenario of the question. Think of yourself actually installing a CPU and heat sink, or imagine that you are upgrading a video card. Picture in your head the steps you must take to accomplish what the question is asking of you. Envision what you do with computers step by step, and the answers will come more easily to you.

Next, read through *all* of the answers. Don't just jump on the first one that seems correct to you. Look at each answer and ask yourself whether it is right or wrong. And if it is wrong, define why it is wrong. Using this approach helps you eliminate wrong answers in the search for the correct answer. When you have selected an answer, be confident in your decision.

Finally, don't get stuck on any one question. You can always mark it and return to it later. This advice especially applies to performance-based questions and longer questions. I offer more tips as we progress through the book, and I summarize all test-taking tips at the end of this book.

Getting Ready for the Practice Exams

The next three chapters feature practice exams based on the 220-1101 exam. Every exam is followed by in-depth explanations. Be sure to read them carefully. Don't move on to another exam until you understand the first one. By that I mean you should be scoring 90% or higher on the exam (without memorizing the answers). Really understand the concepts before moving on to another exam. This makes you an efficient test-taker and allows you to benefit the most from this book.

Consider timing yourself. Give yourself 90 minutes to complete each exam. Write down your answers on a piece of paper. When you are finished, if there is still time left, review your answers for accuracy.

Each exam is more difficult than the one before it. Don't get overconfident if you do well on the first exam; your skills will be tested more thoroughly as you progress. And don't get too concerned if you don't score 90% on the first try.

This just means you need to study more and try the test again later. Keep studying and practicing!

After each exam is an answer key, followed by in-depth answers/explanations. Don't skip the explanations, even if you think you know the concept. I often insert little tidbits of knowledge that are on the periphery of the concept; these tidbits help you build a stronger foundation of knowledge in general. In other words, I might branch off the main topic in order to give you a clearer, bigger picture of the 220-1101 exam and of the tech world in general.

So take a deep breath, and let's go!

CHAPTER TWO

220-1101 Practice Exam A

Welcome to the first 220-1101 practice exam. This is the easiest of the 220-1101 exams. The subsequent exams get progressively harder.

Take this first exam slowly. The goal is to make sure you understand all of the concepts before moving on to the next test.

Write down your answers and check them against the Quick-Check Answer Key, which immediately follows the exam. After the answer key, you will find explanations for all of the answers. Good luck!

Practice Questions

1. Which of the following are components you might find inside a PC? (Select the three best answers.)

   ❏ **A.** CPU

   ❏ **B.** Motherboard

   ❏ **C.** Keyboard

   ❏ **D.** Printer

   ❏ **E.** RAM

   ❏ **F.** Cable modem

Quick Answer: **24**
Detailed Answer: **25**

2. Which device retains data over the long term?

   ○ **A.** CPU

   ○ **B.** RAM

   ○ **C.** Storage drive

   ○ **D.** Video card

Quick Answer: **24**
Detailed Answer: **25**

3. To which type of technology would you install a x16 card?

   ○ **A.** Thunderbolt

   ○ **B.** PCIe

   ○ **C.** USB

   ○ **D.** DisplayPort

Quick Answer: **24**
Detailed Answer: **25**

4. Which computer process checks all your components during boot?

   ○ **A.** CMOS

   ○ **B.** POST

   ○ **C.** BIOS

   ○ **D.** Lithium battery

Quick Answer: **24**
Detailed Answer: **25**

5. You are planning to use an older PC for trade shows in several different countries. The PC only needs to work as a basic kiosk with an Internet browser. Which of the following is the most important factor for you to consider?

   ○ **A.** Maximum wattage

   ○ **B.** Input voltage

   ○ **C.** Number of SATA connections

   ○ **D.** TDP

   ○ **E.** Number of network connections

Quick Answer: **24**
Detailed Answer: **26**

6. Which of the following could cause the POST to fail? (Select the two best answers.)

   ❑ **A.** CPU

   ❑ **B.** Power supply

   ❑ **C.** Memory

   ❑ **D.** Storage drive

7. Which of the following might you find as part of a tablet computer? (Select the two best answers.)

   ❑ **A.** Flash memory

   ❑ **B.** SATA storage drive

   ❑ **C.** Multi-touch touchscreen

   ❑ **D.** 24-inch display

8. Which of the following cloud concepts can allow for scalable services to clients?

   ○ **A.** Metered utilization

   ○ **B.** Shared resources

   ○ **C.** Rapid elasticity

   ○ **D.** High availability

   ○ **E.** SaaS

9. How should you hold RAM when installing it?

   ○ **A.** By the edges

   ○ **B.** By the front and back

   ○ **C.** With tweezers

   ○ **D.** With a punchdown tool

10. You have been tasked with setting up a specialized computer for video editing. Which of the following should you include with the computer? (Select the two best answers.)

    ❑ **A.** Gigabit NIC

    ❑ **B.** Hypervisor

    ❑ **C.** SSD

    ❑ **D.** Docking station

    ❑ **E.** Dual monitors

    ❑ **F.** NAS

11. How many pins are inside an SATA 3.0 data connector?

- ○ **A.** 15
- ○ **B.** 7
- ○ **C.** 24
- ○ **D.** 127

Quick Answer: **24**
Detailed Answer: **27**

12. What is the term for the delay in the RAM's response to a request from the memory controller?

- ○ **A.** Latency
- ○ **B.** Standard deviation
- ○ **C.** Fetch interval
- ○ **D.** Lag

Quick Answer: **24**
Detailed Answer: **27**

13. What is the minimum number of storage drives necessary to implement RAID 5?

- ○ **A.** Two
- ○ **B.** Five
- ○ **C.** Three
- ○ **D.** Four

Quick Answer: **24**
Detailed Answer: **27**

14. A user's time and date keep resetting to January 1, 2015. Which of the following is the most likely cause?

- ○ **A.** The BIOS/UEFI needs to be updated.
- ○ **B.** Windows needs to be updated.
- ○ **C.** The Windows Date and Time Properties window needs to be modified.
- ○ **D.** The lithium battery needs to be replaced.

Quick Answer: **24**
Detailed Answer: **28**

15. Which type of adapter card is normally plugged into a PCIe x16 adapter card slot?

- ○ **A.** Modem
- ○ **B.** Video
- ○ **C.** NIC
- ○ **D.** Sound

Quick Answer: **24**
Detailed Answer: **28**

16. Which of the following is a common type of CPU for a smartphone?

- ○ **A.** LGA 1700
- ○ **B.** SoC
- ○ **C.** Core i9
- ○ **D.** SODIMM

Quick Answer: **24**
Detailed Answer: **28**

17. Which of the following components could cause the POST to beep several times and fail during boot?

- ○ **A.** Sound card
- ○ **B.** Power supply
- ○ **C.** Storage drive
- ○ **D.** RAM
- ○ **E.** LPDDR

18. Which of the following are ports you might find on smartphones and tablets? (Select the two best answers.)

- ❏ **A.** eSATA
- ❏ **B.** USB-C
- ❏ **C.** Lightning
- ❏ **D.** DVI

19. Which of the following has the fastest data throughput?

- ○ **A.** Optical drive
- ○ **B.** Hard disk drive
- ○ **C.** Solid-state drive
- ○ **D.** RAM
- ○ **E.** USB

20. Which of the following CPU cooling methods is the most common?

- ○ **A.** Heat sink
- ○ **B.** Heat sink and fan
- ○ **C.** Liquid cooling
- ○ **D.** Liquid nitrogen

21. You are tasked with fixing a problem with a video editing workstation. An unexpected clicking noise occurs every time the video editing program is started. The case fans have been replaced, but the noise remains. Diagnostics have also been run on the video card, and it appears to be operating normally. What action should you take first?

- ○ **A.** Perform a System Restore.
- ○ **B.** Replace the video card.
- ○ **C.** Replace the hard disk drive.
- ○ **D.** Perform a full data backup.
- ○ **E.** Scan for malware.

22. You are in the process of upgrading a lab's systems from wireless-equipped laptops to thin clients. To support the VDI that you plan to implement, each client needs a 1 Gbps connection. Previously, the laptops connected to the organization's 802.11n wireless network. Which of the following is needed for the thin clients to communicate with each other?

    ◯   **A.**   UPS

    ◯   **B.**   External storage drives

    ◯   **C.**   KVM

    ◯   **D.**   Network cabloc

23. Which of the following cable types should you use to connect a cable modem to a SOHO router?

    ◯   **A.**   RG-6

    ◯   **B.**   USB

    ◯   **C.**   Ethernet

    ◯   **D.**   HDMI

    ◯   **E.**   SATA

24. With which of the following technologies can you have two mobile devices transfer data simply by touching them together?

    ◯   **A.**   USB

    ◯   **B.**   NFC

    ◯   **C.**   Bluetooth

    ◯   **D.**   Wi-Fi

25. What type of power connector is used for a x16 video card?

    ◯   **A.**   Molex 4-pin

    ◯   **B.**   SATA 15-pin

    ◯   **C.**   PCIe 8-pin

    ◯   **D.**   P1 24-pin

26. Which of the following are output devices? (Select the three best answers.)

    ❑   **A.**   Speakers

    ❑   **B.**   Keyboard

    ❑   **C.**   Mouse

    ❑   **D.**   Printer

    ❑   **E.**   Display

    ❑   **F.**   Touchpad

27. What does the b in 1000 Mbps stand for?

    ○ **A.** megabytes

    ○ **B.** bits

    ○ **C.** bytes

    ○ **D.** bandwidth

28. When running cable through drop ceilings, which type of cable do you need?

    ○ **A.** PVC

    ○ **B.** Category 5e

    ○ **C.** Direct burial

    ○ **D.** Plenum

29. Which device connects multiple computers in a LAN?

    ○ **A.** Modem

    ○ **B.** Router

    ○ **C.** Switch

    ○ **D.** Firewall

30. Which of the following is the default subnet mask for IP address 192.168.1.1?

    ○ **A.** 255.255.0.0

    ○ **B.** 255.255.255.0

    ○ **C.** 255.0.0.0

    ○ **D.** 255.255.255.255

31. Which of the following is the minimum cable category needed for a 1000BASE-T network?

    ○ **A.** 802.11ax

    ○ **B.** Category 5

    ○ **C.** Category 5e

    ○ **D.** Category 6

32. Which of the following IP addresses can be routed across the Internet?

    ○ **A.** 127.0.0.1

    ○ **B.** 192.168.1.1

    ○ **C.** 129.52.50.13

    ○ **D.** 10.52.50.13

33. Which port number is used by an HTTPS web server by default?

   ○ **A.** 21

   ○ **B.** 25

   ○ **C.** 80

   ○ **D.** 443

Quick Answer: **24**
Detailed Answer: **32**

34. Which of the following cable types have a copper medium? (Select the three best answers.)

   ❏ **A.** Twisted pair

   ❏ **B.** Coaxial

   ❏ **C.** Fiber optic

   ❏ **D.** Cat 6a

   ❏ **E.** Multimode

   ❏ **F.** 802.11ax

Quick Answer: **24**
Detailed Answer: **32**

35. Which of the following cable types can protect against electromagnetic interference (EMI)? (Select the two best answers.)

   ❏ **A.** UTP

   ❏ **B.** STP

   ❏ **C.** Fiber optic

   ❏ **D.** Cat 6

Quick Answer: **24**
Detailed Answer: **33**

36. You are configuring Bob's computer to access the Internet. Which of the following are required? (Select all that apply.)

   ❏ **A.** DNS server address

   ❏ **B.** Gateway address

   ❏ **C.** Email server name

   ❏ **D.** DHCP server address

   ❏ **E.** Domain name

Quick Answer: **24**
Detailed Answer: **33**

37. Which of the following translates a computer name into an IP address?

   ○ **A.** TCP

   ○ **B.** UDP

   ○ **C.** DNS

   ○ **D.** FTP

Quick Answer: **24**
Detailed Answer: **33**

38. A customer wants to access the Internet from many different locations in the United States. Which of the following is the best technology to enable the customer to do so?

    ○ **A.** Infrared

    ○ **B.** Cellular WAN

    ○ **C.** Bluetooth

    ○ **D.** 802.11ac

Quick Answer: **24**
Detailed Answer: **33**

39. You just configured the IP address 192.168.0.105 in Windows. When you press the Tab key, Windows automatically configures the default subnet mask 255.255.255.0. Which of the following IP addresses is a suitable gateway address?

    ○ **A.** 192.168.1.100

    ○ **B.** 192.168.1.1

    ○ **C.** 192.168.10.1

    ○ **D.** 192.168.0.1

Quick Answer: **24**
Detailed Answer: **33**

40. Which of the following is the name for a wireless network?

    ○ **A.** SSID

    ○ **B.** WPA

    ○ **C.** Screened subnet

    ○ **D.** DHCP

Quick Answer: **24**
Detailed Answer: **34**

41. You configure a mobile device to connect to a Wi-Fi network on channel 165. Which of the following frequencies is the wireless connection using?

    ○ **A.** 2.4 GHz

    ○ **B.** 40 MHz

    ○ **C.** 5 GHz

    ○ **D.** 13.56 MHz

Quick Answer: **24**
Detailed Answer: **34**

42. Which of the following connector types is used by fiber-optic cabling?

    ○ **A.** LC

    ○ **B.** RJ45

    ○ **C.** RG-6

    ○ **D.** RJ11

Quick Answer: **24**
Detailed Answer: **34**

43. Which protocol uses port 53?

- ○ **A.** FTP
- ○ **B.** SMTP
- ○ **C.** DNS
- ○ **D.** HTTPS

44. Which of the following Internet services are wireless? (Select the two best answers.)

- ❏ **A.** Cable Internet
- ❏ **B.** Satellite
- ❏ **C.** DSL
- ❏ **D.** Cellular
- ❏ **E.** Fiber optic

45. Which of the following terms best describes two or more LANs connected over a large geographic distance?

- ○ **A.** PAN
- ○ **B.** WAN
- ○ **C.** WLAN
- ○ **D.** MAN
- ○ **E.** SAN

46. Which device connects to the network and has the sole purpose of providing data to clients?

- ○ **A.** NAS
- ○ **B.** NAT
- ○ **C.** NAC
- ○ **D.** IaaS

47. You are making your own networking patch cable. You need to attach an RJ45 plug to the end of a twisted-pair cable. Which tool should you use?

- ○ **A.** Tone and probe kit
- ○ **B.** Cable tester
- ○ **C.** Crimper
- ○ **D.** Multimeter

48. Which port is used by RDP?

- ○ **A.** 80
- ○ **B.** 110
- ○ **C.** 443
- ○ **D.** 3389

Quick Answer: **24**
Detailed Answer: **35**

49. Which of the following provides for a data plane and a control plane?

- ○ **A.** SDN
- ○ **B.** NIC
- ○ **C.** ONT
- ○ **D.** MAM

Quick Answer: **24**
Detailed Answer: **35**

50. Which of the following printer failures can be described as a condition in which the internal feed mechanism stopped working temporarily?

- ○ **A.** No connectivity
- ○ **B.** Corrupt driver
- ○ **C.** Paper jam
- ○ **D.** Power cycle

Quick Answer: **24**
Detailed Answer: **36**

51. A customer can barely hear sound from a laptop's speakers. What should you do first?

- ○ **A.** Install a new sound driver.
- ○ **B.** Tap the speakers.
- ○ **C.** Search for a volume key.
- ○ **D.** Reinstall Windows.

Quick Answer: **24**
Detailed Answer: **36**

52. After you replace a motherboard in a PC, the system overheats and fails to boot. Which of the following is the most likely cause?

- ○ **A.** The GPU is not compatible with the CPU.
- ○ **B.** The new motherboard's firmware is out of date.
- ○ **C.** Thermal paste was not applied between the heat sink and the CPU.
- ○ **D.** The case fan failed.

Quick Answer: **24**
Detailed Answer: **36**

53. You use your laptop often. Which of the following is a simple, free way to keep your laptop running cool?

- ○ **A.** Keep the laptop on a flat surface.
- ○ **B.** Put the laptop in the freezer when not in use.
- ○ **C.** Direct a fan at the laptop.
- ○ **D.** Keep the laptop turned off whenever possible.

54. Which of the following are important factors when purchasing a replacement laptop AC adapter? (Select the two best answers.)

- ❏ **A.** Current and voltage
- ❏ **B.** Connector size and shape
- ❏ **C.** Battery type
- ❏ **D.** Inverter type

55. Eric uses an external monitor with his laptop. He tells you that his laptop will boot, but the system won't display anything on the external screen. Which of the following solutions enables the display?

- ○ **A.** Connect the laptop to another external monitor.
- ○ **B.** Press the Fn and Screen keys one or more times until an image appears on the screen.
- ○ **C.** Press the Enter and Esc keys while the laptop is booting.
- ○ **D.** Press the Fn key while the laptop is booting.

56. Which type of printer uses a toner cartridge?

- ○ **A.** Inkjet
- ○ **B.** Laser
- ○ **C.** Impact
- ○ **D.** Thermal
- ○ **E.** 3D printer

57. Which of the following should *not* be connected to a UPS?

- ○ **A.** PCs
- ○ **B.** Monitors
- ○ **C.** Laser printers
- ○ **D.** Speakers

68. Terri finishes installing a printer for a customer. What should she do next?

    ◯ **A.** Verify that the printer prints by using Microsoft Word.

    ◯ **B.** Print a test page.

    ◯ **C.** Restart the spooler.

    ◯ **D.** Set up a separator page.

Quick Answer: **24**
Detailed Answer: **38**

59. Which of the following best describes printing in duplex?

    ◯ **A.** Printing on both sides of the paper

    ◯ **B.** Printer collation

    ◯ **C.** Full-duplex printer communication

    ◯ **D.** Printing to file

    ◯ **E.** 1200 DPI

Quick Answer: **24**
Detailed Answer: **38**

60. Special paper is needed to print on which type of printer?

    ◯ **A.** Impact

    ◯ **B.** Thermal

    ◯ **C.** Laser

    ◯ **D.** Inkjet

    ◯ **E.** 3D

Quick Answer: **24**
Detailed Answer: **38**

61. Which of the following channels should you select for an 802.11 wireless network?

    ◯ **A.** 6

    ◯ **B.** 21

    ◯ **C.** 802

    ◯ **D.** 8080

Quick Answer: **24**
Detailed Answer: **38**

62. Which environmental issue affects a thermal printer the most?

    ◯ **A.** Moisture

    ◯ **B.** ESD

    ◯ **C.** Dirt

    ◯ **D.** Heat

Quick Answer: **24**
Detailed Answer: **39**

63. Which of the following occurs last in the laser printing process?

- ○ **A.** Charging
- ○ **B.** Exposing
- ○ **C.** Developing
- ○ **D.** Fusing
- ○ **E.** Cleaning

64. Which type of printer uses impact to transfer ink from a ribbon to the paper?

- ○ **A.** Laser
- ○ **B.** Inkjet
- ○ **C.** Impact
- ○ **D.** Thermal

65. Which of the following steps enables you to take control of a network printer from a remote computer?

- ○ **A.** Installing the printer locally and accessing the Sharing tab
- ○ **B.** Installing the printer locally and accessing the spool settings
- ○ **C.** Installing the printer locally and accessing the Ports tab
- ○ **D.** Connecting to the printer via FTP

66. A color laser printer produces images that are tinted blue. Which of the following steps should be performed to address this problem?

- ○ **A.** Clean the toner cartridge
- ○ **B.** Calibrate the printer
- ○ **C.** Change the fusing assembly
- ○ **D.** Clean the primary corona

67. A laptop cannot access the wireless network. Which of the following statements best describe the most likely causes of this? (Select the two best answers.)

- ❑ **A.** The function key for wireless was pressed by accident.
- ❑ **B.** The user installed a new web browser.
- ❑ **C.** The wireless network was forgotten in Windows.
- ❑ **D.** The computer is obtaining an IP address automatically.

68. A desktop computer does not have a lit link light on the back of the computer. Which of the following is the most likely reason for this?

Quick Answer: **24**
Detailed Answer: **40**

- ○ **A.** Wi-Fi was disabled.
- ○ **B.** USB is malfunctioning.
- ○ **C.** The system did not POST correctly.
- ○ **D.** The network cable is disconnected.

69. Which of the following IP addresses does a technician see if a computer running Windows is connected to a multifunction network device and is attempting to obtain an IP address automatically but is not receiving an IP address from the DHCP server?

Quick Answer: **24**
Detailed Answer: **40**

- ○ **A.** 172.16.10.10
- ○ **B.** 192.168.0.10
- ○ **C.** 169.254.10.10
- ○ **D.** 192.168.10.10

70. For which type of PC component are 80 mm and 120 mm common sizes?

Quick Answer: **24**
Detailed Answer: **40**

- ○ **A.** Case fans
- ○ **B.** CPUs
- ○ **C.** Heat sinks
- ○ **D.** Memory modules

71. An exclamation point next to a device in Device Manager indicates which of the following?

Quick Answer: **24**
Detailed Answer: **41**

- ○ **A.** A driver is not properly installed for this device.
- ○ **B.** The device is disabled.
- ○ **C.** The driver is not digitally signed.
- ○ **D.** The device driver needs to be upgraded.

72. Beep codes are generated by which of the following?

Quick Answer: **24**
Detailed Answer: **41**

- ○ **A.** CMOS
- ○ **B.** RTC
- ○ **C.** POST
- ○ **D.** Windows

73. Which of the following indicates that a printer is network ready?

- ○ **A.** An RJ11 jack
- ○ **B.** A USB connector
- ○ **C.** An RJ45 jack
- ○ **D.** An SCSI connector

Quick Answer: **24**
Detailed Answer: **41**

74. You just turned off a printer to perform maintenance on it. Which of the following should you be careful of when removing the fuser?

- ○ **A.** The fuser being hot
- ○ **B.** The fuser being wet
- ○ **C.** The fuser being fragile
- ○ **D.** The fuser releasing toner

Quick Answer: **24**
Detailed Answer: **41**

75. Which of the following connectors can allow for video, audio, and data?

- ○ **A.** HDMI
- ○ **B.** DVI
- ○ **C.** DisplayPort
- ○ **D.** USB-C

Quick Answer: **24**
Detailed Answer: **42**

76. You are attempting to make a connection to the Internet with a laptop, but there is no Wi-Fi availability. Your smartphone currently has access to the Internet. Which of the following will allow the laptop to connect to the Internet?

- ○ **A.** PRL
- ○ **B.** Hotspot
- ○ **C.** GPS
- ○ **D.** PoE injector

Quick Answer: **24**
Detailed Answer: **42**

77. One of your customers purchased a device that can perform firewall duties, routing tasks, packet inspection, and antivirus scanning. Which of the following devices was purchased?

- ○ **A.** UTM appliance
- ○ **B.** DHCP server
- ○ **C.** Proxy server
- ○ **D.** IDS appliance

Quick Answer: **24**
Detailed Answer: **42**

78. Which of the following is the most important piece of information needed to connect to a specific wireless network?

    ○ **A.** Channel

    ○ **B.** MAC address

    ○ **C.** SSID

    ○ **D.** Administrator password

Quick Answer: **24**
Detailed Answer: **42**

79. You are considering a cloud-based service for file storage and synchronization. Which of the following resources is the most critical to your design?

    ○ **A.** Disk speed

    ○ **B.** RAM utilization

    ○ **C.** CPU utilization

    ○ **D.** I/O bandwidth

Quick Answer: **24**
Detailed Answer: **43**

80. Which of the following statements describes why the display on a laptop gets dimmer when the power supply from the AC outlet is disconnected?

    ○ **A.** The laptop cannot use full brightness when on battery power.

    ○ **B.** Power management settings on the laptop are configured for power saving.

    ○ **C.** To operate properly, laptop displays require an alternating current power source.

    ○ **D.** Security settings on the laptop are configured to dim the display.

Quick Answer: **24**
Detailed Answer: **43**

Quick-Check Answer Key

1. A, B, and E	**28.** D	**55.** B
2. C	**29.** C	**56.** B
3. B	**30.** B	**57.** C
4. B	**31.** C	**58.** B
5. B	**32.** C	**59.** A
6. A and C	**33.** D	**60.** B
7. A and C	**34.** A, B, and D	**61.** A
8. C	**35.** B and C	**62.** D
9. A	**36.** A and B	**63.** E
10. C and E	**37.** C	**64.** C
11. B	**38.** B	**65.** C
12. A	**39.** D	**66.** B
13. C	**40.** A	**67.** A and C
14. D	**41.** C	**68.** D
15. B	**42.** A	**69.** C
16. B	**43.** C	**70.** A
17. D	**44.** B and D	**71.** A
18. B and C	**45.** B	**72.** C
19. D	**46.** A	**73.** C
20. B	**47.** C	**74.** A
21. D	**48.** D	**75.** D
22. D	**49.** A	**76.** B
23. C	**50.** C	**77.** A
24. B	**51.** C	**78.** C
25. C	**52.** C	**79.** D
26. A, D, and E	**53.** A	**80.** B
27. B	**54.** A and B	

Answers and Explanations

1. Answers: A, B, and E

Explanation: Common components inside a PC include the CPU, motherboard, and RAM, along with the power supply, adapter cards, and storage drives.

Incorrect answers: Keyboards (and mice) are input devices that are located outside the PC. Printers (and displays) are output devices that are located outside the PC. A cable modem is an Internet communication device that is outside the PC. *Know the internal components of a PC!*

2. Answer: C

Explanation: The storage drive (or hard drive) stores data over the long term. It stores the OS and data in a nonvolatile fashion, meaning the data won't be erased when the computer is turned off.

Incorrect answers: The CPU calculates data and sends it to RAM for temporary storage; the RAM (which is volatile) is cleared when the computer is turned off. The video card stores temporary video data within its onboard memory, but this, like RAM, is volatile and is cleared when the computer is turned off.

3. Answer: B

Explanation: PCI Express (PCIe) expansion slots accept x1, x4, and x16 cards (pronounced "by one," "by four," and "by sixteen," respectively).

Incorrect answers: PCIe is by far the most common expansion slot for video cards (which are usually x16). Thunderbolt is a technology used primarily with Mac computers for displays and for data transfer. USB stands for Universal Serial Bus; it is a standard for connecting external equipment to a computer, not an expansion bus for use with cards. DisplayPort is a video technology that provides connectivity between the video card and the monitor.

4. Answer: B

Explanation: The POST (power-on self-test) is part of the Basic Input/Output System (BIOS) or Unified Extensible Firmware Interface (UEFI). It runs a self-check of the computer system during boot and stores many of the parameters of the components within the CMOS.

NOTE

In this book I refer to the BIOS and UEFI collectively as BIOS/UEFI.

Incorrect answers: BIOS is known as firmware. The lithium battery powers the CMOS while the computer is off. It remembers settings such as the time and date and passwords. The CMOS, BIOS, and the lithium battery are not processes, but they do work hand in hand with each other.

5. **Answer: B**

   Explanation: The input voltage is the most important thing to consider (of the listed answers at least). Different countries have different standard input voltages. For example, the United States uses 115 volts alternating current as a standard; countries in Europe and elsewhere use 230 volts. In this case, you would want to make sure that the older PC can auto-select voltages or that it at least has a switch to change from 115 V to 230 V.

   Incorrect answers: Because this PC will be used for very basic purposes, the maximum wattage, number of SATA or network connections, and thermal design power (TDP) rating should not make a difference. However, you should make sure that the PC has the correct video connections and appropriate USB connections to work as a kiosk.

6. **Answers: A and C**

   Explanation: The CPU and memory need to be installed properly for the POST to run (and to pass).

   Incorrect answers: Storage drives may or may not be installed properly, but they are not necessary for the POST to complete. If the power supply is defective, the system simply will not boot and will not even get to the POST stage.

7. **Answers: A and C**

   Explanation: A tablet computer often contains flash memory as main storage and a multi-touch touchscreen. Smartphones are similarly equipped.

   Incorrect answers: SATA storage drives and 24-inch displays are more likely to be found on PCs than on tablet computers.

8. **Answer: C**

   Explanation: Rapid elasticity means that a service, compute power, or networking bandwidth can be increased when needed. This kind of scalability is integral to cloud computing.

   Incorrect answers: With metered utilization (or measured services), a cloud provider or an ISP measures the amount of data being sent, received, and stored, as well as network usage and computer usage. Shared resources (or resource pooling) means that multiple systems (or customers) share the same physical hardware, servers, and networking connections. With high availability, a server or service is available with little to no downtime. SaaS stands for software as a service, and SaaS examples include services such as browser-based email.

9. **Answer: A**

   Explanation: Hold RAM by the edges to avoid contact with the pins, chips, and circuitry.

   Incorrect answers: Touching the front and back is not advised because it requires touching the chips on the RAM module. Tools are not needed, and if they are used, metallic ones could be damaging to the module. Plastic tweezers are used to remove screws that fall into tough-to-reach places in the case. A punchdown tool is used to terminate networking cables to patch panels or to punch blocks.

10. **Answers: C and E**

    Explanation: You should incorporate a solid-state drive (SSD) and dual monitors for the video editing workstation. Video files, such as .MP4 and .AVI, are big files that require a decent-size storage drive. An SSD—possibly an M.2 or similar drive—helps work with these files efficiently, especially in the video rendering stage. Having dual monitors (or more than two) is important when editing. You will generally want to have an editing window and a separate playback window.

    Incorrect answers: A gigabit NIC is quite common. Chances are that the computer will have it already, but such NICs—and especially 10 Gbit NICs—are more important for servers than for personal computers. The hypervisor is the type of virtualization software manager that you are using—for example, VMware or VirtualBox. A docking station is a device used with a laptop to charge it and to replicate video and other peripherals. Network-attached storage (NAS) is a multi-drive storage device that connects directly to a network. It often uses magnetic drives but could use SSDs as well. It doesn't use a screen; instead, you remotely administer it, usually from a browser.

11. **Answer: B**

    Explanation: The SATA version 3.0 data connector has 7 pins.

NOTE

SATA *Express* uses a triple connector with 18 pins (7 + 7 + 4).

    Incorrect answers: The SATA power connector has 15 pins. ATX 12 V 2.0 and higher power connections have 24 pins. Among other things, 127 is the maximum number of USB devices you can connect to the computer.

12. **Answer: A**

    Explanation: Memory latency—or CAS (column address strobe) latency—happens when a memory controller tries to access data from a memory module. It is a slight delay (usually measured in nanoseconds) while the memory module responds to the memory controller. It is also known as *CL*. The memory controller (also known as the northbridge) has a specific speed at which it operates. If the CPU asks the chip for too much information at once, this might increase latency time while the memory controller works.

    Incorrect answers: The terms *standard deviation* and *fetch interval* deal with CPUs. *Lag* is similar to latency but is more commonly associated with network connections.

13. **Answer: C**

    Explanation: Because RAID 5 uses striping with parity, a third drive (disk) is needed. You can have more than three drives as well.

    Incorrect answers: Two drives are enough for plain RAID 0 striping, so two is the exact number you need for RAID 1 mirroring. RAID 6 and RAID 10 require four disks at a minimum.

14. **Answer: D**

    Explanation: If the time and date keep resetting—for example, to a date such as January 1, 2015—chances are that the lithium battery needs to be replaced. These are usually nickel-sized batteries; most PCs use a CR2032 lithium battery. You can check the voltage on such a battery by using a multimeter; to work properly, such a battery should register above 3 volts.

    Incorrect answers: Updating the BIOS/UEFI allows the PC to "see" new devices and communicate with them better, but it will not fix the time issue. Updating Windows will not fix this problem, but it should be done often to keep the computer secure. Other date and time synchronization problems can be fixed in the clock settings within the notification area. Windows client computers should be configured to synchronize to a time server.

15. **Answer: B**

    Explanation: The PCI Express (PCIe) x16 expansion slot is used primarily for video.

    Incorrect answers: Modems, network interface cards (NICs), and sound cards usually connect to PCIe x1 slots. Some cards require a minimum of PCIe x4.

16. **Answer: B**

    Explanation: System on a chip (SoC) is a type of CPU used in smartphones and tablet computers. The 64-bit versions are common in mobile devices; they incorporate a variety of functionality within the CPU.

    Incorrect answers: LGA 1700 is a type of CPU socket used in PCs. It is designed to be the replacement for the very common LGA 1200 socket and can work with a variety of Intel CPUs. As of the writing of this book, Core i9 is Intel's latest version of high-powered CPUs. A small outline dual inline memory module (SODIMM) is the most common type of memory in laptops. It is the smaller cousin of the standard DIMM found in PCs.

17. **Answer: D**

    Explanation: RAM is one of the big four factors (along with CPU, motherboard, and video) that can cause the POST to fail. Different RAM errors can cause the POST to make different series of beeps. Consult your motherboard documentation for more information about the different beep codes.

    Incorrect answers: The sound card does not have an effect on the POST. If the power supply has a problem, the computer either will not boot at all (and not even enter POST) or will have intermittent problems (such as shutting down unpredictably). Storage drive problems result in a variety of errors. Although the POST will complete in these cases, the operating system will not boot. Low-Power Double Data Rate (LPDDR) is a common type of RAM used in mobile devices.

18. **Answers: B and C**

    Explanation: Mobile devices such as smartphones and tablets commonly incorporate ports such as USB-C (and microUSB) and Apple's Lightning connector.

    Incorrect answers: eSATA (used by external storage devices) and DVI (used by video cards) are found on some PCs.

19. **Answer: D**

    Explanation: RAM is much faster than the rest of the options listed. For instance, if you have PC4-25600 DDR4 RAM (aka DDR4-3200), your peak transfer rate is 25,600 megabytes per second (MB/s) (which could also be shown as 25.6 GB/s).

    Incorrect answers: The rest of the devices in the incorrect answers are listed in descending order of data throughput:

    ▶ Hard disk drive or solid-state drive: For example, 600 MB/s for SATA 3.0, 1969 MB/s for SATA Express, and 3500 MB/s for typical M.2 drives. M.2 is very fast but still a fraction of RAM speeds (as of the writing of this book in 2022).

    ▶ USB: For example, 5 gigabits per second (Gbps) for version 3.0 and 20 Gbps for version 3.2 (which equates to 2.5 GB/s).

    ▶ Optical drives, though not used often, might still be found in some systems, especially older ones. CD-ROMs typically transfer 7.5 MB/s. DVD-ROMs typically transfer 21 MB/s. Blu-ray discs can typically transfer 72 MB/s.

20. **Answer: B**

    Explanation: The most common CPU cooling method is the heat sink and fan combination. The heat sink helps to disperse the heat away from the CPU, whereas the fan blows the heat down and through the fins; the power supply exhaust fan and possibly additional case fans help the heat escape the case. Heat sink and fan combinations are known as active cooling methods.

    Incorrect answers: A heat sink used by itself provides passive cooling; it requires no power but is not enough to cool most desktop PCs. Liquid cooling is a more extreme method used in custom PCs such as gaming computers and possibly audio/video workstations and virtualization machines. It uses a coolant similar to the way an automobile does. Liquid nitrogen would be plain foolish and is not a legitimate answer.

21. **Answer: D**

    Explanation: The first action you should take is to perform a full data backup. Clicking noises can indicate that the computer's magnetic-based hard drive is damaged and might fail. Immediately back up the drive's contents before taking any other action.

    Incorrect answers: It is less likely, but the clicking noise can also be caused by a fan. However, the case fans have already been replaced, and it is uncommon for a video card fan to make that noise unless a cable is brushing against it (which is also unlikely). As you gain experience, you will find that fan noise and hard disk drive clicking are usually two different sounds. The damage to the hard drive could possibly be caused by malware. After backing up data, scan the drive, and, if necessary, run a System Restore. The video card should not need to be replaced because the diagnostics indicate that it is running normally. After the backup, you should strongly consider replacing the hard drive, for two reasons: (1) The drive is clicking and is probably going to fail, and (2) video editing workstations require faster hard drives. The scenario implies that the system is using a magnetic-based hard drive (also known as a hard disk drive, or HDD). A solid-state drive (SATA or M.2) would run the video editing program more efficiently and would be better in the file-rendering phase. But keep in mind that these drives have no moving parts and therefore will not present any types of clicking sounds if they are about to fail. And know this: All drives fail. It's not a matter of *if* but *when*!

22. **Answer: D**

    Explanation: Network patch cables are required for the thin clients to communicate with each other (and anything else) at 1 Gbps. If the wireless network is 802.11n, its theoretical maximum data transfer rate is only 300 Mbps—which is not fast enough for the VDI requirements.

NOTE

VDI stands for virtual desktop infrastructure. Keep in mind that there are plenty of thin clients with faster wireless connections, but using them would require upgrading the wireless infrastructure at the organization.

   Incorrect answers: An uninterruptible power supply (UPS) is a battery backup for computers. External storage drives are not necessary with thin clients. A thin client has a small internal drive that may include an embedded OS, but the whole purpose of the thin client is to pull all data and possibly the OS/virtual desktop from the network. The faster the network, the better. In this case, KVM refers to a type of switch that can select between two or more systems and allow control from a single keyboard/video/mouse setup.

23. **Answer: C**

    Explanation: Use an Ethernet networking patch cable to connect a cable modem to a SOHO router. This should be a typical straight-through twisted-pair cable that adheres to the T568B standard. It is the same type of cable that you would use to connect a PC to a switch or to an RJ45 jack.

    Incorrect answers: RG-6 is a type of coaxial cable and is often used to connect a cable modem to a *coaxial jack* on the wall and, ultimately, to the network interface device (NID) in the home or office. Universal Serial Bus (USB) cables are used to connect peripherals to PCs, among other things. HDMI is a video standard. SATA is a storage drive standard.

24. **Answer: B**

    Explanation: Near-field communication (NFC) allows you to have two mobile devices such as smartphones transfer data simply by touching them together (or bringing them in very close proximity of each other).

    Incorrect answers: A USB port (for example, microUSB) allows for the transfer and synchronization of data to and from a mobile device and a PC or laptop. Bluetooth and Wi-Fi enable wireless connectivity but do not require that the devices touch or be in close proximity.

25. **Answer: C**

    Explanation: A x16 card is a PCI Express card. It can have one or two PCIe 8-pin (or 6-pin) power connectors.

Incorrect answers: Molex 4-pin power connectors are used by secondary devices, such as fans, monitoring devices, and older IDE hard drives. SATA 15-pin power connections are used by SATA-compliant drives. P1 24-pin power is the main power connection that the motherboard gets from the power supply.

26. **Answers: A, D, and E**

    Explanation: Speakers, printers, and displays are output devices. A speaker outputs sound. A printer outputs paper with text and graphics. A display (or monitor) displays video.

    Incorrect answers: Keyboards, mice, and touchpads are input devices. Another input device used by mobile devices is the stylus.

27. **Answer: B**

    Explanation: The *b* in 1000 Mbps stands for *bits*, and 1000 Mbps is 1000 megabits per second or 1 gigabit per second. Remember that the lowercase *b* is used to indicate bits when measuring network data transfer rates, USB data transfer rates, and other similar serial data transfers.

    Incorrect answers: *Bytes* and *megabytes* refer to parallel data transfers or the calculation and storage of data, where 8 bits equal a standard byte of information. Network data transfer rates are also known as *speed* or *bandwidth*.

28. **Answer: D**

    Explanation: Plenum-rated cable needs to be installed wherever a sprinkler system is not able to spray water. This includes ceilings, walls, and plenums (airways). Plenum-rated cable has a protective covering that burns slower and gives off fewer toxic fumes than regular PVC-based cable.

    Incorrect answers: PVCs in regular cable give off toxic fumes in the event of a fire. Category 5e cable can be obtained in regular or plenum-rated versions. Direct burial is cable that is run underground and should be kept away from electrical cables.

29. **Answer: C**

    Explanation: A switch connects computers together in a local area network (LAN). In SOHO networks, a switch is usually a part of a multifunction network device. In larger networks, a switch is an individual device that has 24, 48, or 96 ports.

    Incorrect answers: A modem connects a PC to the Internet either by way of a coaxial cable connection (as in a cable modem) or a dial-up connection over a plain old telephone service (POTS) line (as in a dial-up modem). A router connects one network to another. Although a SOHO multifunction device is often referred to as a *router*, it is not the router portion of that device that connects the computers in the LAN but the switch portion. A firewall protects all the computers on the LAN from intrusion.

30. **Answer: B**

    Explanation: 192.168.1.1, by default, has the subnet mask 255.255.255.0, which is the standard subnet mask for class C IP addresses. However, remember that some networks are classless, which means that the network can use a different subnet mask.

Incorrect answers: 255.255.0.0 is the class B default subnet mask. 255.0.0.0 is the class A default subnet mask. 255.255.255.255 is the broadcast address for IP. It is not usable as a subnet mask for typical computers on the LAN.

NOTE

For more information about classful and classless IP addresses, see https://dprocomputer. com/?p=2907.

31. **Answer; C**

Explanation: The minimum cable needed for 1000BASE-T networks is Category 5e. Of course, Cat 6 would also work, but it is not the minimum of the listed answers. 1000BASE-T specifies the speed of the network (1000 Mbps), the type (BASE = baseband, a single shared channel), and the cable to be used (T = twisted pair).

Incorrect answers: 802.11ax is a wireless standard, not a cable type. Cat 5 is typically suitable for 100 Mbps networks. Be on the lookout for newer, faster technologies. For example, Category 7 and Category 8 are newer and faster cable types.

32. **Answer: C**

Explanation: The only listed answer that is a public address (needed to get onto the Internet) is 129.52.50.13.

Incorrect answers: All the other answers are private IP addresses, which are meant to be behind a firewall. 127.0.0.1 is the IPv4 local loopback IP address. 192.168.1.1 is a common private IP address used by SOHO networking devices. 10.52.50.13 is a private address. (Note that the 10 network is common in larger networks.)

33. **Answer: D**

Explanation: A server running Hypertext Transfer Protocol Secure (HTTPS) uses port 443 inbound (by default).

Incorrect answers: Port 21 is the default port used by a server running File Transfer Protocol (FTP). (Note that port 20 is used by FTP clients to make connections to the server.) Port 25 is used by the Simple Mail Transfer Protocol (SMTP). Port 80 is used by regular HTTP, which is considered to be insecure and should be avoided whenever possible.

34. **Answers: A, B, and D**

Explanation: Twisted pair, coaxial, and Category 6a cable are all examples of network cables with a copper medium. They all send electricity over copper wire. Twisted pair is the most common type of cabling used in today's networks.

Incorrect answers: Multimode is a type of fiber-optic cable; it uses light to send data over a glass or plastic medium. 802.11ax is not a cable but a standard that defines wireless transmissions over 2.4 and 5 GHz frequencies. It is known as Wi-Fi 6. (Note that Wi-Fi 6E can also transmit over the 6 GHz frequency spectrum.)

35. **Answers: B and C**

Explanation: Shielded twisted pair (STP) and fiber optic can protect against EMI.

Incorrect answers: Unshielded twisted pair (UTP) cannot protect against EMI. Unless otherwise mentioned, Category 6 cable is UTP. STP is shielded twisted pair. Unlike UTP, STP provides an aluminum shield that protects against EMI. UTP and coaxial have no such protection. Fiber optic uses a different medium altogether, transmitting light rather than electricity; therefore, EMI cannot affect fiber-optic cables.

36. **Answers: A and B**

Explanation: To get on the Internet, the DNS server address is required so that the computer can get the resolved IP addresses from the domain names that are typed in. The gateway address is necessary to get outside the network.

Incorrect answers: Email server information is not necessary if the person is just looking to get on the Internet. A DHCP server address is not necessary either; however, using one is an easier method. The beauty of DHCP is that you don't need to know the DHCP server's address to acquire an IP address. The domain name for your network is normally not needed, either; it is necessary only if you want to add the computer to the organization's domain.

37. **Answer: C**

Explanation: The Domain Name System (DNS) protocol translates a computer name into an IP address. Whenever you type a web server name such as dprocomputer.com, a DNS server translates that name to its corresponding IP address.

Incorrect answers: Transmission Control Protocol (TCP) is used to send data from one computer to another, using a guaranteed delivery system. An example of a TCP protocol is HTTPS. User Datagram Protocol (UDP), on the other hand, sends data in a streaming format, without the need for guaranteed delivery. An example of UDP would be the streaming of music over the Internet. File Transfer Protocol (FTP) allows you to send files between computers over the Internet.

38. **Answer: B**

Explanation: With cellular WAN, a phone or other mobile device sends data over standard cellular connections.

Incorrect answers: By themselves, none of the other options offer direct connections to the Internet. Infrared is used more often for very short-distance connections, allowing data to be "beamed" from one device to another. Bluetooth is also for short distances, but not as short as for infrared. Bluetooth headsets are commonly used with smartphones. 802.11ac is a Wi-Fi technology for LANs; a newer version is 802.11ax.

39. **Answer: D**

Explanation: 192.168.0.1 is the only suitable gateway address. Remember that the gateway address must be on the same network as the computer. In this case, the network is 192.168.0, as defined by the 255.255.255.0 subnet mask.

Incorrect answers: 192.168.1.100 is on the 192.168.1.0 network, and so is 192.168.1.1. 192.168.10.1 is on the 192.168.10.0 network. Don't forget that a zero at the end of an IP address denotes the network number.

40. Answer: A

Explanation: The service set identifier (SSID) is the name of the wireless network. This is the name you look for when locating a wireless network.

Incorrect answers: WPA, which stands for Wi-Fi Protected Access, is a connectivity protocol for wireless networks. A screened subnet (also known as a demilitarized zone, or DMZ) is an area between a LAN and the Internet that often houses web, email, and FTP servers. Dynamic Host Configuration Protocol (DHCP) is a service that assigns IP addresses automatically to computers and other devices.

41. Answer: C

Explanation: The wireless connection is using the 5 GHz frequency range. 802.11n, 802.11ac, and 802.11ax use the 5 GHz range. Typical channels for Wi-Fi on 5 GHz include 36, 40, 44, 48, 149, 153, 157, 161, and 165.

Incorrect answers: 2.4 GHz is used by Wi-Fi standards such as 802.11b, 802.11g, and 802.11n. (802.11n can use both 2.4 and 5 GHz.) The standard channels for 2.4 GHz Wi-Fi (in the United States) are between 1 and 11. 40 MHz is a common channel width in Wi-Fi networks when channel bonding is incorporated. 13.56 MHz is a standard channel for near-field communication (NFC).

42. Answer: A

Explanation: The LC connector is used with fiber-optic cabling. Other fiber connectors include SC and ST.

Incorrect answers: RJ45 is the connector used by twisted-pair networks. RG-6 is the cable used by cable Internet and TV; an F type connector is attached to the ends of an RG-6 cable. RJ11 is a standard phone line connector.

43. Answer: C

Explanation: The Domain Name System (DNS) protocol uses port 53 by default.

Incorrect answers: FTP uses ports 20/21. SMTP uses port 25 (or 587 or 465). HTTPS uses port 443.

44. Answers: B and D

Explanation: Satellite and cellular are examples of wireless Internet services.

Incorrect answers: Cable Internet, DSL, and fiber optic all use cabled connections.

45. Answer: B

Explanation: A wide area network (WAN) is a network in which two or more local area networks (LANs) are connected over a large geographic distance—for example, between two cities. The WAN requires connections to be provided by a telecommunications or data communications company.

Incorrect answers: A personal area network (PAN) is a small network made up of short-distance devices such as Bluetooth devices. WLAN stands for wireless local area network. This is the name that the IEEE uses for its 802.11 standards. The reason is that the term *Wi-Fi*, though widely used, is copyrighted. A MAN is a metropolitan (or municipal) area network; it can connect two or more LANs but does so in a small city-based area. A storage area network (SAN) is a network of connected storage devices and controllers that typically uses Fibre Channel technology to connect the hosts together.

46. **Answer: A**

    Explanation: Network-attached storage (NAS) devices store data for network use. They connect directly to a network.

    Incorrect answers: Network Address Translation (NAT) is used on routers to connect a group of computers on a private LAN to the Internet by using a single public IP address. NAC, which stands for network access control, is a group of technologies designed to allow or deny access by authenticating users. IaaS, which stands for infrastructure as a service, is a cloud-based technology organizations can use to offload their network infrastructure to a third party. (This is a tougher one to keep you on your toes!)

47. **Answer: C**

    Explanation: Use an RJ45 crimper tool to permanently attach RJ45 plugs to the end of a cable.

    Incorrect answers: You use a tone generator and probe kit to locate individual phone lines, but you can also use such a kit with network lines. (Note that this tool might also be referred to as a toner probe.) The better tool, however, for testing and locating is a continuity cable tester. A multimeter is great for testing AC outlets and for testing wires inside a computer, but it is not often used in networking applications.

48. **Answer: D**

    Explanation: Remote Desktop Protocol (RDP) uses port 3389 by default. This protocol allows one computer to take control of another remote system.

    Incorrect answers: Port 80 is used by HTTP. Port 110 is used by POP3. Port 443 is used by HTTP Secure (or HTTPS), a protocol used during secure web sessions. It is often required that websites use HTTPS over HTTP whenever possible.

49. **Answer: A**

    Explanation: Software-defined networking (SDN) is a technology in which a controlling server defines how data packets are sent through a network. It uses a data plane (for the actual data packets) and a control plane (for the administrative packets). An example of this is OpenFlow.

    Incorrect answers: NIC stands for network interface card. A NIC is the main networking device in a PC or laptop. ONT stands for optical network terminal; it terminates the signal from a fiber-optic provider. MAM stands for mobile application management, which is a centralized solution that can install and update applications on Android and iOS smartphones and tablets.

50. Answer: C

Explanation: A failure that occurs due to the internal feed mechanism stopping is known as a paper jam. For example, an HP LaserJet might show error code 13.1 (or another number) on the display, which means a paper jam at the paper feed area. You should verify that the paper trays are loaded and adjusted properly.

Incorrect answers: A No Connectivity message means that the printer is not currently connected to the network. A corrupt driver loaded on a workstation would cause any print job from that computer either to fail or to print nonsense. A Power Cycle message means that the self-diagnostic program has encountered a problem and is telling you to shut down the printer and turn it back on. Doing so resets the printer, which can fix many of the issues that may occur.

51. Answer: C

Explanation: Search for the volume keys. They usually share two of the function keys, such as F9 for volume down and F10 for volume up. A mute button is usually included as well (for example, F11). Sometimes, the volume may be muted or set to the lowest position (though there might still be a slight audible noise). The volume is usually controlled by pressing the Fn key and the Volume Up or Volume Down key (or mute) simultaneously.

Incorrect answers: Installing a new sound driver isn't necessary yet. Always check the physical volume first, and then check whether the volume is low or the sound is muted in Windows. Tapping the speakers is an interesting idea, but it has no place in this discussion. If a speaker is loose, it often makes scratchy noises; however, speakers rarely become loose on today's laptops. Reinstalling Windows is the last thing you want to do. Check the simple solutions when troubleshooting problems such as no audio or video.

52. Answer: C

Explanation: If the motherboard was just replaced and the system overheats when booted, there's a good chance that thermal paste was not applied to the CPU. When you install a new motherboard, the CPU must be removed from the old board and installed to the new one, or a new CPU needs to be installed. Either way, the heat sink must come off. Whenever a heat sink is connected (or reconnected) to a CPU, thermal paste (also known as thermal compound), or a thermal pad, should be applied; otherwise, CPU overheating can easily occur.

Incorrect answers: The GPU is the video card's processor; it is not possible for the GPU to be incompatible with the CPU. It is possible for the video card to be incompatible with the expansion bus slots on the new motherboard, though. Even if the new motherboard's firmware has not been updated, the system should not overheat. If the case fan fails, the computer should not overheat. The CPU will still have its own fan, and the power supply will still exhaust hot air.

53. Answer: A

Explanation: Laptops have airflow underneath them; if the unit is not on a flat surface, the airflow will be reduced or stopped altogether, leading to component damage.

> **NOTE**
>
> Most laptops have side exhaust as well. Be sure not to cover up any of these vents as doing so could lead to overheating.

Incorrect answers: The freezer is not a good idea because condensation could build up inside the unit. A fan won't do much good unless the laptop is on a flat surface, and although it is plausible to keep the laptop turned off, doing so negates the reason for using the laptop and is not a proper *solution*.

54. **Answers: A and B**

Explanation: Make sure to purchase an AC adapter that is a true replacement. You can find one on the laptop manufacturer's website. When you enter your model number, the website will tell you everything you need to know about current, voltage, and connector type. (These details are also listed on the brick portion of the power adapter.)

Incorrect answers: The battery and AC adapter do need to work in conjunction with each other; because of this, they both need to be compatible with the laptop. The AC adapter does several things, including reducing voltage and converting from AC to DC, but it does not invert the signal. However, there is an inverter in the laptop; it powers the display. This question does not refer to that, but if you are ever troubleshooting an older CCFL display, the inverter type is very important.

55. **Answer: B**

Explanation: The Screen key (also known as the display toggle) is one of the keys available when you use the Fn (Function) key. It enables you to switch between the laptop display and an external display (or use both). The Fn key is used for a variety of secondary functions, including volume, brightness, and wireless toggle.

Incorrect answers: If the display toggle doesn't work, try another external monitor. No other key combinations perform this task.

56. **Answer: B**

Explanation: Laser printers use toner cartridges.

Incorrect answers: Inkjet printers use ink cartridges. Impact printers (for example, dot-matrix printers) use ribbons. Thermal printers use specially coated paper that is heated. 3D printers use plastic/resin filament to build three-dimensional objects.

57. **Answer: C**

Explanation: Laser printers use large amounts of electricity, which could quickly drain the battery of the UPS. A laser printer should be plugged in to its own individual power strip.

Incorrect answers: PCs, monitors, and speakers can be connected to a UPS. In fact, if you want to have continued use (and protection) during a power outage, they should be!

58. Answer: B

Explanation: Print a test page after installation. If the test page prints properly, printing a page in Word should be unnecessary. Besides, you don't know if the computer has Microsoft Word installed.

Incorrect answers: Restarting the spooler is not necessary if the printer has just been installed. The spooler should already be running. If the spooler has failed, that would be a separate troubleshooting scenario. Separator pages are not necessary; they are optional and can be configured in the Printer Properties window.

59. Answer: A

Explanation: When you are printing "duplex," you are printing on both sides of the paper (if the printer has that capability). Some laser printers can do this, but printing this way creates a longer total paper path, which leads to more frequent paper jams.

Incorrect answers: Collation means that documents are printed in a standard order, usually numerically. Full-duplex in networking means that information can be sent and received simultaneously. A printer can have a full-duplex connection to the network, but this question refers to printing in duplex. Printing to file is a process that Windows can perform. Instead of selecting a physical printer when printing a document, Windows prints to a special file and saves that file with a .prn extension to a location of your choice. 1200 dots per inch (DPI) is the print *quality*. The higher the print resolution, the higher the print quality. 600 DPI or higher is considered to be "letter quality."

60. Answer: B

Explanation: Regular paper can be used on all the listed printers except for thermal printers, which use specially coated paper that is heated to create the image.

Incorrect answers: A dot-matrix printer might use tractor-feed paper, but that is standard for many impact printers; it is also still considered regular paper. A laser printer or dot-matrix printer might use two-part paper, but two-part paper isn't necessary for laser printers or dot-matrix printers to operate; thermal printers won't work unless you use specially coated paper. Inkjet printers normally use standard copy paper for printing. Finally, 3D printers use a plastic filament, not paper.

61. Answer: A

Explanation: Of the listed answers, use channel 6 for 802.11 wireless networks. That would imply a 2.4 GHz connection using either 802.11ax, n, g, or b. The 2.4 GHz frequency range in the United States allows for channels 1 through 11.

Incorrect answers: Of these answers, 21 is outside the allowable 2.4 GHz range for any country. (On a separate note, it is a port number used with FTP.) Here, 802 has no meaning other than being the name of the IEEE protocol suite that includes wireless protocols such as 802.11ac. Also, it is far beyond the range of 5 GHz wireless networks, which are between 36 and 165. 8080 is a less commonly used HTTP port.

62. Answer: D

Explanation: Heat is the number-one enemy of a thermal printer. Keeping a thermal printer or thermal paper in a location where the temperature is too high could cause failure of the printer and damage to the paper.

Incorrect answers: Excessive moisture can cause rubber rollers and separation pads to fail over time, especially in laser printers. Electrostatic discharge (ESD) is always a foe—but only if you are working inside the printer. Dirt can clog up the works over time in any device. Heat is by far the most important factor to watch for with thermal printers.

63. Answer: E

Explanation: In the laser printing process, also known as the imaging process, the cleaning stage happens last.

Incorrect answers: The printing process includes the following steps, in this order: processing, charging, exposing, developing, transferring, fusing, and cleaning.

64. Answer: C

Explanation: Impact is a type of impact printer. It uses a printhead to physically impact the ribbon and transfer ink to the paper.

Incorrect answers: Laser printers apply toner to paper through varying voltages. Inkjet printers spray ink from a cartridge onto the paper. Thermal paper is specially coated and forms text when it is heated properly.

65. Answer: C

Explanation: After you install the driver for the printer locally, you can then take control of it by going to the properties of the printer and accessing the Ports tab. Then click the Add Port button and select the Standard TCP/IP Port option. You have to know the IP address of the printer or the computer that the printer is connected to.

Incorrect answers: The Sharing tab enables you to share the printer so that remote users can use it; however, the remote user would then somehow have to connect to the printer. The spool settings can be set so that the computer spools documents before sending pages to the printer, which helps with less powerful printers and printer congestion. Some printers can be accessed via FTP, but usually they are controlled and accessed in another way. Either way, making a connection to the printer is not taking control of the printer.

66. Answer: B

Explanation: After you install a printer, it is important to calibrate it for color and orientation, especially if you are installing a color laser printer or an inkjet printer. These calibration tools are usually built in to the printer's software and can be accessed from Windows, or you can access them from the printer's display.

Incorrect answers: If a toner cartridge needs to be cleaned, it probably has a leak and should be replaced. The fusing assembly needs to be changed only when it fails. Many printers indicate when the fuser is at 20% life and needs to be replaced soon. If the fuser fails, the toner will fail to stick to the paper. The primary corona wire can be cleaned; it is near the drum. Cleaning it can help with other types of print quality problems, such as lines and smearing, though on many printers this is not necessary.

67. Answers: A and C

Explanation: Most laptops have a special function key (for example, F12) that allows you to enable or disable the Wi-Fi connection with a single key press. Also, a wireless network can be "forgotten" in the operating system. If this happens, the laptop has to be reconnected to the wireless network.

Incorrect answers: After you are connected to a network, you can typically use whatever web browser you want, as long as the browser is compatible with the operating system that is in use. Client computers (such as laptops) normally obtain their IP addresses automatically from a DHCP server, so this is not a likely problem.

68. Answer: D

Explanation: The most likely answer in this scenario is that the network cable is disconnected. If the desktop computer is using a wired connection, it is most likely a twisted-pair Ethernet connection. When this cable is connected to the computer on one end and to a switch or another central connecting device on the other end, it initiates a network connection over the physical link. This link then causes the network adapter's link light to light up. The link light is directly next to the RJ45 port of the network adapter. The corresponding port on the switch (or another similar device) is also lit. If the cable is disconnected, the link light becomes unlit, though there are other possibilities for this link light to be dark (for example, if the computer is off or if the switch port is disabled).

Incorrect answers: The Wi-Fi connection might have its own link light (for example, on the front of a laptop), but this is separate from the wired connection link light. Although it is unlikely, a malfunctioning USB controller or port could possibly be the cause of the unlit link light—but only if the computer is using a USB-based network adapter. Normally, the network adapter (and corresponding RJ45 port) on a PC is either integrated into the motherboard or is installed as a PCIe x1 adapter card. If the system doesn't run the POST properly, it usually indicates a problem with the RAM, video, or other primary component of the system. Generally, a network adapter does not cause a failure during POST.

69. Answer: C

Explanation: If the computer fails to obtain an IP address from a DHCP server, Windows takes over and uses Automatic Private IP Addressing (APIPA). This address will be on the 169.254.0.0 network. APIPA is a type of link-local addressing.

Incorrect answers: All of the other addresses could possibly be obtained from a DHCP server. 172.16.10.10, 192.168.0.10, and 192.168.10.10 are all private IP addresses that could typically be obtained through DHCP.

70. Answer: A

Explanation: Case fans are measured in mm (millimeters); 80 mm and especially 120 mm are very common sizes. A case fan is used to exhaust heat out of the case. Case fans aid in keeping the CPU and other devices cool. The 120 mm is quite common in desktop and tower PCs, and the 80 mm is more common in smaller systems and 1U and 2U rackmount servers.

Incorrect answers: A CPU typically uses a heat sink/fan combination. However, the two are often connected. Memory modules don't use fans, but they can be equipped (or purchased) with heat sinks of their own.

71. **Answer: A**

   Explanation: If you see an exclamation point in Device Manager, it indicates that the device does not have a proper driver. Right-click the device in Device Manager and select Update Driver or install the driver directly from the manufacturer's website.

   Incorrect answers: If the device is disabled, it will have a down arrow next to it. If a driver was not digitally signed, the device might show up in the Unknown Devices category until it is installed properly. If a device has a working driver, upgrading it will be up to you, but you won't necessarily be notified that the driver needs to be upgraded. This question may seem more like a 220-1102 question, but you have to be prepared for some overlap. Remember that some of the concepts of the 220-1101 and the 220-1102 exams are heavily intertwined!

72. **Answer: C**

   Explanation: As the power-on self-test (POST) checks all the components of the computer, it may present its findings on the screen or in the form of beep codes. The POST is a part of the BIOS/UEFI.

   Incorrect answers: The complementary metal-oxide semiconductor (CMOS) stores information such as time and date and BIOS/UEFI passwords. RTC stands for real-time clock; it is the device that keeps time on the motherboard. Windows generates all kinds of error codes but not beep codes. The beep codes come from the POST, which happens before Windows boots.

73. **Answer: C**

   Explanation: The RJ45 jack enables a connection to a twisted-pair (most likely Ethernet) network. A printer with a built-in RJ45 connector is network ready; so is a printer that is Wi-Fi enabled.

   Incorrect answers: RJ11 ports are used by modems and dial-up Internet connections. If a printer has an RJ11 port, it is a multifunction printer acting as a fax machine. USB is the standard port for a printer; it allows the printer to connect to a PC or to a print server. SCSI connectors are not often found on today's printers; such a connector indicates a local connection, not a network connection.

74. **Answer: A**

   Explanation: The fuser heats paper to around 400° Fahrenheit (204° Celsius), which is comparable to the heat of an oven. If you need to replace the fuser, let the printer sit for 10 or 15 minutes after shutting it down and before performing maintenance.

   Incorrect answers: The fuser is not wet or fragile, and it does not contain toner; the cartridge contains toner.

75. Answer: D

Explanation: USB-C can transmit audio, video, and data over one cable. That means it can be used for a variety of peripherals, including monitors.

Incorrect answers: The other three connectors, HDMI, DVI, and DisplayPort, are all video connectors. HDMI and DisplayPort can transmit audio and video (but not data), and DVI sends video only. (Note that VGA sends video only as well.)

76. Answer: B

Explanation: Set up a hotspot on the smartphone. Because the phone has access to the Internet (perhaps a 4G or 5G connection), that connection can be used. Creating a hotspot activates the smartphone's ability to run a wireless network. Then the laptop can simply connect to that Wi-Fi network, and Internet access will pass through the smartphone.

Incorrect answers: Preferred roaming list (PRL) updates are important to have on a smartphone so that the device knows what frequency bands and service providers should be scanned. The Global Positioning System (GPS) is a worldwide system of satellites, towers, and other devices that can locate a device and provide for navigation. A Power over Ethernet (PoE) injector allows for a single device to be powered by way of the network connection; it's handy if there is no AC outlet near the device.

77. Answer: A

Explanation: A unified threat management (UTM) appliance is one that does the work of several security devices. A UTM typically acts as a firewall, router, packet analyzer, and virus scanner, among other functions.

Incorrect answers: A DHCP server is used to automatically assign IP addresses to client computers over the network. A proxy server is used to cache and filter connections to the Internet (HTTPS, FTP, and so on). An intrusion detection system (IDS) appliance is used to detect whether an attacker has attempted to infiltrate a network or an individual device. If the appliance is used on the network, it is known as a network-based IDS (NIDS). If it is installed for a single system, it is known as a host-based IDS (HIDS). Going further, an intrusion *prevention* system (IPS) can detect malicious packets as well as prevent them from entering the network (or individual system).

78. Answer: C

Explanation: The service set identifier (SSID) is the most important piece of information required to connect to a wireless network; it is the name of the wireless network.

Incorrect answers: The wireless channel number isn't necessarily needed as the wireless access point (WAP) might autonegotiate the channel. Also, MAC address filtering is not enabled by default, so the MAC address might not be needed. (In fact, the admin would enter this at the WAP, not from the client computer.) You need the administrator password only if you want to make configuration changes to the wireless access point. For example, if you want to implement MAC filtering, you have to log in to the WAP with an admin password to configure it.

79. Answer: D

Explanation: I/O bandwidth is the most critical of the resources listed in the question. When you are considering file storage and file synchronization, you need to know the maximum input/output operations per second (IOPS) that the cloud provider can deliver. (Get actual reports of previous customers as proof!) IOPS gives you a concrete measurement of data that you can use for analysis.

Incorrect answers: Disk speed is not enough for the planning of file storage. Plus, it might not even be a factor if the cloud provider is using SSDs, NVMEs, and so on. RAM and CPU utilization percentages are important, but they become more vital if you will be working with virtual machines. It's also important to monitor these percentages regularly.

80. Answer: B

Explanation: The power management settings on a laptop can cause the display to automatically dim when the AC adapter is unplugged. In fact, this is the default on many laptops to conserve battery power. These settings can be configured within Power Options in Windows.

Incorrect answers: You can certainly set the display to full brightness when on battery power; doing so just isn't recommended. Laptops can operate properly when connected to the AC power adapter or when using the battery only. The display brightness of a laptop isn't affected by any security settings.

Great Job So Far!

You have completed the first 220-1101 practice exam. This is the easiest of the three 220-1101 practice exams. If you did not get 90% of the answers correct on this exam, I recommend that you study further before doing anything else. If you did answer 90% or better, then take a break before continuing on!

CHAPTER THREE

220-1101 Practice Exam B

Now let's kick it up a notch. This second 220-1101 exam could be considered an intermediate practice test. I've mixed in some more difficult questions this time. You may have noticed that the first exam had some questions grouped together by A+ domain. This exam is more random.

Again, the goal here is to make sure you understand all of the concepts before moving on to the next test. If you didn't take a break already, I suggest taking one between exams. If you just completed the first exam, give yourself a half hour or so before you begin this one. If you didn't score 90% or higher on Exam A do some more studying and then retake Exam A until you pass with a 90% or higher score.

> **NOTE**
>
> If you feel that you are having trouble with more than 25% of the concepts covered on this exam and the first exam, I suggest that you purchase *CompTIA A+ Core 1 (220-1101) and Core 2 (220-1102) Exam Cram* or even consider taking a hands-on A+ course before continuing with this book.

Write down your answers and check them against the answer key that immediately follows the exam. After the answer key, you will find explanations for all of the answers. Good luck!

Practice Questions

1. Which of the following servers is responsible for resolving a name such as dprocomputer.com to its corresponding IP address?

   Quick Answer: **63**
   Detailed Answer: **64**

   - ○ **A.** Web server
   - ○ **B.** FTP server
   - ○ **C.** DNS server
   - ○ **D.** Proxy server
   - ○ **E.** Syslog server

2. Which of the following statements describe advantages of using Dynamic Host Configuration Protocol (DHCP)? (Select the two best answers.)

   Quick Answer: **63**
   Detailed Answer: **64**

   - ❏ **A.** IP addresses can be managed from a central location.
   - ❏ **B.** The network speed can automatically adjust based on the type of traffic being generated.
   - ❏ **C.** The hosts file on the computer can be validated for proper entries.
   - ❏ **D.** Media access control addresses can be changed.
   - ❏ **E.** Computers can automatically get new addressing when moved to different network segments.

3. Which of the following storage technologies is used by hard disk drives?

   Quick Answer: **63**
   Detailed Answer: **64**

   - ○ **A.** Magnetic
   - ○ **B.** Optical
   - ○ **C.** Impact
   - ○ **D.** Solid state

4. A business owner wants to provide the following for laptop users:

   Quick Answer: **63**
   Detailed Answer: **64**

   - ▶ Security
   - ▶ Ability to charge their devices
   - ▶ Ability to access corporate LAN resources
   - ▶ Hardware and peripheral connectivity

Which of the following devices would be the best solution?

○ **A.** Thunderbolt

○ **B.** USB hub

○ **C.** Docking station

○ **D.** Thin client

○ **E.** Cable lock

5. A client brings in a printer that is giving a paper-feed error. Which of the following is the most likely cause?

Quick Answer: **63**
Detailed Answer: **65**

○ **A.** The separation pad

○ **B.** The developing rollers

○ **C.** The paper tray

○ **D.** The pickup rollers

6. Which protocol uses port 389?

Quick Answer: **63**
Detailed Answer: **65**

○ **A.** SMTP

○ **B.** POP3

○ **C.** LDAP

○ **D.** HTTPS

7. What is the maximum distance at which a Class 2 Bluetooth device can receive signals from a Bluetooth access point?

Quick Answer: **63**
Detailed Answer: **65**

○ **A.** 100 meters

○ **B.** 10 meters

○ **C.** 5 meters

○ **D.** 1 meter

8. Which of the following wireless networking standards operates at 5 GHz only? (Select the two best answers.)

Quick Answer: **63**
Detailed Answer: **65**

❑ **A.** 802.11a

❑ **B.** 802.11b

❑ **C.** 802.11g

❑ **D.** 802.11n

❑ **E.** 802.11ac

9. Which of the following types of RAM has a peak transfer rate of 21,333 MB/s?

- ○ **A.** DDR4-2133
- ○ **B.** DDR4-2400
- ○ **C.** DDR4-2666
- ○ **D.** DDR5-4800

Quick Answer: **63**
Detailed Answer: **66**

10. Which of the following types of printers uses a printhead, ribbon, and tractor feed?

- ○ **A.** Laser
- ○ **B.** Impact
- ○ **C.** Inkjet
- ○ **D.** Thermal

Quick Answer: **63**
Detailed Answer: **66**

11. Several users on your network are reporting that a network printer, which is controlled by a print server, is not printing. What is the first action you should take to fix the problem?

- ○ **A.** Have the affected users restart their computers.
- ○ **B.** Replace the USB cable.
- ○ **C.** Clear the print queue.
- ○ **D.** Reinstall the printer drivers on the affected users' computers.

Quick Answer: **63**
Detailed Answer: **66**

12. Which of the following is a possible symptom of a failing CPU?

- ○ **A.** CPU is beyond the recommended voltage range.
- ○ **B.** Computer won't boot.
- ○ **C.** BIOS/UEFI reports low temperatures within the case.
- ○ **D.** Spyware is installed in the browser.

Quick Answer: **63**
Detailed Answer: **67**

13. Which of the following cable types is not affected by EMI but requires specialized tools for installation?

- ○ **A.** Cat 6
- ○ **B.** STP
- ○ **C.** Fiber optic
- ○ **D.** Coaxial

Quick Answer: **63**
Detailed Answer: **67**

14. Setting an administrator password in the BIOS/UEFI accomplishes which of the following?

    ○ **A.** Prevents a user from rearranging the boot order

    ○ **B.** Prevents a user from reading email

    ○ **C.** Prevents a virus from infecting the MBR

    ○ **D.** Prevents an attacker from opening the case

15. Which of the following functions is performed by the external power supply of a laptop?

    ○ **A.** Increases voltage

    ○ **B.** Stores power

    ○ **C.** Converts DC power to AC power

    ○ **D.** Converts AC power to DC power

16. What type of printer driver should you install for a Windows user who needs to print general office documents?

    ○ **A.** PCL

    ○ **B.** PostScript

    ○ **C.** ADF

    ○ **D.** AirPrint

17. Which of the following describes an LCD display's contrast ratio?

    ○ **A.** Power consumption

    ○ **B.** Display resolution and brightness

    ○ **C.** The brightest and darkest outputs

    ○ **D.** Power savings

18. Which of the following tools can protect you in the event of a surge?

    ○ **A.** Torx screwdriver

    ○ **B.** Antistatic strap

    ○ **C.** Voltmeter

    ○ **D.** Antistatic mat

19. Which of the following connectors can have audio *and* video pass through it?

    ○ **A.** VGA

    ○ **B.** RGB

    ○ **C.** DVI

    ○ **D.** HDMI

20. Which of the following devices limits network broadcasts, segments IP address ranges, and interconnects different physical media?

Quick Answer: **63**
Detailed Answer: **69**

- ○ **A.** Switch
- ○ **B.** WAP
- ○ **C.** Firewall
- ○ **D.** Router

21. Many users forget one or more passwords to corporate applications on their mobile devices. You are tasked with creating a simple yet secure solution that will reduce help desk tickets. Which of the following should you do?

Quick Answer: **63**
Detailed Answer: **69**

- ○ **A.** Set up MFA
- ○ **B.** Configure biometric authentication
- ○ **C.** Implement single sign-on
- ○ **D.** Remove password complexity requirements

22. You just upgraded the CPU. Which of the following issues can make your computer shut down automatically after a few minutes? (Select the best answer.)

Quick Answer: **63**
Detailed Answer: **70**

- ○ **A.** The wrong CPU driver is being used.
- ○ **B.** The voltage to the CPU is incorrect.
- ○ **C.** The incorrect CPU has been installed.
- ○ **D.** The CPU has overheated.

23. Which of the following is a valid IPv4 address for a networked host?

Quick Answer: **63**
Detailed Answer: **70**

- ○ **A.** 127.0.0.1
- ○ **B.** 169.254.0.0/16
- ○ **C.** 172.17.58.254
- ○ **D.** 255.10.15.7

24. You want to upgrade memory in your computer. Which of the following is user-replaceable memory in a PC?

Quick Answer: **63**
Detailed Answer: **70**

- ○ **A.** CMOS
- ○ **B.** BIOS
- ○ **C.** DRAM
- ○ **D.** SRAM
- ○ **E.** ROM

25. Which of the following IP addresses is private?

    ○ **A.** 11.58.254.169

    ○ **B.** 169.255.10.41

    ○ **C.** 172.31.1.1

    ○ **D.** 192.169.0.1

Quick Answer: **63**
Detailed Answer: **71**

26. Which of the following is the local loopback IPv6 address?

    ○ **A.** 127.0.0.1

    ○ **B.** ::1

    ○ **C.** 192.168.0.0

    ○ **D.** FE80::/10

Quick Answer: **63**
Detailed Answer: **71**

27. Which of the following statements concerning IPv6 addresses is correct?

    ○ **A.** They cannot be used with IPv4.

    ○ **B.** They are supported by all routers.

    ○ **C.** They represent addressing using 128 bits.

    ○ **D.** They require fiber-optic connections.

Quick Answer: **63**
Detailed Answer: **71**

28. You are working at a DNS server and see the following entry:

```
server1.example.com        IN      10.0.0.1
```

What kind of entry is this?

    ○ **A.** MX record

    ○ **B.** A record

    ○ **C.** AAAA record

    ○ **D.** TXT record

Quick Answer: **63**
Detailed Answer: **71**

29. Which of the following printer technologies should be used to print payroll checks on paper forms that have a carbon backing?

    ○ **A.** Impact

    ○ **B.** Laser

    ○ **C.** Inkjet

    ○ **D.** Thermal

Quick Answer: **63**
Detailed Answer: **71**

30. Which of the following is *not* a configuration that can be made in the BIOS/UEFI?

- ○ **A.** Boot sequence
- ○ **B.** Temperature thresholds
- ○ **C.** Overclocking
- ○ **D.** Driver installation
- ○ **E.** Intrusion detection

Quick Answer: **63**
Detailed Answer: **72**

31. Which of the following traits and port numbers are associated with POP3? (Select the two best answers.)

- ❏ **A.** Receives inbound email on port 110
- ❏ **B.** Receives inbound email on port 25
- ❏ **C.** Sends outbound email on port 110
- ❏ **D.** Sends outbound email on port 25
- ❏ **E.** Receives inbound email on port 995
- ❏ **F.** Sends outbound email on port 587

Quick Answer: **63**
Detailed Answer: **72**

32. Which type of cable should be used to connect a laptop directly to a PC?

- ○ **A.** Cat 6 patch cable
- ○ **B.** Parallel cable
- ○ **C.** Rolled cable
- ○ **D.** Cat 5e crossover cable

Quick Answer: **63**
Detailed Answer: **72**

33. To perform a network installation of Windows, which of the following must be supported by the computer's network interface card?

- ○ **A.** PXE
- ○ **B.** PCIe
- ○ **C.** PCL
- ○ **D.** PnP

Quick Answer: **63**
Detailed Answer: **72**

34. Which of the following devices is the least likely to be replaced on a laptop?

- ○ **A.** CPU
- ○ **B.** RAM
- ○ **C.** M.2 card
- ○ **D.** Keyboard

Quick Answer: **63**
Detailed Answer: **73**

35. If your "bandwidth" is 1000 Mbps, how many bits are you sending/receiving? (Select the two best answers.)

Quick Answer: **63**
Detailed Answer: **73**

- ❏ **A.** 100,000,000 bits per minute
- ❏ **B.** 1000 bits per second
- ❏ **C.** 1,000,000,000 bits per second
- ❏ **D.** 1 gigabit per second

36. Which of the following can send data the farthest?

Quick Answer: **63**
Detailed Answer: **73**

- ◯ **A.** Multi-mode fiber
- ◯ **B.** Single-mode fiber
- ◯ **C.** STP
- ◯ **D.** Coaxial

37. You need to expand the peripherals of a computer, but the system doesn't have enough ports. Which type of card should be installed?

Quick Answer: **63**
Detailed Answer: **73**

- ◯ **A.** Modem
- ◯ **B.** Network adapter
- ◯ **C.** USB card
- ◯ **D.** TV tuner card

38. Which of the following is the typical speed of an SATA hard disk drive?

Quick Answer: **63**
Detailed Answer: **73**

- ◯ **A.** 1000 Mbps
- ◯ **B.** 3.1 GHz
- ◯ **C.** 32 GB
- ◯ **D.** 7200 RPM

39. Which of the following best describes the differences between a switch and a router?

Quick Answer: **63**
Detailed Answer: **74**

- ◯ **A.** A switch interconnects devices on the same network so that they can communicate; a router interconnects one or more networks.
- ◯ **B.** A router broadcasts all data packets that are sent on the network; a switch transmits data directly to a device.
- ◯ **C.** A switch broadcasts all data packets that are sent on the network; a router transmits data directly to a device.
- ◯ **D.** A switch interconnects one or more networks; a router interconnects devices on a network.

40. A group of users in ABC Corp. needs to back up a terabyte of data daily. The data must be stored on durable backup media. Which of the following is the best media for this scenario?

- ○ **A.** DVD
- ○ **B.** RAID 5
- ○ **C.** USB flash drive
- ○ **D.** LTO

41. The organization you work for has three locations within a city that need to be networked together. The network requirement for all three locations is a minimum data throughput of 1 Gbps. Which of the following network types are most likely to be used for internal office and office-to-office communications? (Select the two best answers.)

- ❑ **A.** LAN
- ❑ **B.** PAN
- ❑ **C.** WAN
- ❑ **D.** MAN
- ❑ **E.** SAN
- ❑ **F.** WLAN

42. Which of the following is a popular maker of virtualization software?

- ○ **A.** VDI
- ○ **B.** IaaS
- ○ **C.** Metered utilization
- ○ **D.** VMware

43. You need to replace and upgrade the memory card in a smartphone. Which type of memory is most likely used by the smartphone?

- ○ **A.** SSD
- ○ **B.** NVMe
- ○ **C.** USB flash drive
- ○ **D.** SD

44. You want to use four 16 GB memory modules in your new desktop computer, and you want the RAM to work simultaneously. What kind of technology does your motherboard need to have?

- ○ **A.** DDR
- ○ **B.** SODIMM
- ○ **C.** Quad-channel
- ○ **D.** ECC

45. You are repairing a laser printer because narrow, faded lines run the length of the printed pages. The faded lines are always in the same place. What should you do to fix the problem?

   ○ **A.** Replace the toner cartridge

   ○ **B.** Update the firmware

   ○ **C.** Replace the corona wire

   ○ **D.** Refill the ink cartridge

Quick Answer: **63**
Detailed Answer: **75**

46. Which of the following tools should be used to test a 24-pin ATX 12 V power connector?

   ○ **A.** Torx screwdriver

   ○ **B.** PSU tester

   ○ **C.** Receptacle tester

   ○ **D.** Tone and probe kit

Quick Answer: **63**
Detailed Answer: **76**

47. One of the technicians at your organization is researching various hardware for a new virtualization host. The host's main purpose is to run multiple Linux server virtual machines simultaneously, with good performance for each VM. Which of the following will best ensure good performance?

   ○ **A.** Integrated GPU

   ○ **B.** Liquid cooling

   ○ **C.** Overclocking

   ○ **D.** x86

   ○ **E.** Multicore

Quick Answer: **63**
Detailed Answer: **76**

48. During a mandatory server room inspection, it was found that a couple of server racks were not properly grounded. To pass the inspection and to protect equipment, you must make sure all racks are properly grounded. Which of the following tools should you use in this scenario?

   ○ **A.** Cable tester

   ○ **B.** Tone generator

   ○ **C.** Multimeter

   ○ **D.** Loopback plug

   ○ **E.** Voltmeter

   ○ **F.** SCADA

Quick Answer: **63**
Detailed Answer: **76**

49. Which of the following does a laptop have that a tablet does not have?

- ○ **A.** Touchpad
- ○ **B.** Display
- ○ **C.** Keyboard
- ○ **D.** Wireless network adapter

50. At the beginning of the workday, a user informs you that her computer is not working. When you examine the computer, you notice that nothing is on the display. Which of the following should be done first?

- ○ **A.** Check whether the monitor is connected to the computer.
- ○ **B.** Check whether the monitor is on.
- ○ **C.** Check whether the computer is plugged in.
- ○ **D.** Reinstall the video driver.

51. A customer reports that when his computer is turned on, the screen is blank except for some text and a flashing cursor. He also tells you that there are numbers counting upward when the computer beeps and then freezes. Which of the following is the most likely cause of this problem?

- ○ **A.** The computer has faulty memory.
- ○ **B.** There is a corrupt MBR.
- ○ **C.** The OS is corrupted.
- ○ **D.** The computer is attempting to boot off the network.

52. A computer was working fine for weeks, but now it has suddenly stopped connecting to the Internet. You run the command **ipconfig** and see that the IP address the computer is using is 169.254.50.68. Which of the following statements describes the most likely issue?

- ○ **A.** The computer cannot access the DHCP server.
- ○ **B.** The computer cannot access the POP3 server.
- ○ **C.** The computer cannot access the DNS server.
- ○ **D.** The computer cannot access the AAA server.

53. Which of the following could cause faded print on the paper outputted by a laser printer?

- ○ **A.** Transfer corona wire
- ○ **B.** Primary corona wire
- ○ **C.** Pickup rollers
- ○ **D.** Photosensitive drum
- ○ **E.** Fuser assembly

54. Mary installed a new sound card and speakers; however, she cannot get any sound from the speakers. Which of the following statements describe the most likely cause? (Select all that apply.)

❏ **A.** The speaker power is not plugged in.

❏ **B.** The sound card driver is not installed.

❏ **C.** The sound card is plugged in to the wrong slot.

❏ **D.** The speaker connector is in the wrong jack.

55. A laptop with an integrated 802.11 WLAN card is unable to connect to any wireless networks. Just yesterday the laptop was able to connect to wireless networks. Which of the following statements describes the most likely cause?

○ **A.** The wireless card drivers are not installed.

○ **B.** The wireless card is disabled in BIOS.

○ **C.** The wireless card firmware requires an update.

○ **D.** The wireless hardware button is turned off.

56. The IP address of example.com is 93.184.216.34. You can ping that IP address, but you cannot ping the name example.com. Which of the following statements describes the most likely cause?

○ **A.** example.com is down.

○ **B.** The DHCP server is down.

○ **C.** The DNS server is down.

○ **D.** The AD DS server is down.

57. A newly built computer runs through the POST, but it doesn't recognize the specific CPU that was just installed. Instead, it recognizes the CPU as a generic CPU. Which of the following is the first thing you should check?

○ **A.** Whether the CPU is seated properly

○ **B.** The version of the firmware for the motherboard

○ **C.** Whether it is the correct CPU for the motherboard

○ **D.** The version of Windows installed

58. Which of the following commands displays a network interface card's MAC address?

○ **A.** ping

○ **B.** ipconfig /all

○ **C.** ipconfig

○ **D.** ipconfig /release

59. A customer reports that print jobs sent to a local printer are printing as blank pieces of paper. Which of the following can help you determine the cause?

Quick Answer: **63**
Detailed Answer: **79**

- ○ **A.** Reload the printer drivers.
- ○ **B.** Stop and restart the print spooler.
- ○ **C.** Replace the printer cable.
- ○ **D.** Print an internal test page.

60. Signal strength for a laptop's wireless connection is low (yellow in color and only one bar). The laptop is on the first floor of a house. The wireless access point (WAP) is in the basement. Which of the following can improve signal strength? (Select the two best answers.)

Quick Answer: **63**
Detailed Answer: **79**

- ❏ **A.** Increase the signal strength from low to high.
- ❏ **B.** Move the WAP from the basement to the first floor.
- ❏ **C.** Download the latest driver for the NIC.
- ❏ **D.** Download the latest BIOS/UEFI for the laptop.

61. You are troubleshooting a computer that can't communicate with other computers on the network. The **ipconfig** command shows an APIPA IP address (169.254.21.184). What is the most likely problem?

Quick Answer: **63**
Detailed Answer: **80**

- ○ **A.** DNS resolution
- ○ **B.** Duplicate IP address
- ○ **C.** DHCP failure
- ○ **D.** Cleared ARP cache

62. Which of the following is the first thing you should check when a computer cannot get on the Internet?

Quick Answer: **63**
Detailed Answer: **80**

- ○ **A.** NIC driver
- ○ **B.** Disk defrag
- ○ **C.** Patch cable
- ○ **D.** Firewall settings

63. You have just built a PC, and when it first boots, you hear some beep codes. If you don't have the codes memorized, which of the following are the best devices to examine first? (Select the two best answers.)

Quick Answer: **63**
Detailed Answer: **80**

- ❏ **A.** RAM
- ❏ **B.** Storage drive
- ❏ **C.** Video card
- ❏ **D.** CPU

64. A customer reports a problem with a PC located in the same room as cement testing equipment. The room appears to have adequate cooling. The PC will boot up but locks up after 5–10 minutes of use. After a lockup, it will not reboot immediately. Which the following statements best describes the most likely problem?

    ○ **A.** The PC has a virus.

    ○ **B.** The PC air intakes are clogged with cement dust.

    ○ **C.** The CPU heat sink is underrated for the CPU.

    ○ **D.** The power supply is underrated for the electrical load of the PC.

Quick Answer: **63**
Detailed Answer: **80**

65. A coworker needs to print to a printer from a laptop running Windows. The printer has USB and Ethernet connectors. Which of the following is the easiest way to connect the printer directly to the laptop?

    ○ **A.** Use the Thunderbolt port.

    ○ **B.** Use the network connection.

    ○ **C.** Use the USB connector.

    ○ **D.** Use the Ethernet connector.

Quick Answer: **63**
Detailed Answer: **81**

66. You have had several support requests related to a PC located in a school cafeteria kitchen that is experiencing problems. You have already reseated the PCIe and PCI cards and replaced the storage drive in the PC. Computers located in the business office or the classrooms have not had the same problem as the computer in the cafeteria. Which of the following is the most likely issue?

    ○ **A.** Excessive heat

    ○ **B.** Faulty RAM

    ○ **C.** 240 V outlets

    ○ **D.** Under-voltage events

Quick Answer: **63**
Detailed Answer: **81**

67. A telecommuter complains that his network interface card (NIC) is not functioning and has no link lights. The user often works from home on a screened porch. The weather has been changing drastically over the past few days, and humidity and temperature have been rising and falling every day. Which of the following could be the direct cause of this problem? (Select the best answer.)

    ○ **A.** Thermal expansion and contraction

    ○ **B.** Thermal sublimation

    ○ **C.** Chip creep

    ○ **D.** POST errors

Quick Answer: **63**
Detailed Answer: **81**

68. Which network type enables high-speed data communication and is the most difficult to eavesdrop on?

- ○ **A.** Satellite
- ○ **B.** DSL
- ○ **C.** Fiber optic
- ○ **D.** Cable

Quick Answer: **63**
Detailed Answer: **82**

69. Which of the following properties of a heat sink has the greatest effect on heat dissipation?

- ○ **A.** Connection type
- ○ **B.** Shape
- ○ **C.** Surface area
- ○ **D.** Proximity to the power supply

Quick Answer: **63**
Detailed Answer: **82**

70. A home customer wants to run several IoT devices, including a Wi-Fi thermostat, a doorbell camera, and a mobile robot. The customer has read articles that say many IoT devices are insecure out of the box. The customer is concerned and does not want smartphones or PCs to be "hacked." What can you do to help in this situation? (Select the two best answers.)

- ❏ **A.** Upgrade the firmware of the SOHO router.
- ❏ **B.** Disable wireless access on the IoT devices.
- ❏ **C.** Enable the SSID for the wireless network.
- ❏ **D.** Place the IoT devices on a guest network.
- ❏ **E.** Disable MAC filtering.

Quick Answer: **63**
Detailed Answer: **82**

71. Your boss can receive email but can't seem to send email with the installed email client software. Which protocol is not configured properly?

- ○ **A.** SMTP
- ○ **B.** POP3
- ○ **C.** FTP
- ○ **D.** HTTPS

Quick Answer: **63**
Detailed Answer: **82**

72. Which of the following technologies can be used for wireless payments? (Select the two best answers.)

- ❏ **A.** RFID
- ❏ **B.** Bluetooth
- ❏ **C.** 5G
- ❏ **D.** NFC

Quick Answer: **63**
Detailed Answer: **82**

73. One of your customers is running Windows on a PC that has a 3.0-GHz CPU, 16-GB RAM, and an integrated video card. The customer tells you that performance is slow when editing video files. Which of the following solutions would increase performance on the computer?

    ○ **A.** Increasing system RAM

    ○ **B.** Upgrading the video card

    ○ **C.** Increasing the storage drive capacity

    ○ **D.** Upgrading the CPU

Quick Answer: **63**
Detailed Answer: **83**

74. Which of the following are configured in the BIOS/UEFI? (Select the four best answers.)

    ❏ **A.** Time and date

    ❏ **B.** The registry

    ❏ **C.** Boot sequence

    ❏ **D.** Passwords

    ❏ **E.** USB drivers

    ❏ **F.** WOL

Quick Answer: **63**
Detailed Answer: **83**

75. You want to test whether IPv4 *and* IPv6 are working properly on a computer. Which of the following commands should be issued?

    ○ **A.** **ipconfig ::1** and **ping ::1**

    ○ **B.** **ping 127.0.0.0** and **ping :1**

    ○ **C.** **ping 127.0.0.1** and **ping ::1**

    ○ **D.** **ipconfig 127.0.0.1** and **ping 127::1**

Quick Answer: **63**
Detailed Answer: **83**

76. Which of the following is the typical latency of an SATA hard disk drive?

    ○ **A.** 600 MB/s

    ○ **B.** 10,000 RPM

    ○ **C.** 64 MB

    ○ **D.** 4.2 ms

Quick Answer: **63**
Detailed Answer: **83**

77. The marketing printer in an organization has been used for four years. Which of the following is a best practice for ensuring that the printer remains in good working order?

    ○ **A.** You should clean the printer.

    ○ **B.** You should install a maintenance kit.

    ○ **C.** You should clear the counter.

    ○ **D.** You should print a test page.

Quick Answer: **63**
Detailed Answer: **84**

78. Your organization is planning a technology refresh on all mobile phones and PCs in the marketing department. A marketing manager is concerned that personal data on the smartphone, such as contacts, pictures, and videos, will be replaced. In an effort to save the data without compromising security, which of the following should be performed before a device is refreshed?

- ○ **A.** Synchronize the device to a flash drive at a remote location.
- ○ **B.** Synchronize the data across the network to a shared public folder.
- ○ **C.** Synchronize the data to a VM in the company's data center.
- ○ **D.** Synchronize the device to a private cloud.

79. You are troubleshooting a computer that is no longer able to browse the Internet. The user says that the computer worked before he went on vacation. Now the user is able to navigate the local intranet but cannot connect to any outside sites. You ping a well-known website on the Internet by name, but you receive no replies. Then you ping the website's IP address, and you do receive a reply. Which of the following commands will fix the problem?

- ○ **A.** ipconfig /flushdns
- ○ **B.** ipconfig /all
- ○ **C.** ipconfig /release
- ○ **D.** ipconfig /setclassid

80. Which of the following units is used to measure TDP?

- ○ **A.** Volts
- ○ **B.** Watts
- ○ **C.** Ohms
- ○ **D.** Amps

Quick-Check Answer Key

1. C	**28.** B	**55.** D
2. A and E	**29.** A	**56.** C
3. A	**30.** D	**57.** B
4. C	**31.** A and E	**58.** B
5. D	**32.** D	**59.** D
6. C	**33.** A	**60.** A and B
7. B	**34.** A	**61.** C
8. A and E	**35.** C and D	**62.** C
9. C	**36.** B	**63.** A and C
10. B	**37.** C	**64.** B
11. C	**38.** D	**65.** C
12. A	**39.** A	**66.** A
13. C	**40.** D	**67.** A
14. A	**41.** A and D	**68.** C
15. D	**42.** D	**69.** C
16. A	**43.** D	**70.** A and D
17. C	**44.** C	**71.** A
18. B	**45.** A	**72.** A and D
19. D	**46.** B	**73.** B
20. D	**47.** E	**74.** A, C, D, and F
21. C	**48.** C	**75.** C
22. D	**49.** A	**76.** D
23. C	**50.** B	**77.** B
24. C	**51.** A	**78.** D
25. C	**52.** A	**79.** A
26. B	**53.** D	**80.** B
27. C	**54.** A, B, and D	

Answers and Explanations

1. Answer: C

Explanation: A Domain Name System (DNS) server is responsible for resolving (or converting) hostnames and domain names to their corresponding IP addresses. To see this in action, open the command line and try connecting to a domain (such as dprocomputer.com) and run the command **ping**, **tracert** (or **traceroute** in Linux and macOS), **nslookup**, or **dig** (or all of those) against the domain name. These commands can supply you with the IP address of the host. Remember, it is important to practice in a hands-on manner on real computers to reinforce your knowledge!

Incorrect answers: A web server is in charge of storing websites and presenting them to users on the Internet or an intranet. File Transfer Protocol (FTP) servers are used to upload and download files. A proxy server facilitates web page caching for client computers. A syslog server is used to send out log file information of networking devices in real time to an administrator's workstation for analysis. Know your server roles!

2. Answers: A and E

Explanation: Advantages of using DHCP include the following: IP addresses can be managed from a central location, and computers can automatically get new addressing when moved to a different network segment (perhaps one that uses a different DHCP server).

Incorrect answers: Quality of service (QoS) can be used to adjust the network speed based on the type of traffic generated. DHCP has nothing to do with the hosts.txt file, which contains static entries of hostname-to-IP address conversions. Media access control addresses are usually not changed on a network adapter, although they can be masked. MAC filtering maintains a list of MAC addresses that are allowed to access a network, but once again, this is a different concept from DHCP.

3. Answer: A

Explanation: Hard disk drives (HDDs) are magnetic disks and have moving parts. In contrast, solid-state drives (SSDs) have no moving parts.

Incorrect answers: Examples of optical drives include CD, DVD, and Blu-ray drives. Impact refers to a type of printer, such as a dot-matrix or daisywheel printer. A solid-state drive does not have a *disk* and therefore has no moving parts, is quiet, and works as fast as (if not faster than) a traditional magnetic hard drive. However, an SSD can be more expensive per byte than a magnetic-based hard disk drive.

4. Answer: C

Explanation: Use docking stations for the laptops in this scenario. A docking station stays at the user's desk, and the laptop can be plugged, or "docked," right into the station. Docking stations can provide security because they often have locking capability. They also have the ability to charge devices because they plug into an AC outlet. This makes it more convenient because a user doesn't have to hunt for an AC outlet to plug a laptop into. Docking stations also provide access to corporate resources—often via an RJ45 connection. Finally, docking stations have multiple USB ports for hardware and peripheral connectivity. Companies such as Kensington and Lenovo offer docking stations. Keep in mind that a docking station has more functionality than a port replicator, which might only allow for additional USB and video ports.

Incorrect answers: Thunderbolt is not a device but rather a technology that can allow for video or data transmission; it is common in Apple computers. A USB hub is a device that simply allows for more USB ports. A USB hub can be passive or active, meaning that it can rely solely on the computer for power or can be connected to an AC outlet, respectively. Docking stations actually have the equivalent of a USB hub built in. A thin client is a basic computer that has a CPU, RAM, and sometimes a small SSD, with a "thin" (or small-footprint) operating system. It is meant to be a basic client on a network that allows for the download of virtual desktops. Using a cable lock is a good idea for securing laptops, but it won't meet the customer's connectivity requirements in this case.

5. **Answer: D**

   Explanation: Paper-feed errors are often related to the pickup rollers, which are in charge of feeding the paper into the printer.

   Incorrect answers: If a separation pad fails, it might cause more than one sheet of paper to be entered into the printer. The developing rollers transfer ink to the imaging drum. The paper tray simply holds the paper; it should not cause paper-feed errors unless the constraining tabs are too tight.

6. **Answer: C**

   Explanation: Port 389 is the default port, and it is used by Lightweight Directory Access Protocol (LDAP). Port 636 is used for secure LDAP.

   Incorrect answers: Port 25 is the default port for Simple Mail Transfer Protocol (SMTP). Port 110 or 995 is used by POP3. Port 443 is used by HTTPS.

7. **Answer: B**

   Explanation: Class 2 Bluetooth devices have a maximum range of approximately 10 meters. Class 2 devices (such as Bluetooth headsets) are the most common.

   Incorrect answers: Class 1 has a 100-meter range, and Class 3's range is approximately 1 meter. The maximum length of a standard USB 2.0 cable is 5 meters. USB 3.0 through 3.2 have lengths that range from 1 to 3 meters—but with varying results in terms of data transfer rate, latency, dropped frames, and so on. Note that twisted-pair cable such as Category 5e or Category 6 can also transmit data up to 100 meters (328 feet), but don't confuse the two!

8. **Answers: A and E**

   Explanation: 802.11a operates at 5 GHz only; so does 802.11ac. 802.11ac is also known as Wi-Fi 5.

   Incorrect answers: 802.11b and g operate at 2.4 GHz. 802.11n operates at either 2.4 or 5 GHz. The IEEE 802.11 wireless standards are collectively known as 802.11x. Note that 802.11ax is a newer Wi-Fi standard that can work on 2.4 GHz and 5 GHz (known as Wi-Fi 6) as well as 6 GHz (known as Wi-Fi 6E).

9. Answer: C

Explanation: DDR4-2666 has a peak transfer rate of 21,333 MB/s. It runs at an I/O bus clock speed of 1333 MHz and can send 2666 megatransfers per second (MT/s). It is also known as PC4-21333.

The math: To figure out the data transfer rate of DDR4 from the name "DDR4-2666," simply multiply the 2666 by 8 (bytes) and solve for megabytes: 21,333 MB/s. (If you are wondering how I got to that number, it is because the 2666 is actually 2666.66—repeating decimal.) To figure out the data transfer rate of DDR4 from the consumer name "PC4-21333," just look at the number within the name and add "MB/s" to the end. To figure out the data transfer rate when given only the I/O bus clock speed (for example, 1333 MHz), multiply the clock speed by 2 and then multiply that number by 8 and solve for megabytes: 1333 MHz × 2 × 8 = 21,333 MB/s. However, keep in mind that a RAM module such as DDR4-2666 is often inaccurately referred to as a 2666-MHz RAM module when really that is the MT/s.

Incorrect answers: DDR4-2133 has a peak transfer rate of 17,066 MB/s; it is also known as PC4-17000. DDR4-2400 has a peak transfer rate of 19,200 MB/s; it is also known as PC4-19200. Be prepared for systems with DDR5 as well. A DDR5-4800 module has a peak transfer rate of 38,400 MB/s.

10. Answer: B

Explanation: An impact printer uses a printhead, ribbon, and tractor feed. An example of an impact printer is a dot matrix printer.

Incorrect answers: Laser printers are much more complex and use more parts than do impact printers. Inkjet printers use a printhead but use an ink cartridge instead of a ribbon and don't use a tractor feed. Thermal printers use a printhead and a special heating element.

11. Answer: C

Explanation: The first thing you should try (of the listed answers) is to clear the print queue. How this is done will vary depending on the type of print server being used. For example, if the printer is being controlled by a Windows Server machine, that server will have the Print Management role installed. From the Print Management console window, you can access the printer in question and locate the queue. In most client Windows operating systems (such as Windows 10 or 11), you can find the queue simply by double-clicking the printer. Regardless of the OS, it is where you would normally go to manage print jobs. Then, after you have found the queue, delete any pending or stalled jobs. One of those print jobs might have been causing a delay, possibly if the print job was too big or was corrupted. Of course, you will have to notify users that any jobs as of *x* time frame have been deleted and will need to be printed again. On some printers, you can clear the print queue from the onscreen display (OSD) directly on the printer; an OSD is also known as an OCP (operator control panel). Or, if the print server is built into a SOHO router or similar device, you have to access it from a browser.

Incorrect answers: If at all possible, try to solve problems centrally, without getting users involved. Having the affected users restart their computers is probably a waste of time in this case. If only one user were affected, restarting could be a viable solution, but when multiple users are affected, the problem is more likely located centrally—at a server or a network device. You don't even know if the printer is connected with a USB cable. It might be if it is connected directly to the server, but it could be wired to the network with a twisted-pair patch cable. Either way, cables don't usually fail out of nowhere. This potential solution should be further down your list. Reinstalling the print drivers is not the best answer because several users were affected. Again, if only one user were affected, this might be a valid option, but if several were affected, the problem is probably more centralized.

12. Answer: A

Explanation: If the CPU is running beyond the recommended voltage range for extended periods of time, it can be a sign of a failing CPU. The problem could also be caused by overclocking. Check in the BIOS/UEFI to see whether the CPU is overclocked.

Incorrect answers: If the computer won't boot at all, another problem might have occurred, or the CPU might have already failed. Low case temperatures are a good thing (if they aren't below freezing!), and spyware is unrelated to this issue.

13. Answer: C

Explanation: Fiber-optic cable is the only answer listed that is not affected by electromagnetic interference (EMI). Fiber does not use copper wire or electricity but instead uses glass or plastic fibers and light.

Incorrect answers: Any copper cable is susceptible to EMI to a certain degree. Regular UTP cable such as Cat 5e or Cat 6 is very susceptible, coaxial slightly less, and shielded twisted pair (STP) even less than that. STP is difficult to install and must be grounded; because of this, it is found less commonly in networks. To truly protect against EMI, fiber optic is the best way to go. Special tools are typically used during installation to splice the fibers properly and test the connection effectively.

14. Answer: A

Explanation: Setting an admin password in the BIOS/UEFI prevents a user from rearranging the boot order. The idea behind this is to stop a person from attempting to boot off an optical disc or USB flash drive. As an administrator, you should change the BIOS/UEFI boot order to the bootable storage drive first (meaning the one with the operating system on it). Then apply an administrative password. That'll stop 'em right in their tracks!

Incorrect answers: The administrator password does not prevent any of the other listed answers. To prevent a user from reading email, you would have to remove email applications (such as Outlook) and probably take away the browser, too (which doesn't sound feasible). To prevent a virus from infecting the boot sector/MBR, you could turn on boot sector scanning in the BIOS/UEFI (if the motherboard supports it). To prevent an attacker from opening the case, use a case lock. To find out if someone attempted to physically get into the computer, turn on the chassis intrusion alert in the BIOS/UEFI.

15. Answer: D

Explanation: The external power supply of the laptop converts AC to DC for the system to use and for charging the battery. It is known as the power adapter, and it needs to run at a very specific voltage. In fact, power adapters of different makes and models usually do not work with different laptops, even if the voltages are only slightly different.

Incorrect answers: The adapter does not increase voltage. It also does not store power; that is the responsibility of the laptop battery. It is also accomplished by a UPS, though you probably wouldn't lug one of those around with your laptop while traveling.

16. Answer: A

Explanation: Printer Command Language (PCL) drivers are used for general office applications: printing typical documents, spreadsheets, and so on. They are more commonly used than PostScript drivers.

Incorrect answers: PostScript drivers are used for professional graphics and presentations. They are designed for higher-end printers but can be supported by lesser models as well. Be sure to use the correct driver type for your work environment. ADF, which stands for automatic document feeder, refers to a wonderful contraption that allows you to scan, copy, or fax multiple page documents without having to feed each page individually. AirPrint is an Apple technology that helps you create full-quality printed output without the need to download or install drivers.

17. Answer: C

Explanation: Contrast ratio is the brightness of the brightest color (measured as white) compared to the darkest color (measured as black). Static contrast ratio measurements are static; they are performed as tests using a checkerboard pattern. But there is also the dynamic contrast ratio—a technology in LCD displays that adjusts dynamically during darker scenes in an attempt to give better black levels. It usually has a higher ratio, but it should be noted that there is no real uniform standard for measuring contrast ratio.

Incorrect answers: Power consumption deals with the number of watts that the display uses. Display resolution is the number of pixels on the screen, measured horizontally by vertically. Displays often have a brightness setting as well as a contrast setting. The brightness setting is used to increase or decrease the amount of light put out by the display. Power savings is another concept altogether and can be adjusted by enabling the power-saving features of the operating system, ultimately using fewer watts and conserving energy while increasing the life span of the display.

18. Answer: B

Explanation: Most antistatic straps come with a 1 megaohm resistor, which can protect against surges. However, the best way to avoid a surge is to (1) make sure the computer is unplugged before working on it, (2) avoid touching any components that hold a charge, and (3) stay away from live electricity sources. In other words, don't open power supplies or CRT monitors; don't touch capacitors on any circuit boards such as motherboards; and, of course, stay away from any other electrical devices, wires, and circuits when working on computers.

Incorrect answers: A Torx screwdriver is used to remove specialized screws from laptops and other mobile devices. A voltmeter (or a multimeter) is used to find out how many volts are being generated by a battery or are being cycled through an AC outlet. An antistatic mat is used to keep a computer and components at the same electrical potential as the person working on the computer.

19. **Answer: D**

    Explanation: High-Definition Multimedia Interface (HDMI), as the word *multimedia* implies, can transmit video and audio signals. DisplayPort and USB-C can also transfer video and audio (and USB-C can also transfer data).

    Incorrect answers: VGA, RGB, and DVI are video-only standards.

20. **Answer: D**

    Explanation: A router can limit network broadcasts through segmentation and programmed routing of data. This is part of a router's job when connecting two or more networks. It is also used with different media. For example, you might have a LAN that uses twisted-pair cable, but the router connects to the Internet via a fiber-optic connection. That one router will have ports for both types of connections.

    Incorrect answers: A switch connects multiple computers on the LAN; it does not limit IP-based network broadcasts. However, the switch does not segment by IP address; it communicates with computers and segments the network via MAC addresses. Also, the switch normally uses one type of media—twisted pair—and connects to RJ45 ports. However, it is possible that a switch might connect to another switch by way of a specialized fiber-optic connector. A wireless access point (WAP) connects the computers on a wireless LAN (WLAN). It often has only one connection, a single RJ45 port. A hardware-based firewall usually connects to the network via RJ45; regardless, it has only one or only a few connections. It doesn't deal with routing or broadcasts; instead, it prevents intrusion to a network.

21. **Answer: C**

    Explanation: Of the listed answers, the best one is to implement single sign-on (SSO). With SSO, a user can type a single password and get access to multiple programs, systems, or networks. There are several open source and free options for SSO and federated identity management.

    Incorrect answers: Setting up multifactor authentication (MFA) would require a second method of authentication. While this is a good idea in general, it is not a simple solution to the problem. Configuring biometric authentication is a possibility, but to work in connection with multiple corporate apps, it will probably require more work than simply enabling mobile device facial recognition. Plus, there could be a cost involved in using third-party software. In addition, some apps are not written to accept biometric authentication. Removing password complexity requirements would probably reduce the number of help desk tickets, but It would also be much less secure, which is not desirable in this scenario.

NOTE

In general, the CompTIA A+ exams are looking for answers that are relatively easy to implement and have the lowest cost.

22. Answer: D

Explanation: The CPU could overheat if thermal paste (compound) has not been applied correctly (which is common) or if the CPU is not seated properly (which is rare).

Incorrect answers. As part of the boot process, power needs to be verified to the CPU. If the wrong voltage is running to the CPU, the system won't even boot. If an incorrect CPU has been installed, the system will probably not boot, especially if the BIOS/UEFI doesn't recognize it. Finally, the CPU doesn't use a driver; instead, the BIOS/UEFI recognizes it (or doesn't, if it needs a BIOS/UEFI update) and passes that information to the operating system.

23. Answer: C

Explanation: Of the answers listed, 172.17.58.254 is the only valid IPv4 address for a network host. A host on the network is any computer or network device that uses an IP address to communicate with other computers or devices. 172.17.58.254 is a class B private IP address, so it fits the description of a valid IPv4 address for a network host.

Incorrect answers: 127.0.0.1 is the IPv4 local loopback address. Every computer using TCP/IP gets this address, which is used for testing. This address cannot be used to communicate with other hosts on the network. 169.254.0.0/16 means the IP address 169.254.0.0 with the default subnet mask 255.255.0.0, indicating that the network number is 169.254; it is not a valid host IP address because it ends in 0.0. The first IP address of a network is always reserved for the network number; it cannot be used by a host. Otherwise, if the address were, say, 169.254.0.1, the address would work, but because it is an APIPA address, it would be able to communicate only with other systems using APIPA addresses. 255.10.15.7 is not valid. That address is within the class E reserved range. For normal host IP addresses, the first octet is either between 1 and 126 or between 128 and 223, but it cannot be between 224 and 255.

24. Answer: C

Explanation: Dynamic random-access memory (DRAM) is a module (or stick) of memory that you can install into a motherboard. DDR (for example, DDR4 and DDR5) and LPDDR are examples of DRAM.

Incorrect answers: A complementary metal-oxide semiconductor (CMOS) is a chip soldered onto the motherboard that works in conjunction with the Basic Input/Output System (BIOS), another chip soldered onto the motherboard. Static RAM (SRAM) is memory that is nonvolatile (as opposed to DRAM); it is also soldered to the circuit board. Read-only memory (ROM) is usually not serviceable. The BIOS resides on a ROM chip—specifically on an electrically erasable programmable ROM (EEPROM) chip.

25. **Answer: C**

   Explanation: 172.31.1.1 is the only address listed that is private. It is within the class B range of private addresses: 172.16.0.0–172.31.255.255.

   Incorrect answers: 11.58.254.169 is not private because it is on the class A 11 network. The class A private range is within the 10.0.0.0 network. 169.255.10.41 is not private either. Microsoft's APIPA, however, uses the 169.254.0.0 network, which is private. 192.169.0.1 is public because of the second octet: 169. The class C private range is 192.168.0.0–192.168.255.255.

26. **Answer: B**

   Explanation: The IPv6 loopback address used for testing is ::1. This determines if IPv6 is working correctly on the network card but does not generate network traffic. It exists on every computer that runs IPv6.

   Incorrect answers: 127.0.0.1 is the IPv4 loopback address. 192.168.0.0 is simply a private IP network number. FE80::/10 is the link-local prefix—a range of auto-assigned addresses in IPv6.

27. **Answer: C**

   Explanation: The only statement that is correct concerning IPv6 is that it uses 128-bit addresses. In contrast, IPv4 uses 32-bit addresses.

   Incorrect answers: IPv6 and IPv4 can cohabit a computer with no problems. IPv6 is not necessarily supported by all routers. Some routers still support only IPv4. IPv6 is a logical concept. The physical cable that connects to the computer has no bearing on which IP version is used.

28. **Answer: B**

   Explanation: This is an example of an A record (address record). An A record contains the fully qualified domain name (FQDN) of the host and the IPv4 address of that same host. In this case, they are *server1.example.com* and *10.0.0.1*, respectively. In a normal DNS server, this record would also say A in the entry, telling you that it is an address record that resolves from name to IPv4 address.

   Incorrect answers: An MX record means a mail exchange record, which deals with mail servers. An AAAA record is a name-to-IPv6 address record. A TXT record is informational (basic text).

29. **Answer: A**

   Explanation: The impact printer technology is what you want. Such a printer strikes a ribbon and consequently the paper with a printhead. The physical hammering action causes the carbon backing to apply text to the next layer of paper. Multipart forms such as these are commonly used for receipts.

   Incorrect answers: Laser printers can print to special multipart forms, but not ones with carbon backing. Inkjet and thermal printers are not usually used with multipart forms.

30. Answer: D

Explanation: You cannot install drivers to the BIOS/UEFI. Drivers are software that allows the operating system to communicate with hardware; they can be configured in Device Manager in Windows.

Incorrect answers: The rest of the answers can be configured in the BIOS/UEFI. The boot sequence (also known as boot priority or boot order) allows you to select which device will be booted off first. (The storage drive with OS is the most secure.) Temperature thresholds allow you to set alerts and possibly shut down the system if the CPU runs too hot. Overclocking occurs when the CPU's voltage is raised and the speed is increased. Overclocking is not recommended, but if you do configure it, you should set temperature thresholds. Intrusion detection can be enabled and will log when a person opens the computer case.

31. Answers: A and E

Explanation: POP3 is a protocol used by email clients to receive email. It makes use of either port 110 (considered insecure) or port 995 (a default secure port).

Incorrect answers: SMTP is used by email clients to send email. It uses port 25 and the more secure port 587.

32. Answer: D

Explanation: To connect one computer to another directly by way of network adapter cards, use a crossover cable. (The category, such as 5e or 6, doesn't matter.) A crossover cable is designed to connect *like* devices. It is wired as T568B on one end and T568A on the other. Those standards are ratified by the Telecommunications Industry Association/Electronic Industries Alliance (TIA/EIA).

Incorrect answers: A regular (and more common) Cat 6 patch cable is known as a straight-through cable. It is used to connect *unlike* devices, such as a computer to a switch. Normally, it is wired with the 568B standard on each end. A parallel cable might be used to connect an older printer to a computer or an external hard drive to a SCSI card. *Rolled cable* is a less commonly used term for a cable that administrators use to connect from a serial port on a PC to a console port on a router. Its proper name is a *null-modem cable*, but it might also be referred to as a *rollover cable* or a *console cable*.

33. Answer: A

Explanation: Network installations require that the network card be configured for Preboot Execution Environment (PXE). This allows the network card to boot off the network, locate a network installation server, and request that the installation begin. This configuration might be done in the BIOS/UEFI of the computer (if the network adapter is integrated into the motherboard), within a special program in Windows, or in a program that boots from disc or other removable media (if the network adapter is an adapter card).

Incorrect answers: Peripheral Component Interconnect Express (PCIe) is an expansion bus that accepts video cards, network adapter cards, sound cards, and so on. PCL, which stands for Printer Command Language, was developed by HP so that a computer can properly communicate with impact or thermal printers. PnP, which stands for plug and play, is a Windows technology that allows devices to be located and installed automatically.

34. Answer: A

Explanation: The CPU is the least likely component to be replaced. You would probably need to replace other equipment, too, in this case. Just like PCs, though, the CPU should rarely fail.

Incorrect answers: You might upgrade, replace, or add to RAM. M.2 cards are internal cards that can be added or upgraded to incorporate better video or WLAN and Bluetooth. Laptop keyboards fall victim to spilled coffee, overuse, and other damage over time and sometimes need to be replaced.

35. Answers: C and D

Explanation: 1000 Mbps is 1000 megabits per second, which can also be notated as 1,000,000,000 bits per second or 1 gigabit per second.

Incorrect answers: Data transfer is measured in bits per second (bps), not bits per minute. Consequently, 1000 bits per second would be very slow. At their peak, dial-up modems would transfer 56,000 bits per second, and that is considered the slowest Internet access you could find in the United States.

36. Answer: B

Explanation: Single-mode fiber-optic cable can send data up to hundreds of kilometers, which is farther than any of the other answers.

Incorrect answers: Multi-mode fiber-optic cable can send data about 600 meters. STP is a type of twisted pair; all twisted pair is limited to 100 meters, or 328 feet. Coaxial cable is limited to 200 or 500 meters, depending on the type.

37. Answer: C

Explanation: You should install a USB add-on card. This will give you more ports than the computer already has for use with peripherals. Another option—and a more common option at that—would be to purchase a USB hub.

Incorrect answers: Modems, network adapters, and TV tuner cards all have their own purposes and do not allow additional peripherals.

38. Answer: D

Explanation: A typical speed of a magnetic hard disk drive (HDD) is 7200 revolutions per minute (RPM). Other common speeds include 5400 RPM, 10,000 RPM, and 15,000 RPM. Note that a solid-state drive (SSD) does not have a magnetic disk and therefore is not given an RPM rating or a latency rating.

Incorrect answers: A common network data transfer rate is 1000 Mbps. SATA drives commonly have a DTR of 6 Gb/s (600 MB/s). Note that 3.1 GHz is a common CPU frequency, and 32 GB might be the amount of RAM you install in a computer or the size of a USB flash drive.

39. Answer: A

Explanation: A switch interconnects devices on the same network so that they can communicate, whereas a router interconnects one or more networks.

Incorrect answers: All the other answers are incorrect. Remember that a switch is in charge of connecting devices on a LAN, but a router is in charge of connecting a LAN to another LAN, to the Internet, or to both. Multifunction network devices make matters confusing; they combine the functionality of a switch, a router, a wireless access point, and a firewall. Physically, the four-port section of such a device is the switch portion, and the single port that leads to the Internet is the router portion.

40. Answer: D

Explanation: In a large corporation (or an enterprise environment), tape backup such as Linear Tape-Open (LTO) or Digital Linear Tape (DLT) is the best media for backing up. These tapes can contain lots of data before they fill up. For example, an LTO 5 data cartridge can contain 5 TB of data. Also, LTO tapes are much more durable than USB flash drives.

Incorrect answers: LTO and DLT tapes have large capacity, allowing for a huge amount of backup compared to DVDs and dual-layer DVDs (4.7–17 GB) and USB flash drives (typically 32 to 512 GB as of the writing of this book). USB flash drives are not known for longevity; tape backup is more durable. While RAID 5 can contain a lot of data, it is an expensive proposition for a backup solution. Generally, backups are made to tape rather than to storage drives.

41. Answers: A and D

Explanation: The organization will most likely use a local area network (LAN) for each office and a metropolitan area network (MAN) to connect the three networks. The LANs meet the requirements for each office's internal communications. Most LANs operate at 1 Gbps or faster. The MAN meets the requirement for the connection between the offices within the city. A MAN is the right choice because it can harness the power of fiber-optic cables and other technologies that already exist in the city limits and can provide for 1 Gbps or more throughput.

Incorrect answers: A personal area network (PAN) is a group of Bluetooth devices that communicate with each other. A wide area network (WAN) connects multiple LANs but usually over longer distances—often between cities. Also, a WAN does not typically have as much data throughput as a MAN. A storage area network (SAN) is a group of storage arrays, network-attached storage (NAS) devices, and so on. It could be that the offices might use one, but just having a SAN does not meet the throughput requirements; plus, a SAN can be within a LAN, cross over to a MAN, or move beyond to a WAN, so it is somewhat vague when considering the scenario. A wireless local area network (WLAN) might be incorporated as well, but as of the writing of this book (2022), you'd be hard-pressed to get it to meet the 1 Gbps data throughput requirement for all computers.

42. Answer: D

Explanation: VMware is an example of virtualization software. Actually, VMware is the company, and it makes a multitude of software, including virtualization software such as VMware Workstation (type 1 hypervisor) and VMware ESXi (type 2 hypervisor).

Incorrect answers: VDI stands for virtual desktop infrastructure. It's a technology by which operating system desktops can be delivered to PCs, laptops, and thin clients over the network. VMware also happens to make VDI software. Infrastructure as a service (IaaS) is a type of cloud model that allows a company to use the cloud to host networking infrastructure, routing, and VM hosting (which includes various types of virtualization software). In metered utilization, the provider monitors the services rendered so that the provider can properly bill the customer and make sure that the customer's use of services is being handled in the most efficient way.

43. Answer: D

Explanation: Smartphones typically use Secure Digital (SD) cards—especially microSD cards.

Incorrect answers: SSD stands for solid-state drive. This technology is implemented as flash-based drives or as adapter cards with DDR memory and a battery. NVMe drives are high-performance drives used in PCs and laptops. USB flash drives don't fit inside a typical smartphone and so are relegated to hanging on people's key chains and acting as mobile transporters of data.

44. Answer: C

Explanation: The motherboard in the desktop computer will have to have at least four RAM slots that can work as a quad-channel configuration—meaning all four memory modules can work together, creating a 256-bit memory bus.

Incorrect answers: Double Data Rate (DDR) is the technology that most memory modules use today (for example, DDR4 or DDR5). Small outline dual inline memory module (SODIMM) technology is used in laptops, not in desktops. Error correcting code (ECC), which is used to detect and correct errors in memory, is more common in servers than in desktop computers.

45. Answer: A

Explanation: In this case, you should most likely replace the toner cartridge. Faded lines usually mean that something is wrong with the toner cartridge (or, if separate, the transfer drum). Also replace the toner cartridge if there is faded print, streaks, smearing, or speckling. Know the main steps of the laser printer imaging process: processing, charging, exposing, developing, transferring, fusing, and cleaning. For example, in the charging step, the drum is conditioned/charged by the primary corona wire (negatively charging it) and is prepared for writing. In the transferring step, the paper is positively charged by the transfer corona wire, preparing it to accept the toner from the drum. In the fusing step, the toner is fused to the paper with heat and pressure. In the cleaning step (the last step), the receptacle, rollers, and other items are cleaned and readied for the next print job.

NOTE

See the book *CompTIA A+ Core 1 (220-1101) and Core 2 (220-1102) Exam Cram* for more information about laser printer troubleshooting.

Incorrect answers: If there were a firmware issue, you would probably have more severe errors in printing, or you might not get any printing at all. "Replace the corona wire" is somewhat vague. Which corona wire—the charging wire or the transferring wire? Either way, it is more likely that you would simply replace the toner cartridge or the transfer drum and not actually replace any "wires." In today's modern workplace, you will usually not refill any type of cartridge; however, an incorrect answer is "ink cartridge," which implies an inkjet printer, whereas the printer in the scenario is a laser printer.

46. Answer: B

Explanation: When testing the main 24-pin ATX power connector that leads from the power supply to the motherboard, use a power supply unit (PSU) tester or a multimeter. The multimeter can test each individual wire's voltage, and the PSU tester can test them all in one shot.

Incorrect answers: A Torx screwdriver is used to open computers and laptops that have special Torx screws; T-10 is a common size. A receptacle tester is used to test an AC outlet, and multimeters can be used for that as well. A tone and probe kit is used to test telephone and network connections for continuity. However, it can test only one pair of the wires in the cable. For better results when testing network cables, use a proper network cable testing kit. Testing tools are a key ingredient in a computer technician's toolkit.

47. Answer: E

Explanation: Be sure that the virtualization host has multiple cores. A good rule of thumb is to use two cores per Linux VM, but that will vary depending on the scenario. So, for example, if you are going to run three Linux VMs, you would want six cores for those VMs. Don't forget that you will need at least a couple of cores for the hosting OS. That means that the host should have a multicore CPU with at least eight cores. Note that it's also important to have enough RAM for each VM. In the case of Linux, at least 1 to 2 GB of RAM is required.

Incorrect answers: An integrated GPU is probably not necessary here because you are running virtual machines (and as Linux servers, they will most likely be command line only). Liquid cooling and overclocking are okay for gaming computers and other enthusiast performance systems, but they are not commonly used for virtualization hosts at an organization. x86 refers to a 32-bit CPU architecture that can access only 4 GB of RAM. That is an old technology that you want to avoid; instead use a system with a newer x64 (x86-64) CPU.

48. Answer: C

Explanation: Use a multimeter to verify that the server racks are properly grounded. You need to check the resistance of the grounding wire that attaches from the server rack(s) to a grounding source. To do that, set the multimeter to impedance (Ω). A multimeter can usually verify voltage, amperage, and impedance (and possibly more).

NOTE

Remember that in some municipalities, a licensed electrician must perform the work and be present at the inspection.

Incorrect answers: A cable tester (or cable certifier) is used to check the continuity of the individual wires in a twisted-pair cable. A tone generator is used to find an individual cable among a group or bundle of cables. A loopback plug is a device used to test the network connectivity of a PC or switch RJ45 port. A voltmeter *only* checks voltage and does not check for resistance. SCADA, which stands for supervisory control and data acquisition, is a control system that offers high-level management of machines and processes.

49. **Answer: A**

    Explanation: A tablet does not have a touchpad; instead, you use your finger(s) or a stylus to tap on the display (known as a *touchscreen*).

    Incorrect answers: A tablet has a display and a wireless network adapter. It also has an onscreen keyboard. The question does not specify physical or virtual keyboard. Be ready for vagaries like this on the A+ exam.

50. **Answer: B**

    Explanation: When troubleshooting a computer system, always look for the most likely and simplest solutions first. The fact that the user might not have turned on her monitor when she first came in is a likely scenario.

    Incorrect answers: If the monitor *is* on, you can move on down the troubleshooting list. Next, you could check whether the computer is on, whether the computer and monitor are plugged into the AC outlet, and whether the monitor is plugged into the computer. Reinstalling the video driver is much further down the list.

51. **Answer: A**

    Explanation: Chances are that the computer has faulty memory or a memory module that needs to be reseated properly. The flashing cursor on the screen tells you that the system is not posting properly. The numbers counting up are the system checking the RAM. If the system beeps and freezes during this count-up, there is an issue with the RAM. (Note that, depending on the system and how the BIOS/UEFI is configured, you might not see the POST counting upward.) It could also be incompatible with the motherboard.

    Incorrect answers: A corrupt MBR would either give a message stating "missing OS" or "the MBR is corrupt." However, most systems today are GPT based, not MBR based, so you won't often see these types of boot sector issues. If the OS is corrupted, you get a message to that effect. If the computer attempts to boot off the network, you see gray text and a spinning pipe sign as the machine attempts to find a DHCP server.

52. **Answer: A**

    Explanation: If you get any address that starts with 169.254, the computer has self-assigned that address. It is known as an APIPA (Automatic Private IP Addressing) address, which is a type of link-local address. Normally, DHCP servers do not use this network number. Using the commands **ipconfig /release** and **ipconfig /renew** might fix the problem if a DHCP server is actually available.

    Incorrect answers: The POP3 server is for incoming mail. The DNS server is for resolving domain names to IP addresses. AAA means authentication, authorization, and accounting. An example of an AAA server would be a RADIUS server used for wireless authentication.

53. Answer: D

Explanation: Faded print, ghosted images, or blurry marks could be a sign that the drum has some kind of imperfection or is dirty, especially if the image reappears at equal intervals. Replace the toner cartridge (or, less commonly, the drum only). Another possibility is that the fuser assembly has been damaged and needs to be replaced.

Incorrect answers: Blank pages might indicate a problem with the transfer corona wire or primary corona wire; if this is the issue, replace the toner cartridge. Stuck pages, jams, or problems with feeding the paper could be due to the pickup rollers. If the fuser assembly is having problems, you might encounter toner not fusing to the paper, or the paper that exits the printer may be too hot.

54. Answers: A, B, and D

Explanation: Always make sure that the speaker power cord (if any) is plugged into an AC outlet and that the speakers are turned on (if they have a power button). When a sound card is first installed, Windows should recognize it and either install a driver through plug and play or ask for driver media. For best results, use the manufacturer's driver, the latest of which you can find on its website. Make sure that you plug the speakers into the correct 1/8-inch jack. The speaker out is the one with concentric circles and an arrow pointing out. Or you might have 5.1 (or 7.1) surround sound; in this case, you would use the standard front speaker jack, which is often a green jack.

Incorrect answers: It's quite hard to plug a sound card into the wrong slot. For example, if you have a PCI Express (PCIe) x1 sound card (a common standard), you can plug that sound card into any of the available PCIe slots on your motherboard, and it will be recognized. (Word to the wise: If you ever remove the sound card when upgrading other components, make sure you put it back in the same slot.) PCIe cards will not fit in the older PCI slot, though you will rarely use that type of slot anyway.

55. Answer: D

Explanation: The wireless hardware button is disabled. Always check whether Wi-Fi is enabled. Often this occurs via a key that shares one of the function keys of a laptop. To enable it, press the Fn key and the appropriate function key (such as F12) at the same time. If Wi-Fi is already enabled, make sure that the wireless adapter is enabled in Windows. Also, check whether the laptop is within range of the wireless access point.

Incorrect answers: The drivers and the firmware should not be an issue because the laptop was able to connect yesterday. However, you never know what might have happened, so check those later on in your troubleshooting process.

56. Answer: C

Explanation: The purpose of a DNS server is to resolve (convert) hostnames and domain names to IP addresses. Computers normally communicate via IP addresses, but it is easier for humans to type in names. If example.com is down, you cannot ping the corresponding IP address at all.

Incorrect answers: If the DHCP server is down, your workstation will probably not have an IP address on the network and will not ping the corresponding IP address. AD DS stands for Active Directory Domain Services, which is a domain controller and doesn't have much to do with this scenario except that in many smaller companies, the domain controller and DNS server are one and the same.

57. Answer: B

Explanation: You must have the correct firmware to recognize the latest CPUs. A BIOS/UEFI flash can fix many problems related to unidentified hardware.

Incorrect answers: If the CPU is not seated properly or if you have an incorrect CPU, the system simply won't boot. Windows does not affect the POST at all. In some cases, you might purchase a motherboard that says it can support a specific new processor. However, there might not yet be firmware to actually work with that processor.

58. Answer: B

Explanation: **ipconfig /all** shows a lot of information, including the MAC address, as well as the DNS server, DHCP information, and more.

Incorrect answers: Plain old **ipconfig** shows only the IP address, subnet mask, and gateway address. **ping** tests whether other computers are alive on the network. **ipconfig/ release** is used to troubleshoot DHCP-obtained IP addresses and is often used in conjunction with **ipconfig/renew**.

59. Answer: D

Explanation: First, try printing an internal test page (that is, from the printer's onscreen display). If that doesn't work, you need to start troubleshooting the printer. Perhaps the toner cartridge is empty, or maybe a corona wire is malfunctioning.

NOTE

A printer's onscreen display (OSD) is also known as an operator control panel (OCP).

Incorrect answers: If the test page prints fine, you can check the printer drivers and other settings at the computer that uses the printer. Restarting the spooler should not help in this situation. If the spooler stalled, no paper should come out of the printer. Likewise, the printer cable should not have to be replaced.

60. Answers: A and B

Explanation: The easiest and (probably) cheapest way is to move the WAP. Basements are usually the worst place for access points because of concrete foundations and walls, electrical interference, and so on. Many WAPs come with the ability to change the signal level. Typically the device will have low, mid, and high options. Boosting the power to the wireless signal can also fix the problem. External signal boosters might also work, but often the cost of a signal booster is the same as the cost of buying a newer, more powerful WAP.

Incorrect answers: Unfortunately, new drivers and firmware usually do not help the situation. It's possible that a new driver can make better use of the wireless network adapter hardware, but it won't necessarily offer a better connection. It's a good idea in any event, but it's not one of the best answers listed.

61. Answer: C

Explanation: The most likely issue is a DHCP failure. Link-local IP addresses such as APIPA on 169.254.0.0 usually kick in when the client computer cannot locate a DHCP server. There are several possible reasons this might happen: lack of network connectivity, incorrect client configuration, DHCP server failure, and so on. The best way to troubleshoot this situation would be to start at the client and check its network cable (or wireless connection) and then its TCP/IP configuration. You could also try configuring a static IP address on the client to see if it allows the client to communicate over the network. If those things don't solve the problem or give you any clues, you can look at the network switch, DHCP server, and so on.

Incorrect answers: DNS resolution has to do with translation between hostnames and IP addresses. No hostnames are a part of this scenario; you are troubleshooting at the IP level. Duplicate IP addresses happen when two computers are statically configured with the same IP address; they are uncommon (if not rare) in DHCP environments or when APIPA is involved. Address Resolution Protocol (ARP) is responsible for converting IP addresses to MAC addresses. The ARP cache is built off the current IP address and the IP and MAC addresses of other computers. Clearing the cache won't solve the problem, but it won't make things any worse either. However, you might consider clearing the ARP cache after the problem is fixed; you might also restart the computer.

62. Answer: C

Explanation: The simplest solution is often the most common. Check cables and see whether the power is on for your devices and computers.

Incorrect answers: After checking cables and power, you can check the driver (for example, within Device Manager in Windows) and check the firewall settings. Whether a hard disk drive (HDD) is fragmented should not affect the Internet connection.

63. Answers: A and C

Explanation: It is common for a RAM stick or video card to be unseated. These are the most common culprits of beep codes during the POST.

Incorrect answers: If the CPU is not installed properly, you might not get any beep codes at all. The storage drive's functionality has little bearing on the POST unless it does not have a bootable OS.

64. Answer: B

Explanation: The PC air intakes are probably clogged with cement dust. This would stop fresh, cool air from entering the PC and would cause the CPU to overheat. That would explain why the system doesn't reboot immediately and the CPU needs some time to cool down. You should install a filter in front of the PC air intake and instruct the customer to clean the filter often. While you are working on the computer, you should clean out the inside of the system and vacuum out the exhaust of the power supply (without opening the power supply, of course).

Incorrect answers: If the PC had a virus, that might cause it to lock up or shut down, but you would be able to reboot the computer right away. Plus, there would probably be other indicators of a virus. The CPU heat sink could be an issue and could cause the same results, but this scenario is less likely. Companies often buy computers from popular manufacturers such as Dell and HP; these computer manufacturers spend a lot of time designing their heat sink/fan combinations to work with the CPU. If the power supply were underrated, it would cause intermittent shutdowns but not lockups. Nothing in the scenario would lead you to believe that the computer uses enough powerful components to make the power supply underrated.

65. Answer: C

Explanation: Use the USB connector. This is by far the easiest method. Windows will sense the USB connection and attempt to install the print driver automatically (though you should still install the latest proper driver from the printer manufacturer's website).

Incorrect answers: Yes, the printer has an Ethernet connection as well (that is the network connection), but using it will require you to connect it to the network. What if there is no network? And even if there is, the printer would have to be configured for the network, and then the laptop would have to connect to the printer over the network. If the laptop is the only system that will use the printer, connecting via USB is much easier than connecting via Ethernet. Thunderbolt often uses Mini DisplayPort for the transmission of data or video, especially (but not exclusively) on Apple computers. Though Thunderbolt can be used for printing, the scenario doesn't state that the laptop has a Thunderbolt port.

66. Answer: A

Explanation: Excessive heat is the most likely cause of the problem. This could be an unfortunate result of proximity to ovens and other equipment. Computers in environments such as these are often prone to dirt collecting inside the CPU fans and other devices inside the case.

Incorrect answers: Faulty RAM wouldn't cause storage drives to fail or unseat expansion cards. The cards probably moved around due to thermal expansion and contraction. You are most likely going to find 240-volt outlets in this environment, but the computer shouldn't use those; in the United States, the computer should be connected to a 120-volt outlet. The computer should be changed to 240 V only if it is brought to another country—such as a country in Europe. Under-voltage events (brownouts) could cause failures of the power supply and maybe even the storage drive, but they would not cause the adapter cards to be unseated.

67. Answer: A

Explanation: Thermal expansion and contraction happen when humidity changes quickly. It can lead to what some technicians refer to as "chip creep" or "card creep."

Incorrect answers: Although there might have been chip creep, the direct cause of the problem was most likely thermal expansion/contraction. POST errors would not be the cause of the error, but in some cases could give you diagnostic information leading to the cause. Thermal sublimation refers to a specific type of printing process and is not involved in the problem. While in the computer, you might want to check other adapter cards to determine whether they were also affected by this phenomenon.

68. Answer: C

Explanation: Fiber-optic networks use fiber-optic cables that have a core of plastic or glass fibers. They are much more difficult to eavesdrop on than any copper cable.

Incorrect answers: Satellite connections and cable Internet use RG-6. DSL uses a standard phone line or other twisted-pair cable. These other options are copper based.

69. Answer: C

Explanation: The surface area of the heat sink has the greatest effect on heat dispersion. The more solid the bond between the heat sink and CPU cap, the better the transition of heat out of the CPU. To aid in this transition, you must use thermal compound.

Incorrect answers: The other answers have little or nothing to do with heat dispersion. The shape of the heat sink is somewhat important, but most CPUs have the same shape. The key is to get the appropriate heat sink for the type of CPU you are using.

70. Answers: A and D

Explanation: You should upgrade the firmware of the SOHO router and place the IoT devices on a guest network. By upgrading the firmware on the router, you update the system to the latest security protocols, making the system more difficult to breach. By placing the IoT devices on a guest network (or screened subnet/DMZ), you separate those devices from the main devices in the home, creating an extra level of defense from attack. Then, for an attacker who does gain access to an IoT device, it will be difficult to gain access to the main portion of the network.

> **NOTE**
>
> You should also upgrade the firmware and software of any IoT devices on the network and make sure the customer is using strong passwords or other forms of authentication.

Incorrect answers: Disabling wireless access on IoT devices will make them non-functional—and the whole point of many IoT devices is to allow for easy wireless connectivity. Enabling the SSID makes it visible to scans—and less secure. To make a Wi-Fi network more secure, *disable* the SSID after the devices have been connected. Disabled MAC filtering is the default state of most SOHO routers. To increase security, *enable* MAC filtering or IP filtering.

71. Answer: A

Explanation: Simple Mail Transfer Protocol (SMTP) is not configured properly. This is the protocol that is used to send mail.

Incorrect answers: POP3 receives email. FTP enables two computers to upload and download files. HTTPS is a protocol used in web browsers for surfing the Internet and accessing web servers.

72. Answers: A and D

Explanation: Near-field communication (NFC) and radio-frequency identification (RFID) technologies can be used in contactless payment processing. NFC is commonly used by mobile devices with mobile wallets such as Apple Pay, Google Pay, and contactless cards. Some credit cards can be "tapped" to pay. Many of these have tiny RFID chips inside them that allow for this functionality.

Incorrect answers: Bluetooth is a technology for connecting wireless peripherals to mobile devices over short distances (for example, 10 meters). It uses public frequencies to transmit data. 5G is a type of cellular technology for sending data and making voice calls on mobile devices.

73. **Answer: B**

Explanation: The only solution listed is to upgrade the video card. This is the main way that computer performance can be increased while editing video files.

Incorrect answers: The CPU and RAM can make the system faster when dealing with applications and calculations of many kinds, but when it comes to video editing and rendering, an integrated video card is inadequate. No matter how much RAM you add or what CPU you put in, the video will still perform like an actor on a late, late, late movie—badly. Increasing the storage drive capacity will have no effect on video but can definitely help in other areas of system performance, such as with pagefile access and general data access.

74. **Answers: A, C, D, and F**

Explanation: The time/date, boot priority (boot sequence), passwords, and Wake-on-LAN (WOL) can all be configured in the BIOS/UEFI.

Incorrect answers: The registry and USB drivers are configured in the operating system—which in this case would be Windows because macOS and Linux don't use a registry.

75. **Answer: C**

Explanation: To test IPv4, use the command **ping 127.0.0.1**. To test IPv6, use the command **ping ::1.**

Incorrect answers: You don't run **ipconfig** commands to particular IP addresses. The commands **ping :1** or **ping 127::1** are not valid.

76. **Answer: D**

Explanation: The typical latency of an SATA magnetic-based hard disk drive is 4.2 ms (milliseconds). When you are dealing with magnetic drives, latency is the delay in time before a particular sector on the platter can be read. It is directly linked to rotational speed. For example, a hard disk drive with a rotational speed of 7200 RPM has an average latency of 4.2 ms.

Incorrect answers: Note that 600 MB/s is the data transfer rate of an SATA revision 3.0 hard drive; it is also expressed as 6.0 Gb/s. 10,000 RPM is the rotational speed of a drive, and 64 MB is a common amount of cache memory on a hard drive (usually DRAM).

77. Answer: B

Explanation: A maintenance kit includes a new fuser assembly, rollers, and more. Installing a maintenance kit is like changing a car's oil (although it typically isn't done as often).

Incorrect answers: Cleaning the printer might not be necessary. If you have a toner spill or work in a dirty environment, cleaning it might be a good idea. Clearing the counter is something you might do on an inkjet printer; this process clears the counter indicating how much ink goes through the cartridge. Printing a test page is important when first installing a printer and when you finish installing a maintenance kit.

78. Answer: D

Explanation: The marketing manager (or the technician) should synchronize the device to a private cloud. This will ensure that the data can be restored later, after the refresh. It also ensures that the process will be done with a certain level of security. A private cloud is a cloud the company uses that is not used by other parties. It is a more secure cloud option.

Incorrect answers: Synchronizing to a flash drive is not secure as the device could easily be lost or stolen. "At a remote location" is somewhat ambiguous. Regardless, it should not be done at any location. Synchronizing data to a shared public folder is very insecure because other users will be able to see and access that data. In most cases, the marketing manager should not have access to a VM in the company's data center. However, the private cloud could actually use resources in the organization's data center.

79. Answer: A

Explanation: You should run **ipconfig /flushdns** in an attempt to fix the problem. The problem could be that the DNS cache on the client computer is outdated and cannot associate Internet domain names with their corresponding IP addresses. So you run **ipconfig /flushdns** and potentially **ipconfig /registerdns** (or restart the computer) to fix the problem. That clears the DNS cache of name resolutions and forces the client to request new DNS information from a DNS server either on the Internet or within the company.

Incorrect answers: **ipconfig /all** shows in-depth information about the network adapter's TCP/IP configuration. If there is an incorrect DNS server configuration, this information will help you identify it but won't help to solve the problem. **ipconfig /release** is used to remove a DHCP-obtained IP address from a network adapter. (**ipconfig /renew** is often run afterward to get a new IP address.) **ipconfig /setclassid** is a potential solution because it allows for an additional set of DHCP options for each class ID, including gateway address, DNS server address, and so on. These options are often set at the DHCP server, and you would need to know the class ID number to use. However, it is unlikely from this scenario that the class ID was ever changed. Due to the time the user was away from the computer (on vacation), it is more likely that the DNS cache needs to be purged.

80. **Answer: B**

   Explanation: The thermal design power (TDP) of a CPU is measured in watts. For example, a typical Core i7 CPU might be rated at 140 watts or less. The lower the wattage rating, the less the computer's cooling system needs to dissipate heat generated by the CPU.

   Incorrect answers: Volts is the measurement used for potential energy; it is a measurement commonly associated with internal PC components running at 5- or 12-volt DC and with typical household and business AC outlets running at 120 volts or 240 volts. Ohms is the measurement used for impedance, or the resistance to electricity. Amps is the measurement for electric current. A typical computer might use 4 amps of current if it has a 500-watt power supply.

CHAPTER FOUR

220-1101 Practice Exam C

This time let's turn up the gas a little further. I've increased the level of difficulty once more. This third 220-1101 exam could be considered an advanced practice exam. Be ready for more scenario-oriented and troubleshooting-based questions.

If you didn't take a break already, I suggest taking one between exams. If you did not score 90% or higher on the first two 220-1101 practice exams, do not take this one yet. Go back and study and then retake those exams until you pass with a 90% or higher score. Then come back to this exam.

Write down your answers and check them against the Quick-Check Answer Key that immediately follows the exam. After the answer key, you will find the explanations for all of the answers. Good luck!

Practice Questions

1. You just installed a maintenance kit on a laser printer. Which of the following steps should you take next?

   Quick Answer: **107**
   Detailed Answer: **108**

   ○ **A.** You should restore the printer to factory settings.

   ○ **B.** You should print a test page.

   ○ **C.** You should refill the paper trays.

   ○ **D.** You should restart the printer.

2. Which of the following is indicated by repetitive flashing lights on the keyboard during POST?

   Quick Answer: **107**
   Detailed Answer: **108**

   ○ **A.** A software error

   ○ **B.** A hardware error

   ○ **C.** A password is required

   ○ **D.** An external peripheral error

3. Which of the following protocols are associated with the following TCP or UDP port numbers, in order?

   Quick Answer: **107**
   Detailed Answer: **108**

   21, 22, 25, 53, 443, 3389

   ○ **A.** FTP, Telnet, SMTP, DNS, HTTP, RDP

   ○ **B.** FTP, SSH, SMTP, DNS, HTTP, RDP

   ○ **C.** FTP, SSH, SMTP, POP3, HTTPS, RDP

   ○ **D.** FTP, SSH, SMTP, DNS, HTTPS, RDP

4. Which of the following multimeter settings should be used only when there is no electrical flow through the part being tested? (Select the two best answers.)

   Quick Answer: **107**
   Detailed Answer: **108**

   ❑ **A.** Continuity

   ❑ **B.** Wattage

   ❑ **C.** Voltage

   ❑ **D.** Amps

   ❑ **E.** Resistance

5. When a PC is first booted, which of the following tests the processor, RAM, video card, storage drive controllers, drives, and keyboard?

   Quick Answer: **107**
   Detailed Answer: **109**

   ○ **A.** CMOS chip

   ○ **B.** BIOS/UEFI setup

   ○ **C.** POST

   ○ **D.** BSOD

6. Which of the following should you use to manage a smart thermostat?

- ○ **A.** RDP
- ○ **B.** SFTP
- ○ **C.** NFC
- ○ **D.** Wi-Fi
- ○ **E.** SMTP

7. You have purchased a motherboard for your new audio workstation. You have opened the computer case and are ready to install. What are the first and last things you should do? (Select the two best answers.)

- ❏ **A.** Select a motherboard.
- ❏ **B.** Install the CPU.
- ❏ **C.** Put on an antistatic strap.
- ❏ **D.** Test the motherboard.
- ❏ **E.** Connect the main power cable.

8. Which of the following tools should be used to determine why a computer fails to boot?

- ○ **A.** Cable tester
- ○ **B.** Loopback plug
- ○ **C.** PSU tester
- ○ **D.** Tone and probe kit

9. Which of the following types of DIMMs have 288 pins? (Select all that apply.)

- ❏ **A.** DDR3
- ❏ **B.** DDR4
- ❏ **C.** DDR5
- ❏ **D.** ECC
- ❏ **E.** Quad-channel

10. You are configuring a new desktop and need to implement full disk encryption. As you begin the process, you get an error that says the device cannot be encrypted. Without adding any hardware, which of the following should you enable on the desktop computer so that the drive can be encrypted?

Quick Answer: **107**
Detailed Answer: **110**

- ○ **A.** TPM
- ○ **B.** Secure Boot
- ○ **C.** UEFI
- ○ **D.** HSM
- ○ **E.** BIOS
- ○ **F.** EFS

11. You are tasked with plugging a network patch cable into an inactive drop in a user's cubicle. Which of the following tools enables you to find the correct network drop in the wiring closet so that you can make the port hot?

Quick Answer: **107**
Detailed Answer: **110**

- ○ **A.** PSU tester
- ○ **B.** Multimeter
- ○ **C.** Cable tester
- ○ **D.** Tone and probe kit

12. You think that the power supply in your PC might be failing, causing issues with an SATA drive. You decide to test the SATA drive. Which of the following are the standard voltages of an SATA connection on an ATX power supply?

Quick Answer: **107**
Detailed Answer: **111**

- ○ **A.** 3.3 V, 5 V, 12 V
- ○ **B.** −3.3 V, 5 V, −12 V
- ○ **C.** −5 V, 5 V, 12 V
- ○ **D.** 5 V and 12 V

13. Which of the following is defined as the movement of electrical charge?

Quick Answer: **107**
Detailed Answer: **111**

- ○ **A.** Voltage
- ○ **B.** Wattage
- ○ **C.** Amperage
- ○ **D.** Impedance

14. Which of the following should be used to clean a laser printer's rubber rollers?

Quick Answer: **107**
Detailed Answer: **111**

- ○ **A.** Soap and water
- ○ **B.** WD-40
- ○ **C.** Isopropyl alcohol
- ○ **D.** A moist cloth

15. You are in charge of deploying a home customer's access point that will be used for streaming 4K videos and online gaming. Of the listed answers, which wireless frequency would be most appropriate?

Quick Answer: **107**
Detailed Answer: **111**

- ○ **A.** 13.56 MHz
- ○ **B.** 1300 MHz
- ○ **C.** 2.4 GHz
- ○ **D.** 5 GHz

16. A coworker at a satellite office reports that a new replacement shared workgroup printer has arrived. It is the same model as the old one. Your coworker replaced the old printer and connected all the cables to the new printer. Which of the following is the easiest way to ensure that all the client computers can connect to the new printer via IPP?

Quick Answer: **107**
Detailed Answer: **112**

- ○ **A.** Name the new printer with the old printer name.
- ○ **B.** Allow the printer to acquire a DHCP address.
- ○ **C.** In DHCP, set a reservation by MAC address.
- ○ **D.** Have your coworker print the configuration page.

17. Which of the following communications protocols is used to connect to websites over secure communications links?

Quick Answer: **107**
Detailed Answer: **112**

- ○ **A.** SSH
- ○ **B.** SFTP
- ○ **C.** HTTPS
- ○ **D.** Kerberos

18. Which of the following protocols can be used to configure and monitor network printer device status?

Quick Answer: **107**
Detailed Answer: **112**

- ○ **A.** SMTP
- ○ **B.** SNMP
- ○ **C.** TCP/IP
- ○ **D.** IPP
- ○ **E.** DNS

19. Which of the following symptoms would indicate a power supply issue?

    ○ **A.** The CPU is overclocking.

    ○ **B.** The Wi-Fi range is reduced.

    ○ **C.** The storage drives fail frequently.

    ○ **D.** USB drives are not recognized by Windows.

20. Which of the following systems requires a powerful CPU and maximum RAM to run multiple operating systems at the same time?

    ○ **A.** Gaming computer

    ○ **B.** Layer 3 switch

    ○ **C.** Virtualization workstation

    ○ **D.** NAS

21. You need to install a device that can read groupings of parallel lines. Which of the following devices should be selected?

    ○ **A.** Biometric scanner

    ○ **B.** Image scanner

    ○ **C.** Barcode reader

    ○ **D.** Touchpad

22. You are building a new gaming PC and want to select a motherboard that supports the Scalable Link Interface (SLI) technology so you can install two SLI video cards connected by a bridge. Which of the following expansion slots should the motherboard have for your two video cards?

    ○ **A.** Two PCIe version 3 slots

    ○ **B.** Two PCIe version 4 slots

    ○ **C.** A PCIe x1 slot and a PCIe x16 slot

    ○ **D.** A USB port and PCIe slot

23. Which of the following RAID arrays is fault tolerant and allows you to do striping with parity?

    ○ **A.** RAID 0

    ○ **B.** RAID 1

    ○ **C.** RAID 5

    ○ **D.** RAID 10

24. Which of the following are possible reasons that an optical mouse cursor erratically jumps around the screen? (Select the two best answers.)

Quick Answer: **107**
Detailed Answer: **114**

- ❏ **A.** It is using an incorrect mouse driver.
- ❏ **B.** The mouse trackball needs to be removed and cleaned.
- ❏ **C.** There's a conflict with the keyboard.
- ❏ **D.** It is on an uneven surface.
- ❏ **E.** The mouse needs to be charged.

25. A customer wants you to "daisychain" three monitors. When purchasing the monitors, which of the following video types should you make sure is available?

Quick Answer: **107**
Detailed Answer: **114**

- ○ **A.** DisplayPort
- ○ **B.** VGA
- ○ **C.** HDMI
- ○ **D.** DVI
- ○ **E.** USB-C

26. When you are dealing with a power issue, which of the following should be checked first?

Quick Answer: **107**
Detailed Answer: **115**

- ○ **A.** Input devices
- ○ **B.** Network cabling
- ○ **C.** Wall outlet
- ○ **D.** Power supply

27. When a computer receives the IP address 169.254.127.1, which of the following has failed?

Quick Answer: **107**
Detailed Answer: **115**

- ○ **A.** DHCP
- ○ **B.** DNS
- ○ **C.** VPN
- ○ **D.** APIPA

28. Emergency! Your boss forgot the password to the BIOS/UEFI on a PC. Which of the following methods helps you to reset the password?

Quick Answer: **107**
Detailed Answer: **116**

- ○ **A.** Removing the RAM from the motherboard
- ○ **B.** Removing the CMOS battery from the motherboard
- ○ **C.** Removing the RAM jumper from the motherboard
- ○ **D.** Removing the main power connection from the motherboard

29. In a RAID 5 array of eight storage drives, how many can fail without losing the entire array?

Quick Answer: **107**
Detailed Answer: **116**

- ○ **A.** Zero
- ○ **B.** One
- ○ **C.** Two
- ○ **D.** Five

30. A company laptop has a cracked display, and it is under warranty. Which of the following steps should be taken before shipping the laptop to the manufacturer for repair?

Quick Answer: **107**
Detailed Answer: **116**

- ○ **A.** You should remove the display panel.
- ○ **B.** You should clean the laptop thoroughly.
- ○ **C.** You should remove the storage drive.
- ○ **D.** You should remove the WLAN card.

31. You are trying to deploy multiple VMs to several Intel-based desktop computers. Some of the installations are failing because a CPU function is disabled in the BIOS/UEFI. Which of the following should be enabled so that the installations will succeed?

Quick Answer: **107**
Detailed Answer: **116**

- ○ **A.** TPM
- ○ **B.** Hyperthreading
- ○ **C.** Intel virtualization
- ○ **D.** VNC

32. A thin client in a VDI environment receives an operating system by connecting through the network using a number of devices. If you begin at the thin client, which of the following is the first physical networking device in the chain?

Quick Answer: **107**
Detailed Answer: **117**

- ○ **A.** Router
- ○ **B.** Switch
- ○ **C.** NIC
- ○ **D.** VPN

33. Which of the following video connectors accepts digital and analog video signals only?

Quick Answer: **107**
Detailed Answer: **117**

- ○ **A.** DVI-D
- ○ **B.** DVI-A
- ○ **C.** DVI-I
- ○ **D.** HDMI Type B

34. Which of the following refers to a mobile device sharing its Internet connection with other Wi-Fi–capable devices?

- ○ **A.** USB tethering
- ○ **B.** Wi-Fi sharing
- ○ **C.** VLAN
- ○ **D.** Mobile hotspot

35. Which of these printers would display an error that says "replace filament"?

- ○ **A.** Laser
- ○ **B.** 3D
- ○ **C.** Inkjet
- ○ **D.** Thermal

36. Which of the following steps should be taken first when a printer fails to print very large documents but still prints smaller documents without a problem?

- ○ **A.** Check whether the correct type of paper is being used.
- ○ **B.** Replace the communications cable.
- ○ **C.** Change the toner cartridges.
- ○ **D.** Add memory to the printer.

37. You are working on a device that shows the following information:

```
Management Interface
IPv4 Interface
        IP Address:        10.50.0.1
        Network Mask:      255.255.0.0
        Management VLAN:   1
```

What kind of device are you most likely working on?

- ○ **A.** Sandbox
- ○ **B.** Managed switch
- ○ **C.** NID
- ○ **D.** Spam gateway

38. A coworker notices that the battery light on a laptop is flashing when the laptop is In a docking station. Which of the following steps should be performed first to fix the problem?

- ○ **A.** Replace the laptop battery.
- ○ **B.** Reinstall the operating system.
- ○ **C.** Reseat in the docking station.
- ○ **D.** Remove and reseat the battery.

39. A tablet device is having trouble accessing the wireless network. Which of the following steps should be taken to troubleshoot the problem? (Select the three best answers.)

- ❏   **A.**   Power cycle the device.
- ❏   **B.**   Use GPRS instead.
- ❏   **C.**   Ensure that the SSID is correct.
- ❏   **D.**   Set up a static IP address.
- ❏   **E.**   Forget the network and reconnect to it,

40. Which of the following steps should be taken to connect a Bluetooth headset to a smartphone? (Select the two best answers.)

- ❏   **A.**   Pair the device to the phone.
- ❏   **B.**   Install Bluetooth drivers.
- ❏   **C.**   Enter a passcode.
- ❏   **D.**   Disable Wi-Fi.

41. A computer's CPU overheats and shuts down the system inter-mittently. Which of the following steps should be taken to fix the problem? (Select the two best answers.)

- ❏   **A.**   Ensure that the heat sink is secure.
- ❏   **B.**   Check the BIOS/UEFI temperature threshold.
- ❏   **C.**   Ensure that the fan is connected.
- ❏   **D.**   Reseat the RAM, if needed.

42. A burning smell comes from a computer. Which of the following is the most likely source?

- ○   **A.**   Thermal paste
- ○   **B.**   Keyboard
- ○   **C.**   Power supply
- ○   **D.**   AC outlet

43. A user recently purchased a new wireless 802.11ac router. After connecting a laptop with an 802.11ac wireless adapter to the wire-less network, he notices that the signal strength on the laptop is poor, and the laptop only connects at 300 Mbps. The user moves the laptop nearer the WAP but is still experiencing the same issue. Which of the following is most likely the cause?

- ○   **A.**   The cable modem is faulty.
- ○   **B.**   The laptop is connecting to the incorrect wireless network.
- ○   **C.**   The router's wireless card drivers are faulty.
- ○   **D.**   The wireless antennas on the router need to be replaced.

44. Which of the following disk arrays provide for fault tolerance? (Select the two best answers.)

    ❏ **A.** Spanned volume

    ❏ **B.** RAID 0

    ❏ **C.** RAID 1

    ❏ **D.** RAID 5

Quick Answer: **107**
Detailed Answer: **120**

45. You have been tasked with upgrading a desktop computer's internal storage to allow enough storage space for backups, videos, and photos. The storage solution should be large enough that you won't have to scale it again in the next six months. Which of the following is the appropriate solution?

    ○ **A.** 500 TB SAN

    ○ **B.** 50 GB NAS

    ○ **C.** 3 TB HDD

    ○ **D.** 512 GB SSD

Quick Answer: **107**
Detailed Answer: **120**

46. Which of the following terminates a coaxial cable?

    ○ **A.** F connector

    ○ **B.** DB-9

    ○ **C.** RJ11

    ○ **D.** RJ45

Quick Answer: **107**
Detailed Answer: **121**

47. Mary's printer is printing hundreds of pages, and she can't get it to stop. She has tried to delete the job by double-clicking the printer and deleting the print job. Which of the following steps would be the best way to stop the printer?

    ○ **A.** Clear the print spooler.

    ○ **B.** Unplug the printer.

    ○ **C.** Reset the printer.

    ○ **D.** Turn off the printer.

Quick Answer: **107**
Detailed Answer: **121**

48. You are troubleshooting a coworker's computer. When you ping the loopback address, you receive no response. Which of the following is the most likely cause of this problem?

    ○ **A.** The LAN is unresponsive.

    ○ **B.** The DHCP server is down.

    ○ **C.** The Ethernet cable needs to be replaced.

    ○ **D.** The TCP/IP protocol is not functioning.

Quick Answer: **107**
Detailed Answer: **121**

49. Which of the following steps should be performed when trouble-shooting a Bluetooth connection that is malfunctioning? (Select the two best answers.)

    ❏ **A.** Verify that the WLAN is enabled.

    ❏ **B.** Ensure that you are in range.

    ❏ **C.** Unpair the devices.

    ❏ **D.** Turn Bluetooth off and on.

50. A customer brings in a computer that doesn't display anything when it is turned on. You verify that the computer and monitor are receiving power and that the monitor is securely connected to the computer's only video port. Which of the following is the most likely cause of this problem? (Select all that apply.)

    ❏ **A.** Motherboard

    ❏ **B.** RAM

    ❏ **C.** Storage drive

    ❏ **D.** DVD-ROM

    ❏ **E.** CPU

    ❏ **F.** Power supply

    ❏ **G.** Video card

    ❏ **H.** SATA data cable

51. While troubleshooting a network problem, you discover that one set of LED lights on a switch is blinking rapidly even when all other nodes are disconnected. Which of the following is the most likely cause of this problem? (Select the two best answers.)

    ❏ **A.** A switch that is not plugged into a server

    ❏ **B.** A defective storage drive in the computer

    ❏ **C.** A defective network card in the computer

    ❏ **D.** An unplugged server

    ❏ **E.** A defective port on the network switch

52. A user with an Android phone is attempting to get email to work properly. The user can send email but cannot receive it. The user is required to connect to a secure IMAP server, as well as an SMTP server that uses SSL/TLS. To fix the problem, which port should you configure?

    ○ **A.** 25

    ○ **B.** 110

    ○ **C.** 143

    ○ **D.** 443

    ○ **E.** 993

53. You are called to a school lab to fix a computer. The computer supposedly worked fine yesterday, but now it does not power on. The computer is plugged into a power strip with another computer. The other computer works fine. Which of the following are the most likely causes of this problem? (Select the two best answers.)

- ❏ **A.** The power cable is unplugged from the computer.
- ❏ **B.** The power strip is overloaded.
- ❏ **C.** The monitor is unplugged.
- ❏ **D.** The voltage switch on the power supply is set incorrectly.
- ❏ **E.** The power strip is unplugged.

54. Tracy cannot connect to the network and asks you to help. Which of the following steps should be performed first?

- ○ **A.** Replace the NIC.
- ○ **B.** Reconfigure TCP/IP.
- ○ **C.** Check for a link light on the NIC.
- ○ **D.** Install the latest NIC drivers.

55. You have been tasked with setting up a Wi-Fi thermostat for a customer. The customer has concerns about IoT devices getting hacked and possibly acting as gateways to other devices and computers on the network. Which are the *best* ways to address the customer's concern? (Select the two best answers.)

- ❏ **A.** Upgrade the customer's router to the latest firmware version.
- ❏ **B.** Disable wireless access to the thermostat to make it unhackable.
- ❏ **C.** Upgrade the customer's wireless network to WPA.
- ❏ **D.** Separate the IoT thermostat by placing it in a screened subnet.
- ❏ **E.** Use the latest encryption standard on the wireless network and set a strong password.
- ❏ **F.** Enable two-factor authentication for the IoT device's cloud account.

Quick Check

Quick Answer: **107**
Detailed Answer: **123**

56. Your coworker's tablet is having trouble connecting to email. Which of the following steps should be performed to troubleshoot this problem? (Select the three best answers.)

❏ **A.** Verify Internet access.

❏ **B.** Check for Bluetooth connectivity.

❏ **C.** Check port numbers.

❏ **D.** Make sure GPS is enabled.

❏ **E.** Verify the username and password.

Quick Answer: **107**
Detailed Answer: **124**

57. You just installed Microsoft Windows on a computer with three internal SATA storage drives and one external USB flash drive. SATA storage drive 1 contains the operating system. SATA drive 2 contains the user profiles. SATA drive 3 and the external USB flash drive are empty. Where should you place the pagefile to maximize performance?

○ **A.** The external USB flash drive

○ **B.** Internal SATA storage drive 1

○ **C.** Internal SATA storage drive 2

○ **D.** Internal SATA storage drive 3

Quick Answer: **107**
Detailed Answer: **124**

58. One of your customers is having difficulty with two network connections in the accounting office. The accounting office is adjacent to the building's mechanical room. Network cables run from the accounting office through the drop ceiling of the mechanical room and into the server room next door. Which of the following solutions should be recommended to the customer?

○ **A.** UTP

○ **B.** Plenum-rated cable

○ **C.** T568B

○ **D.** Fiber optic

Quick Answer: **107**
Detailed Answer: **124**

59. A customer reports that a computer freezes after booting into the operating system. The customer has replicated the problem by rebooting the system three times. You analyze the computer and see the following results:

```
CPU:    3.0 GHz quad-core
                Vcore:          1.25 V
                Overclocking:   Enabled
                Fan speed:      5000 rpm
                Temperature:    90° C
        GPU:    PCI Express
                Memory:         2 GB
                GPU voltage:    1.022 V
                Temperature:    60° C
```

```
Drive:   NVME (SMART data)
                 Read error:    200
                 Seek error:    200
PSU:     600 W
                 3.3 V rail:    3.36 V
                 5 V rail:      4.97 V
                 12 V rail:     11.98 V
```

Which of the following should you research further as a potential cause of the freeze-ups?

○ **A.** The integrity of the storage drive

○ **B.** The CPU temperatures

○ **C.** The power supply voltages

○ **D.** The GPU temperatures

60. Michelle's laptop powers on only when the AC adapter is connected to it. Which of the following is the most likely cause of this problem?

Quick Answer: **107**
Detailed Answer: **125**

○ **A.** Bad transformer

○ **B.** Bad AC port on the laptop

○ **C.** Bad battery

○ **D.** Bad CMOS battery

61. A user reports that a laser printer is printing poorly. You observe that the pages have wrinkles and random patterns of missing print. Which of the following is the most likely cause of this problem?

Quick Answer: **107**
Detailed Answer: **125**

○ **A.** The fuser needs to be replaced.

○ **B.** The toner cartridge is defective.

○ **C.** The corona wire is frayed.

○ **D.** There is high humidity in the room.

62. A user asks you to explain a message that comes up on the computer display before the operating system boots. The message states that the BIOS/UEFI logged a chassis intrusion. Which of the following would be your explanation to the user?

Quick Answer: **107**
Detailed Answer: **125**

○ **A.** The laptop combination lock has been picked.

○ **B.** The CPU is loose.

○ **C.** A malicious individual has hacked the system.

○ **D.** The computer case has been opened.

63. Jim attempts to plug a scanner into the front USB port of a Windows PC, but the scanner does not power on. Which of the following solutions should be recommended to Jim?

- ○ **A.** Use a different USB cable.
- ○ **B.** Run Windows Update on the computer.
- ○ **C.** Upgrade the computer's drivers.
- ○ **D.** Use the onboard USB ports.

64. One of your coworkers just installed a newer, more powerful video card in a customer's computer. The computer powers down before it completes the boot process. Before the installation, the computer worked normally. Which of the following is the most likely cause of this problem?

- ○ **A.** The video card is not compatible with the CPU.
- ○ **B.** The monitor cannot display the higher resolution of the new video card.
- ○ **C.** The computer's RAM needs to be upgraded.
- ○ **D.** The power supply is not providing enough wattage for the new video card.

65. One of the users at your organization will be attending several day-long conferences and wants to make sure a mobile device will have enough power for the events. There will be a lack of AC outlet availability, and the user needs to continuously use the mobile device throughout the events. The user also needs to access the mobile device's USB port to access flash drives. In addition, the user needs to access the Internet to get updates. What should you recommend to the user?

- ○ **A.** Purchase a built-in battery case.
- ○ **B.** Use a wireless charging pad.
- ○ **C.** Bring extra charging cords.
- ○ **D.** Put the mobile device into airplane mode.

66. You want your computer to boot from the network and have the capability to be brought out of sleep mode over the network. Which two technologies should be implemented in the BIOS/UEFI?

- ○ **A.** WAP and WPA3
- ○ **B.** WDS and a magic packet
- ○ **C.** PXE and WOL
- ○ **D.** Ghost and Unattend.xml

67. A customer tells you that a networked printer is not printing documents. You successfully ping the printer's IP address. Which of the following is the most likely cause of this problem? (Select the two best answers.)

- ❑ **A.** The printer is low on toner.
- ❑ **B.** The network cable is unplugged.
- ❑ **C.** The printer is out of paper.
- ❑ **D.** The gateway address on the printer is incorrect.
- ❑ **E.** The spooler is not functioning.

68. A customer has a home office. Which of the following technologies would benefit from the use of QoS?

- ○ **A.** SSID
- ○ **B.** Instant messaging
- ○ **C.** Email
- ○ **D.** VoIP

69. A PC's monitor has no display after a power failure. The LED light on the monitor is on. Which of the following steps should be performed first?

- ○ **A.** Power cycle the PC.
- ○ **B.** Power cycle the peripherals.
- ○ **C.** Power cycle the UPS.
- ○ **D.** Power cycle the breaker switches.

70. Which of the following should be checked when a laptop fails to turn on? (Select the four best answers.)

- ❑ **A.** Power LED
- ❑ **B.** Sound port
- ❑ **C.** AC adapter
- ❑ **D.** Inverter
- ❑ **E.** Hibernate mode
- ❑ **F.** Function key
- ❑ **G.** Power button

71. A computer just had a memory upgrade installed. After the computer is booted, it does not recognize the new memory, even though it is listed as being compatible on the manufacturer's website. Which of the following steps should be performed to resolve the issue?

Quick Answer: **107**
Detailed Answer: **128**

- ○ **A.** BIOS/UEFI update
- ○ **B.** Adjust jumper settings
- ○ **C.** OS update
- ○ **D.** New CMOS battery

72. A computer has a RAID 1 array. SATA drive 0 failed, and now the computer will not boot. You need to boot the computer temporarily to get access to data quickly. Which of the following steps would most likely allow the computer to boot again?

Quick Answer: **107**
Detailed Answer: **128**

- ○ **A.** Replace SATA drive 1.
- ○ **B.** Mark SATA drive 1 as active.
- ○ **C.** Replace SATA drive 0.
- ○ **D.** Replace the array's controller.

73. You are troubleshooting what you believe to be a power issue. Which of the following should be tested first?

Quick Answer: **107**
Detailed Answer: **128**

- ○ **A.** Power supply
- ○ **B.** 24-pin power connector
- ○ **C.** IEC cable
- ○ **D.** AC outlet
- ○ **E.** Circuit breaker

74. A CAD/CAM workstation running AutoCAD is displaying rotating 3D images very slowly. The customer needs the images to rotate quickly and smoothly. Which of the following should be upgraded on the computer? (Select the best answer.)

Quick Answer: **107**
Detailed Answer: **128**

- ○ **A.** CPU
- ○ **B.** RAM
- ○ **C.** Video card
- ○ **D.** Storage drive

75. Which of the following devices is used to implement network security for an IT environment?

Quick Answer: **107**
Detailed Answer: **129**

    ○ **A.** Managed switch

    ○ **B.** Repeater

    ○ **C.** Gateway

    ○ **D.** Firewall

76. Your end users work with a web-based calendar app. Which of the following cloud-based technologies are they using?

Quick Answer: **107**
Detailed Answer: **130**

    ○ **A.** SaaS

    ○ **B.** IaaS

    ○ **C.** PaaS

    ○ **D.** DaaS

77. You are a manager of a technical services team. One of your technicians notices that a printer is jamming just above the printer tray. Which of the following steps should the technician first perform to resolve the issue?

Quick Answer: **107**
Detailed Answer: **130**

    ○ **A.** Clean the feeder rollers.

    ○ **B.** Clean the pickup rollers.

    ○ **C.** Replace the fuser.

    ○ **D.** Replace the drum.

78. You configured a customer's router to automatically assign only five IP addresses in an attempt to make the network more secure. Now you notice that the wireless printer is intermittently losing connections when there are multiple users on the wireless network. Which of the following would be the best solution?

Quick Answer: **107**
Detailed Answer: **130**

    ○ **A.** Increase the wireless router IP lease times.

    ○ **B.** Install another access point.

    ○ **C.** Configure the printer to use a static IP address.

    ○ **D.** Configure the printer for DHCP.

79. Which of the following steps can be performed to ensure that all external traffic to your website is directed through a firewall to the right computer?

Quick Answer: **107**
Detailed Answer: **130**

- O **A.** Configure port forwarding.
- O **B.** List in the exceptions the IP address of the local website.
- O **C.** Configure NAT.
- O **D.** Configure all interior traffic appropriately.

80. You are troubleshooting an Internet connectivity issue. Several laptop users cannot connect to any websites. Users with desktop PCs do not have any trouble. Which of the following is most likely causing the problem?

Quick Answer: **107**
Detailed Answer: **131**

- O **A.** Router
- O **B.** Cable modem
- O **C.** WAP
- O **D.** Encryption
- O **E.** Firewall
- O **F.** UTM
- O **G.** IPv6 link-local address

Quick-Check Answer Key

1. B	28. B	55. D and E
2. B	29. B	56. A, C, and E
3. D	30. C	57. D
4. A and E	31. C	58. D
5. C	32. C	59. B
6. D	33. C	60. C
7. C and D	34. D	61. A
8. C	35. B	62. D
9. B and C	36. D	63. D
10. A	37. B	64. D
11. D	38. C	65. B
12. A	39. A, C, and E	66. C
13. C	40. A and C	67. C and E
14. D	41. A and C	68. D
15. D	42. C	69. A
16. C	43. B	70. A, C, E, and G
17. C	44. C and D	71. A
18. B	45. C	72. B
19. C	46. A	73. C
20. C	47. A	74. C
21. C	48. D	75. D
22. B	49. B and D	76. A
23. C	50. A, B, E, and G	77. B
24. A and D	51. C and E	78. C
25. A	52. E	79. A
26. C	53. A and D	80. C
27. A	54. C	

Answers and Explanations

1. **Answer: B**

   Explanation: Print a test page after doing preventive maintenance on a laser printer.

   Incorrect answers: Normally, when you maintain a laser printer, you power it down and unplug it before any work begins. So, you do not need to restart the printer; when you finish, you simply start it. You also do not need to restore a printer to factory settings unless it fails. Your preventive maintenance will hopefully stave off that dark day. The paper trays probably still have paper in them; anyway, part of preventive maintenance is to fill the trays. Printing the test page should be last.

2. **Answer: B**

   Explanation: Most likely, repetitive flashing lights on a keyboard indicate the presence of a hardware error, probably internal to the computer. If nothing comes up on the display, and all you have to go by are flashing lights on the keyboard, you can probably ascertain that the POST has failed, and the problem lies within the big four (as I like to call them): CPU, RAM, video, or motherboard.

   Incorrect answers: Software errors can't occur until the operating system attempts to boot, and without the POST finishing successfully, that won't happen. Passwords are required when you see a repetitive flashing light on the screen, not on the keyboard—and even then, only if you are attempting to access the BIOS (or UEFI) or if someone configured a user password in the BIOS. External peripherals don't need to post properly for the computer to boot to the OS. Even the keyboard isn't necessary. The POST is more interested in the guts of the computer, especially the big four and the storage drive.

3. **Answer: D**

   Explanation: The port numbers 21, 22, 25, 53, 443, and 3389 correspond to the protocols FTP, SSH, SMTP, DNS, HTTPS, and RDP.

   Incorrect answers: The Telnet protocol uses port 23. Telnet is deprecated, insecure, and outdated; plus, it isn't even installed or enabled on newer versions of operating systems. Use SSH in its place for a more secure connection. HTTP uses port 80. This also is considered deprecated and is mostly used only for testing purposes as of 2022. It is important to use HTTPS (on port 443), which makes use of Transport Layer Security (TLS). POP3 uses port 110. However, this is considered insecure as well; it is recommended to use port 995 and TLS security instead. Know your port numbers!

4. **Answers: A and E**

   Explanation: Of the listed answers, continuity and resistance are the settings that you should use when there is no electrical flow through the part being tested, and you want to be sure that there is no electrical flow when doing these tests. Examples of continuity or resistance tests include testing a fuse's impedance (measured in ohms) and testing a network cable for continuity. In each example, you don't want any electricity flowing through the device or line. It would give erratic results and could possibly cause damage to your testing equipment and even you.

   Incorrect answers: When testing for watts, volts, and amps, you need to have electricity flowing through the item you want to test.

5. **Answer: C**

    Explanation: The power-on self-test (POST) checks the CPU, memory, video card, and so on when the computer first boots and displays error messages if any errors occur.

    Incorrect answers: BIOS/UEFI setup is the program you can access to configure the system. The BIOS is more than just the setup program that you can access, and the POST is a part of the BIOS. The CMOS chip retains settings that the BIOS records during the POST. (Note that the bootstrap loader is within the ROM chip as well. When the computer is turned on, it automatically reads the storage drive boot sector to continue the process of booting the operating system.) A blue screen of death (BSOD) error is a Windows error that means the operating system has failed to boot.

6. **Answer: D**

    Explanation: Use a Wi-Fi connection from a laptop or another mobile device to manage IoT devices such as smart thermostats. (You might also use Zigbee or Z-wave technologies.)

    Incorrect answers: Remote Desktop Protocol (RDP) is used to remotely control Windows systems. Secure File Transfer Protocol (SFTP) is used to get and put files to and from an FTP server. Near-field communication (NFC) is used to transmit files and data between two mobile devices (or a mobile device and a point-of-sale device) that are in close proximity to each other. Simple Mail Transfer Protocol (SMTP) is used to send email.

7. **Answers: C and D**

    Explanation: The first thing you should do is put on your antistatic strap. The last thing you should do is test the motherboard. Always remember to test!

    Incorrect answers: You already selected the motherboard. Technically, installing the CPU isn't part of the motherboard installation process, but you can't really test the motherboard without it. Either way, the CPU would be installed before testing. Cables need to be connected during the installation and prior to testing. But anything that deals with power or circuit boards should not be touched unless you are wearing an antistatic strap.

8. **Answer: C**

    Explanation: Use a power supply unit (PSU) tester to determine why a computer fails to boot. One of the culprits could be a faulty power supply.

    NOTE

    You should also make use of a POST tester if the motherboard has an integrated one.

    Incorrect answers: A cable tester checks network cables only to see if they are wired correctly and have continuity. Loopback plugs are used to test network cards and serial ports. A tone and probe kit (also known as a toner probe) is used to test phone lines and network connections for continuity. So, the rest of the answers are all tools that are used externally from the computer, whereas the PSU tester is the only one used inside the computer.

9. **Answers: B and C**

    Explanation: DDR4 and DDR5 DIMMs both have 288 pins—but they are not compatible with each other!

    Incorrect answers: DDR3 DIMMs have 240 pins. Error correction code (ECC) in RAM can detect *and* correct errors. Real-time applications might use ECC RAM. When using ECC, additional information needs to be stored, and more resources are used in general. Quad-channel means that the address bus uses four 64-bit channels simultaneously, resulting in a 256-bit bus that is often inhabited by four separate RAM modules.

10. **Answer: A**

    Explanation: The Trusted Platform Module (TPM) chip should be enabled. This can be done in the BIOS/UEFI. Once it is enabled, you can configure full disk encryption with BitLocker (in Windows) or another provider's tool. Many motherboards come with a built-in TPM chip.

    Incorrect answers: Secure Boot is enabled in the BIOS/UEFI as well, but it verifies that the system is booted securely by validating special cryptographic keys. Newer versions of Windows (such as Windows 11) require Secure Boot. Unified Extensible Firmware Interface (UEFI) is the firmware that is meant to replace the older Basic Input/Output System (BIOS). However, we often just refer to these together—for example, as "BIOS/ UEFI." A hardware security module (HSM) is a device that manages digital keys and performs encryption as well. This is a device that is separate from the desktop computer or is installed as a PCIe card. While this could do the job (and can meet stringent security requirements), the scenario says not to add any hardware. The Encrypting File System (EFS) in Windows is designed to encrypt individual files or folders but not the entire drive. Use BitLocker or another third-party tool to do that.

11. **Answer: D**

    Explanation: A tone and probe kit (also known as a toner probe) allows you to find the network drop in the wiring closet. Here's how this works: You connect the tone generator portion of the tone and probe kit via RJ45 to the network port in the user's cubicle. Then you switch it on so that it creates tone. Then you go to the wiring closet (or network room or server room) and use the probe (an inductive amplifier) to find the tone. You do this by pressing the probe against each of the cables. This is an excellent method when there are dozens or hundreds of cables in the wiring closet. When you find the right cable, plug it into the patch panel or directly into a network switch. (Or terminate it with an RJ45 plug if it is not already terminated.) When you return to the user's cubicle, the RJ45 jack should be "hot," meaning it can be used to send and receive data.

    Incorrect answers: A PSU tester tests the power supply of a computer. A multimeter can test the voltage of any wire or AC outlet. *Cable tester* is somewhat of a vague term, but it usually means either a network patch cable tester or a LAN tester, which checks the individual wires of longer network cable runs.

12. **Answer: A**

    Explanation: SATA power connections have 3.3-, 5-, and 12-volt wires.

    Incorrect answers: There are no negative voltage wires on SATA power connections. However, the main 24-pin power connection of a power supply has positive *and* negative wires. Molex power connections use 5 V and 12 V only, but SATA includes the 3.3 V line. In this scenario, you should test the SATA power connector and the main power connector from the power supply with your trusty PSU tester. (Most PSU testers have an SATA power port in addition to the main 24-pin power port.)

13. **Answer: C**

    Explanation: Amperage can be defined as electric current or the movement of electrical charge. It is measured in amps (A). You should know the circuits in your office. The more you know, the less chance of overloading them. For example, a standard 15-amp circuit might be able to handle three or four computers and monitors. But a 20-amp circuit can handle one or two additional computers. Circuit breakers, electrical cable, and outlets all must comply with a certain number of amps. If you connect a power strip or surge protector, make sure that it is specified to work with your circuit's amp rating.

    Incorrect answers: Voltage is a representation of potential energy, measured in volts (V). Wattage is electric power, the rate of electric energy in a circuit, measured in watts (W). Impedance is the amount of resistance to electricity, measured in ohms (Ω).

14. **Answer: D**

    Explanation: Use a simple moist cloth that is not too wet; you don't want to get any liquid inside the printer.

    Incorrect answers: Soap and water can be used to clean the outside of a computer case (or the outside of a printer case). WD-40 can, over time, cause damage to various components within a printer. (Have you ever sprayed WD-40? It's somewhat hard to contain in a small area.) Alcohol is too strong and can dry out the rollers, making them ineffective over time. However, in some dirtier environments, you might need something stronger once in a while. Your best bet in these uncommon situations is to mix standard 70% isopropyl alcohol with water so that there is 50% alcohol and 50% water. This reduces the potency of the alcohol. (I do this for cleaning monitor screens and mobile devices as well.)

15. **Answer: D**

    Explanation: The most appropriate frequency listed is 5 GHz. This is used by faster Wi-Fi such as 802.11n, 802.11ac, and 802.11ax. You might also be interested in the 6 GHz wireless range, which is just being released as of the writing of this book (in 2022) and works with the 802.11ax Wi-Fi standard. Always be on the lookout for better, stronger, and faster technologies!

    Incorrect answers: 13.56 MHz is used by near-field communication (NFC). The 1300–1350 MHz frequency range is used by long-range radar systems. 2.4 GHz is used by Wi-Fi but generally doesn't allow for the same type of speed/bandwidth as 5 GHz.

2.4 GHz was very common with older and slower Wi-Fi technologies such as 802.11b and 802.11g. While it can be used on 802.11n and 802.11ax Wi-Fi standards, it does not have the frequency range (or channel bonding) required to achieve maximum data rates. 802.11ac works on 5 GHz only.

16. **Answer: C**

    Explanation: In DHCP, set a reservation based on the MAC address. In this scenario, the clients are most likely connecting to the printer by using the IP address. Internet Printing Protocol (IPP) can be used in this manner. By default, the moment the new printer is connected to the network, it acquires an IP address from the DHCP server; this is a new IP address that is different from the one used by the old printer. This causes the clients to fail when attempting to connect and print to the new printer. To prevent this problem, you can go to the router (or another DHCP device) and configure a MAC address reservation. The MAC address of the printer (which might be on a label or might be accessible from the onscreen display) can be plugged into the DHCP server and reserved to a specific IP address. Of course, a better option would be to simply configure the printer to use a static IP address.

    Incorrect answers: Renaming the printer with the old name doesn't help because the client computers are most likely connecting via IP address, not via name. Printing the configuration page is great and might help you to figure out what the problem could be, but it doesn't actually solve the problem!

17. **Answer: C**

    Explanation: Hypertext Transfer Protocol Secure (HTTPS) is used to make secure connections to websites. It uses the Transport Layer Security (TLS) protocol to encrypt connections and make logins, purchases, and so on safe. HTTPS relies on port 443 by default.

    Incorrect answers: SSH, which stands for Secure Shell, is used to make secure remote connections between computers for the purposes of command execution and remote control, and it replaces the deprecated Telnet protocol. It uses port 22. SFTP is SSH File Transfer Protocol, a more secure version of FTP that is built on SSH. Kerberos is a network authentication protocol used by various systems, including Microsoft domains. It uses port 88.

18. **Answer: B**

    Explanation: Simple Network Management Protocol (SNMP) can be used to monitor remote computers and printers. This requires the installation of SNMP on the appropriate hosts. Be sure to use the latest version of SNMP across all devices!

    Incorrect answers: SMTP, which stands for Simple Mail Transfer Protocol, deals with the sending of email. TCP/IP is the entire suite of protocols that you use when you connect to an IP network. IPP, which stands for Internet Printing Protocol, allows hosts to print documents to a remote printer without the need for UNC paths. It is the basis for Apple's AirPrint technology and is supported by most printers. DNS, which stands for Domain Name System, resolves domain names to their corresponding IP addresses.

19. Answer: C

Explanation: An indication of a power supply issue is frequent failure of storage drives. If the power supply fails to provide clean power to the 3.3 V, 5 V, and 12 V lines to the drives, those drives will fail frequently. These are often the first devices to fail when a power supply starts having intermittent problems. You should test such issues with a power supply tester or multimeter.

Incorrect answers: If the power supply fails, the CPU does not overclock; on the contrary, it might lose power and turn off the computer altogether. Overclocking is controlled in the BIOS/UEFI, and there are thresholds in place to stop the CPU from overclocking too far. The wireless adapter would either work or not work. Reduced range could be due to obstruction or distance from the wireless access point (WAP). If USB drives are not recognized by Windows (or any other OS), the USB host controller driver might need to be updated.

20. Answer: C

Explanation: Virtualization workstations require powerful CPUs with multiple cores— as many cores as possible, as well as maximized RAM. This allows the system to run virtualization software that can house multiple virtual machines (VMs), each with its own OS, with all the VMs running simultaneously. While it is helpful for any computer, such as a gaming computer, to have a powerful CPU and loads of RAM, the virtualization workstation especially needs them to run multiple VMs at the same time.

Incorrect answers: The other systems are not reliant on CPUs and RAM *to run multiple VMs*. A gaming computer isn't used to run multiple operating systems at the same time; it's used to play games. This means that while the CPU (and overclocking) and RAM are important, the most important component is the video card. Note that an actual PCIe *card* should be used, and it should not be integrated with the motherboard. A Layer 3 switch is a network switch that is managed and assigned an IP address. While it has a CPU and RAM, it is not a device that you would upgrade in the way that you would a PC. Also, it does not run virtual machines. A network-attached storage (NAS) device relies on a RAID array, a good network adapter, and sometimes increased RAM. While you can run basic VMs on a NAS device, their CPU power is usually limited.

21. Answer: C

Explanation: You should select a barcode reader. This tool reads barcodes such as UPC barcodes that have groupings of parallel lines of varying widths. (Note that you might also use a magnetic reader.)

Incorrect answers: A biometric scanner authenticates individuals by scanning physical characteristics such as fingerprints. There are many types of image scanners; multifunction printers have them and allow you to scan photos or make copies of documents. A touchpad is a device that takes the place of a mouse. It is often used in laptops but can be purchased as an external peripheral for desktop PCs as well.

22. **Answer: B**

    Explanation: The best answer is two PCI Express (PCIe) version 4 slots (that is, version 4 minimum). For SLI to work properly, you need two identical PCIe slots. SLI is an NVIDIA technology; AMD CrossFire (CF) is a similar multi-GPU technology.

    Incorrect answers: Version 3 PCIe is an older version. For a new gaming computer, you would most likely want to go with the latest standards (and new standards are always being released!). The SLI technology cannot span different expansion slots. Video cards are normally placed into larger slots (such as x16) only, not x1 slots. USB is not an expansion slot at all; it is a port, as mentioned, and does not work together with PCIe in an SLI configuration. It doesn't have nearly the bandwidth or capabilities of PCIe.

23. **Answer: C**

    Explanation: RAID 5 is fault tolerant and allows for striping with parity (if you have at least three drives to dedicate to the array). It's the parity information that makes it fault tolerant.

    Incorrect answers: RAID 0 is simply striping of data. It is not fault tolerant, meaning that it cannot re-create data after a failure or continue to function after a failure. RAID 1 is mirroring; it requires two drives and is fault tolerant. (With advanced version of RAID 1 called disk duplexing, each drive in the mirror is connected to its own storage drive controller.) RAID 10 is a stripe of mirrors. It requires four drives and is fault tolerant. It stripes the mirrors but does not stripe with parity.

24. **Answers: A and D**

    Explanation: The mouse can move erratically due to an incorrect driver or an uneven surface. Remember to visit the website of the device manufacturer to get the latest and greatest driver. That should fix the problem. But an optical mouse is very sensitive and needs to be on an even, flat surface. Also, it helps if that surface is nonreflective.

    Incorrect answers: An optical mouse doesn't have a trackball. Older ball mice had trackballs, and they had to be cleaned to fix this problem. (Good luck finding one!) The mouse should not conflict with the keyboard. Every USB device gets its own resources; this is taken care of by the USB controller. Finally, if the mouse needs to be charged or needs new batteries, it should simply stop working.

25. **Answer: A**

    Explanation: Use monitors with DisplayPort connections to "daisychain" monitors together. As of the writing of this book (2022), DisplayPort is the only video technology that can do this. Daisychaining means to run the monitors in series: Computer > Monitor1 > Monitor2 > Monitor3. This means that Monitor1 and Monitor2 would need to have DisplayPort inputs and outputs (which not all DisplayPort-ready monitors have). The monitors would have to be equipped with DisplayPort version 1.2 or higher or Thunderbolt. The computer's GPU would have to support DisplayPort 1.2 or higher as well as Multi-Stream Transport (MST). Some GPUs can handle three monitors, and others can handle up to six.

Incorrect answers: As of the writing of this book, VGA, HDMI, DVI, and USB-C cannot perform monitor daisychaining. Note that USB-C can support video signals (as well as audio and, of course, data), but the monitor and the PC/laptop would have to be equipped with a USB-C connector.

26. **Answer: C**

Explanation: You should check the wall outlet first if you are dealing with a power issue. Because power comes from the AC outlet, it should be foremost on your mind.

NOTE

Before checking the AC outlet, check the system's power button and power cable!

Incorrect answers: If you have already deduced that the wall outlet is not causing a problem, check the power supply next. Input devices don't often cause power issues unless they are active devices, meaning they plug into an AC outlet. But once again, you should unplug them and check the AC outlet where they are plugged in. Phone and network cabling can carry power surges and spikes, especially if they are not installed or grounded properly. However, it is less likely that the power issue emanates from a networking or telecommunications cable. After checking the wall outlet and power supply, unplug them from the computer when troubleshooting power issues.

27. **Answer: A**

Explanation: If a computer is attempting to obtain an IP address automatically and it receives the IP address 169.254.127.1—or any other IP address starting with 169.254—DHCP has failed at either the client or the server. When this happens, Windows automatically assigns an APIPA address. Then the computer will be able to communicate only with other computers on the 169.254 network, which is pretty worthless if that is not your main network number. What went wrong? The problem could be one of several things. Perhaps the DHCP client service on the client computer needs to be restarted. Or maybe the computer is not connected to the right network. It could even be a problem with the server: It may lack IP addresses, the DHCP service may have failed, the DHCP server may be down, and so on. Put on your problem-solving hat and start troubleshooting!

Incorrect answers: DNS deals with resolving domain names to IP addresses; it doesn't affect DHCP address assignment. A virtual private network (VPN) is a private connection from a host to other locations that runs over the Internet in a secure manner. VPNs are often reliant on DHCP, but they are not in charge of distributing IP addresses automatically the way DHCP is. DNS could fail, and a computer could still obtain an IP address from a DHCP server. If APIPA failed, the computer wouldn't be able to get an address on the 169.254 network. If DHCP and APIPA were both to fail, the client computer would effectively have the IP address 0.0.0.0 (or nothing would be listed in the **ipconfig** screen), placing the computer in the Twilight Zone.

NOTE

If you do not understand any of the acronyms used in this explanation, or if you are having trouble with any of the concepts listed (besides the Twilight Zone), it is a strong indicator that you need to study more.

---

28. **Answer: B**

    Explanation: Remove the CMOS battery from the motherboard. Normally, this trick resets any variable settings in the BIOS/UEFI, such as the password and time/date. On some older systems you need to move a BIOS configuration jumper to another position in addition to removing the battery. You can perform essentially the same thing on some laptops by powering down the system, removing the battery, and pressing and holding the power button for 30 seconds.

    Incorrect answers: Removing the RAM doesn't do anything. When the computer is turned off, the contents of RAM are emptied. Today's motherboards usually don't have RAM jumpers. Removing the main power connection from the motherboard will have no effect if the computer was already turned off and unplugged. By the way, RAM and power connections should not be removed unless the power has been shut off and the AC cable has been unplugged.

29. **Answer: B**

    Explanation: One drive can fail in a RAID 5 array, and the array can rebuild that drive's data from the remaining drives. However, if a second drive fails, the array is toast. The reason is that the array requires the parity information from all the other drives.

    Incorrect answers: One—and only one—drive can fail in a RAID 5 array. However, with a RAID 6 array (which includes another parity stripe), you could lose as many as two drives and still continue to function. In other systems, such as RAID 10, you could lose additional drives and still function. With any type of RAID, be sure to have a backup plan in place.

30. **Answer: C**

    Explanation: Remove the storage drive before releasing a computer to a third party. There could very well be confidential company data on the drive. Store the drive in a locking cabinet. Don't worry; the manufacturer of the laptop has plenty of drives it can use to test the laptop! Another option would be to image the drive, store the copied image in a secure location, and then sanitize the drive before shipping out the system.

    Incorrect answers: You don't need to remove the display panel or WLAN card because they do not contain confidential information. Also, if the laptop is under warranty, you should not remove the display yourself; instead, send it to the manufacturer for repair and set up a temporary laptop for the user in question. Finally, you could clean it if you want, but do you really have time for that?

31. **Answer: C**

    Explanation: To ensure that the virtual machines (VMs) can be installed to the various desktops, make sure that Intel virtualization is enabled in the BIOS/UEFI. Without it, Hyper-V, VMware Workstation, VirtualBox, and other virtualization platforms will not function.

> **NOTE**
>
> Intel CPU virtualization is named VT-x. AMD CPU virtualization is named AMD-V. However, on newer systems, the BIOS/UEFI might simply say "Virtualization."

Incorrect answers: A TPM chip, which stands for Trusted Platform Module chip, is a chip on the motherboard that, if enabled, allows for encryption of an entire drive. Hyperthreading is built into most CPUs today; it allows two concurrent threads per CPU core. VNC, which stands for Virtual Network Computing, is a graphical desktop sharing system.

32. **Answer: C**

Explanation: If you start at the thin client, the first link in the networking chain is the thin client itself—specifically, the thin client's network interface card (NIC).

Incorrect answers: The next step would be the network switch. If the OS image is stored on another network, then the next link in the chain would be the router (or routers). It is unlikely that an OS image will be transferred over a VPN connection, but you never know. Regardless, that would require VPN software at the thin client, so this wouldn't be a physical networking device. You might have some sort of physical VPN concentrator device, but that would be outside the thin client and therefore not the first link in the chain.

33. **Answer: C**

Explanation: DVI-I accepts analog and digital video signals. All DVI ports are video only; they do not support audio.

Incorrect answers: DVI-D is digital only, as you may guess from the *D*, and DVI-A is analog only. HDMI can accept video *and* audio signals. While not common, HDMI type B—known as *double bandwidth*—supports higher resolutions than type A.

34. **Answer: D**

Explanation: A mobile hotspot, when enabled, allows a mobile device to share its Internet connection with other Wi-Fi–capable devices. This might also be referred to as "Wi-Fi tethering."

Incorrect answers: In USB tethering, a mobile device shares its Internet connection with a PC or laptop via USB. The term *Wi-Fi sharing* is not typically used. A virtual local area network (VLAN) is an isolated area of a LAN; it refers to the partitioning of a network, not Internet sharing.

35. **Answer: B**

Explanation: Three-dimensional (3D) printers use filaments (often made of plastic) to build three-dimensional objects.

Incorrect answers: Laser printers use toner cartridges. Inkjet printers use ink cartridges. Thermal printers use specially coated paper that is super-heated.

36. **Answer: D**

    Explanation: Add memory to the printer. Large documents, especially those with graphics, require more memory to print. A printer's memory can be upgraded in a similar manner to a PC's.

    Incorrect answers: The paper doesn't have an effect on large documents, but it could be an issue if the entry rollers are grabbing more than one piece of paper at a time; that would indicate that the paper is too thin (that is, the pound size is too low). If the communications cable were faulty, no pages would print at all; you would probably get a message on the printer's display warning of a bad connection. If a toner cartridge began to fail, you would see white lines, smearing, or faded ink.

37. **Answer: B**

    Explanation: In this scenario, you are most likely working on a managed switch. A managed switch allows an administrator to log in and view/modify the configuration of the switch, including items such as the IP address. The management interface is common in Cisco switches. This scenario was based on the Cisco SG200 smart switch.

    > **NOTE**
    >
    > For practice, check out the Cisco switch emulators at https://community.cisco.com/t5/small-business-support-documents/200-series-smart-switches-online-device-emulators/ta-p/3173055.

    Incorrect answers: A sandbox isn't really a device. It's an isolated area where a program can be run and tested without interfering with other programs or the host's operating system. NID stands for network interface device; a common example of a NID is the termination point for a household's cable Internet connection. A spam gateway is often software based; it is used to identify and quarantine spam emails before they are delivered to users on the network.

38. **Answer: C**

    Explanation: You should first attempt to reseat the laptop in the docking station; the laptop probably doesn't have a sturdy connection, and the blinking battery light is telling you that the laptop is not charging properly (or at all).

    Incorrect answers: Charge the laptop before you attempt to reseat or replace the battery. This is a hardware issue; the operating system does not have an effect on the blinking battery light.

39. **Answers: A, C, and E**

    Explanation: You can try power cycling the device, ensuring that the SSID is correct, and forgetting the network and then reconnecting to it. You should also check whether the device is within range of the wireless access point, whether the device supports the necessary encryption, and whether Internet passthrough or other Internet sharing technologies are conflicting. Furthermore, you can power cycle the Wi-Fi program, check whether any Wi-Fi sleep is enabled, and try enabling best Wi-Fi performance if the device offers it.

Incorrect answers: Using the cellular GPRS connection is not a valid option when troubleshooting the Wi-Fi connection. Setting up a static IP address on a mobile device is usually not a good idea and not necessary; in fact, this is one of the things you should check in the Advanced settings of the device. A static IP address applied to the Wi-Fi adapter could prevent the device from connecting to all wireless networks except the one that uses that IP address network number.

40. **Answers: A and C**

    Explanation: To connect a Bluetooth headset to a smartphone, you must pair the device to the phone; then, if necessary, you enter a passcode into the phone to use the device. Here is the CompTIA Bluetooth pairing process:

    ▶ Enable Bluetooth.

    ▶ Enable pairing.

    ▶ Find a device for pairing.

    ▶ Enter the appropriate PIN code.

    ▶ Test connectivity.

    Incorrect answers: Drivers are usually not necessary; most mobile devices have Bluetooth installed and usually recognize devices automatically. If this phone does not recognize devices automatically, you might have to update Bluetooth on the device or update the device's OS. Disabling Wi-Fi is not necessary; however, Wi-Fi and Bluetooth have been known to have conflicts, and sometimes one must be disabled to use the other.

41. **Answers: A and C**

    Explanation: You should make sure that the heat sink is secure and that the fan is connected. Either of these issues could cause the CPU to overheat. Also, make sure that thermal compound was applied to the heat sink. If you didn't log in writing somewhere that you did this, you will have to take the heat sink off and inspect it. It's a good idea to log when you apply thermal compound because if you remove the heat sink, you will need to reapply thermal compound before reinstalling it.

    Incorrect answers: The BIOS/UEFI temperature threshold is what tripped, causing the system to shut down. You could increase the threshold, which would fix the problem temporarily but could cause permanent damage to the CPU. The threshold is there to protect the CPU; therefore, "Check the BIOS/UEFI temperature threshold" is not the best answer. If the RAM needed to be reseated, you might get one of several errors or beeps, but the system should not automatically shut down.

42. **Answer: C**

    Explanation: The power supply is the most likely source of a burning smell. If it is a very slight smell, the power supply could be brand new. New power supplies have a "burn-in" period of 24–48 working hours. However, you should be very cautious. If the power supply is about to fail, or if it does fail, it could burn up the motor that drives the fan. This situation could be an electrical and/or fire hazard. So, to be safe, you should remove the power supply and test it in your lab or call the manufacturer for a replacement.

Incorrect answers: It is possible but unlikely that the thermal paste would cause a burning smell; however, if this were to occur, it would be much less noticeable and more chemical in nature. The keyboard should not present a burning smell no matter how fast you type on it. The AC outlet could possibly be the cause of a burning smell, and that would be very bad news. In that case, disconnect devices from that outlet, turn off the circuit breaker immediately, and call an electrician. However, the AC outlet is not part of the computer.

43. **Answer: B**

Explanation: The laptop is probably connecting to a different wireloss network, either in the home next door or in an adjacent business—and that network does not have encryption, it would seem. Based on the speed—300 Mbps—you can safely assume that the connection being made is to an 802.11n network (or something similar). The best course of action is to verify the SSID name of the 802.11ac router, forget the current wireless network, and connect to the new network. You might find that in some cases a laptop connects at a slower speed (such as 802.11n), even though faster speeds (such as 802.11ac and 802.11ax) are available. The reason could be due to the configuration of the WAP or the wireless adapter on the laptop. That's not one of the listed answers and is not the case here because of the poor signal strength mentioned in the scenario.

Incorrect answers: The cable modem isn't part of the equation in this scenario. You are only interested in connecting to the wireless network to start. A router (wireless access point) doesn't have a wireless card like the ones in desktops and laptops. Also, you don't know whether the device is faulty yet because the laptop never connected to it. The same goes for the wireless antennas.

44. **Answers: C and D**

Explanation: RAID 1 (mirroring) provides fault tolerance by copying information to two drives. RAID 5 (striping with parity) provides fault tolerance by keeping a compressed copy of the data (in the form of parity) on each of the disks other than where the original data is stored. (Note that RAID 6 and RAID 10 would also provide for fault tolerance.)

Incorrect answers: RAID 0 is striping only, and a spanned volume is one that stores data on two or more drives—but as whole files rather than as stripes of data.

45. **Answer: C**

Explanation: The best of the listed answers is 3 TB HDD, meaning a 3 terabyte magnetic-based hard disk drive. It can be installed internally to the computer, is relatively inexpensive, and offers a good storage size that probably won't be exceeded in the next six months (although anything can happen!).

Incorrect answers: A 500 TB storage area network (SAN) is an entire network of storage devices that exists outside the desktop computer. Also, for a typical PC, it is much bigger than needed. A 50 GB network-attached storage (NAS) device also exists outside the desktop computer. In addition, the storage size is quite limited. A 512 GB SSD is a possibility, but it doesn't have as much space as the 3 TB HDD, and it will be more expensive per megabyte. A good rule of thumb is to use SSDs for the OS, apps, and working projects and use an HDD for backup and long-term storage. Keep in mind that this does not take into account any fault tolerance.

46. **Answer: A**

    Explanation: The F connector (also known as F-type) is commonly used to terminate coaxial cable that is used for television or cable Internet. Generally, it is used to terminate RG-6 cable, but it might also be seen with RG-59 cable, which has a thinner conductor and therefore isn't used as much. (Note that RG-59 cable may also be terminated with BNC connectors for professional video applications.)

    Incorrect answers: The DB-9 connector (more accurately named the DE-9) is used for serial connections between computers. RJ11 plugs are used with telephone lines. RJ45 plugs are commonly found as the terminators of patch cables in twisted-pair networks.

47. **Answer: A**

    Explanation: Clear the printer spooler. You do this by stopping the Print Spooler service in Computer Management (or in the PowerShell/Command Prompt by entering **net stop spooler**) and then deleting the files in the path C:\Windows\System32\Spool\Printers.

    Incorrect answers: Try not to turn off or unplug the printer unless absolutely necessary. The answer "Reset the printer" is somewhat vague, but doing that would most likely result in a need for printer reconfiguration.

48. **Answer: D**

    Explanation: Pinging the loopback address should return results even if you are not physically connected to the network. This trick deals with the computer internally and doesn't even require a LAN. You can ping the local computer with the commands **ping loopback** and **ping localhost**; however, the best option is to ping the IPv4 loopback IP address by typing **ping 127.0.0.1** (or **ping ::1** for IPv6). This eliminates any possible name resolution that might occur in Windows. Note that name resolution happens whenever you connect to a system by name (such as computerA, workstationB, and so on); the name must ultimately be translated to its corresponding IP address. So, to avoid any name resolution issues, we computer techs like to go right to the source and ping the IP address directly. This way, we can troubleshoot whether the TCP/IP protocol suite is functioning properly, without being concerned about any other services and name resolution getting in the way. It's a good general practice for connecting to systems directly.

    Incorrect answers: Pinging the loopback address doesn't make use of the network, so the LAN, DHCP servers, and Ethernet cable do not play into the scenario.

49. **Answers: B and D**

    Explanation: Determine whether you are within range. The range of Bluetooth devices is limited; for example, Class 2 devices are limited to 10 meters. Also try power cycling the Bluetooth program by turning Bluetooth off and on. In addition to those correct answers, you can try charging the device, restarting the device, working with a known good Bluetooth device, attempting to forget the device, and reconnecting it.

    Incorrect answers: WLAN is a separate wireless technology from Bluetooth, and it should not have any bearing on how Bluetooth functions. If devices are paired within Bluetooth, they should work; unpairing and re-pairing should not have any effect.

50. Answers: A, B, E, and G

Explanation: If the computer is receiving power, everything is hooked up properly, and there is no display, you need to consider the big four: motherboard, CPU, video card, and RAM. These are the four components of the computer that could cause a no-display issue. The most common is the video card. Check whether it is seated properly into the expansion slot. You should also check whether that card works in one of your test systems. Next, check whether the RAM and then the CPU are properly installed and compatible. Finally, check the motherboard, if necessary. Of course, at the beginning of this process, you should ask the customer when this computer failed and whether anything was recently modified on the system. The answers might help you troubleshoot the problem. You would question the user during step 1 of the CompTIA A+ troubleshooting process: Identify the problem.

Incorrect answers: The storage drive won't even be accessed if the system's RAM, motherboard, or CPU fails because the system won't even run the POST. There will be little to no activity on the storage drive LED. If the video card failed, the system might still boot, but it would do so without video, and you would see some drive LED activity. However, some systems will not boot; lack of video will cause the system to stop at the POST. In the unlikely event that your computer has one, the DVD-ROM drive won't cause a no-display issue because it is a secondary device. The power supply is not the cause of the problem in this case. The scenario says that the computer was receiving power. If the power supply failed, nothing would happen when you press the computer's power-on button. If the SATA data cable were disconnected (and if that were the only problem), you would get video, the system would POST (and most likely record a drive error), and when the system attempted to boot to the drive, you would get a "missing OS" error or a similar message.

51. Answers: C and E

Explanation: If only one computer is connected to the switch, there shouldn't be much activity. Rapidly blinking LED lights might lead you to believe that the computer's network card (NIC) or the port on the switch is faulty. The problem could be that the person is sending a lot of data to himself while you are testing the network, but that would be strange and rare.

Incorrect answers: Switches are not plugged into servers; however, they facilitate network connections between many computers. A defective drive would cause some kind of boot failure. The server doesn't have anything to do with this scenario.

52. Answer: E

Explanation: What should have been port 993 was probably configured incorrectly if the person can send but not receive email. To securely send email over Internet Message Access Protocol (IMAP), use port 993.

Incorrect answers: Simple Mail Transfer Protocol (SMTP) uses port 25 by default to send mail but uses port 587 (or 465) if SSL or TLS security is implemented. Port 110 is the POP3 email port. POP3 also is used to receive email, but not in this question's scenario. IMAP can receive email on port 143, but it is not considered secure. Port 443 is commonly used by HTTPS. Configuring email on mobile devices such as Android phones can be a little more difficult than configuring email on PCs. Be sure to work with mobile devices and go through the steps of setting up email on both Android and iOS.

53. **Answers: A and D**

    Explanation: Check the basics first! Make sure the power cable isn't disconnected from the computer and verify that the voltage switch on the power supply is in the correct position (if the PSU is not auto-switching). Kids like to play tricks on lab computers!

    Incorrect answers: A standard power strip should not overload with just two computers connected to it, but if it does, press the reset switch on the power strip. The monitor being unplugged could be a separate problem, but it won't prevent the computer from powering on. If the second computer works fine, that tells you the power strip is plugged in.

54. **Answer: C**

    Explanation: Start with the physical! Of the listed answers, check for a link light on the NIC first. This light tells you whether there is physical connectivity. Note that, before this, you should check the network icon within the operating system to see if there are any errors.

    Incorrect answers: If necessary, you can, in this order, test the patch cable, reconfigure TCP/IP, install drivers (from the manufacturer's website), and, finally, replace the NIC.

55. **Answers: D and E**

    Explanation: Start securing the IoT device by separating it (and other IoT devices). Do this by moving it to a screened subnet (DMZ) or a guest network (or both). Also, use the latest encryption standards for the wireless network—that is, WPA2/WPA3 or higher and AES.

    Incorrect answers: You should definitely upgrade the router to the latest firmware, but that is not the best answer listed because it does not directly affect the IoT device. More importantly, update the IoT device's firmware—often! Disabling wireless access would render the thermostat nonfunctional. Upgrading to WPA is not enough. Newer versions of WPA are available. Two-factor authentication (if it is even available) would provide good security, but that is something that concerns the account that accesses the thermostat—but only if the thermostat can be controlled over the cloud. You don't know that this thermostat allows cloud-based access based on the information in the scenario. If this feature does exist, you should secure the login as much as possible, but the device itself can still be accessed via Wi-Fi.

56. **Answers: A, C, and E**

    Explanation: First, make sure that the tablet has a connection to the Internet. Then check that the email settings—including port numbers, server names, username/password, and any security settings—were entered properly.

    Incorrect answers: Bluetooth can be off while email is being used. GPS tracks where a mobile device is located, and it too can be turned off when accessing email.

57. **Answer: D**

Explanation: Use internal SATA drive 3 for the pagefile (pagefile.sys). By separating the pagefile from the operating system and the user profiles, you maximize the system's performance.

Incorrect answers: If the pagefile were on either of the other SATA drives, the constant accessing of the pagefile would slow down the OS performance or would slow down the access to user files. SATA drive 3 is a better option than the external USB flash drive for a variety of reasons: it is probably faster; it is subject to less latency; and, in general, internal drives perform more efficiently than external drives.

58. **Answer: D**

Explanation: Of the listed answers, you should recommend fiber-optic cables. Another option would be shielded twisted pair (STP). Furthermore, you could rerun the cables through a metal conduit or reroute the cables around the mechanical room. In this scenario, it is likely that the mechanical room's contents are causing interference on the network cables. Electromagnetic interference (EMI) can be prevented with STP or fiber-optic cables.

Incorrect answers: UTP (unshielded twisted pair) is the most common type of cable, and it is probably what the customer is using currently. Plenum-rated cable is used in areas where sprinklers cannot get to. It has a coating that makes it burn much more slowly than regular cable. T568B is the most common network cabling wiring standard.

59. **Answer: B**

Explanation: You should investigate the CPU temperatures first. 90° Celsius is very high for a CPU. For example, the maximum operating temperature of many Intel Core i7 CPUs is 68°C (154°F). You'll note that the fan speed is very high as well. It is apparently at the maximum in an attempt to cool the CPU. But with the temperature that high, the fan won't be enough. The BIOS/UEFI has a built-in safeguard that either freezes or shuts down the system if the CPU temperature reaches a certain threshold for a period of time. The CPU could be overheating because it was not installed properly, there is not enough airflow, or there is overclocking involved (which appears to be the case here). Troubleshoot right away. You don't want a fried CPU!

Incorrect answers: The integrity of the drive is okay. A value of 200 for the raw read error rate and seek error rate is normal and should also display with the status "OK." The power supply unit (PSU) voltages are within specifications. Generally, you want a reading that is within ±5% of the normal voltage. So for example, the 3.3 V rail should be within 3.135 and 3.465 volts. Anything beyond that standard deviation should be analyzed further. This situation is okay, because at the rail is at 3.36 volts. 60°C is a decent temperature for a GPU. GPUs consistently run in that temperature range.

NOTE

To analyze (and benchmark) your computer's hardware, use tools such as CPU-Z, GPU-Z, HWiNFO, AIDA64, HWMonitor, or others.

60. Answer: C

Explanation: If the laptop gets power when plugged in but doesn't work when disconnected from AC power, the battery must be dead or defective.

Incorrect answers: A bad transformer means that the AC adapter needs to be replaced. That and a bad AC port would cause the laptop to fail when plugged into the AC adapter, but the laptop should work fine on battery power (until the battery fully discharges, that is). A bad CMOS battery causes the time, date, and passwords to be reset in the BIOS/UEFI.

61. Answer: A

Explanation: The wrinkled pages are the number-one indicator that the fuser needs to be replaced. Random patterns of missing print further indicate that the fuser is not working properly. Toner not being fused to the paper is the last clue. The fuser usually needs to be replaced every 200,000 pages or so on a laser printer.

Incorrect answers: If the toner cartridge were defective, either you would get blank printouts or you would see lines or smears, but there wouldn't be page wrinkles. If the transfer corona wire were defective, it might result in blank paper. Damage to the primary corona wire can also result in black lines or smearing. High humidity could cause the separation pads or rollers to fail.

62. Answer: D

Explanation: A chassis intrusion means that the computer case has been opened. On some motherboards, the BIOS/UEFI program has the capability to detect this. This is a security feature that informs the user of a possible breach. As a PC/laptop technician, you should check the computer inside and out for any possible tampering.

Incorrect answers: The BIOS/UEFI program will not detect if a laptop's combination lock has been compromised. These are external locking cables that connect to the laptop and can be used to secure the laptop to a stationary item like a desk or pole. Regardless, generally, you are more concerned with chassis intrusion on PCs. (Also, a person wouldn't "pick" a combination lock, but I digress.) If the CPU were loose, the computer would not boot, and there would be nothing to display. It is possible that a malicious individual has hacked—or attempted to hack— the system. However, this is not necessarily the case, although you should check to make sure.

63. Answer: D

Explanation: Tell the customer to use the onboard ports—that is, the ports that are integrated directly into the motherboard on the back of the PC. This is a quick, temporary fix, but it should work because these ports are hardwired to the board. The front USB plugs are part of the computer case; they were probably never connected to the motherboard properly. You would want to connect those case wires to the USB headers on the motherboard. You should also check whether the USB scanner needs to be plugged into an AC outlet.

Incorrect answers: If the *back* USB ports don't work, you could try a different USB cable. Software shouldn't affect the USB device getting power. If a device has a proper USB connection, it should power up. But, after that, if Windows doesn't recognize the USB device, try updating drivers and Windows.

64. Answer: D

Explanation: Today's video cards can be very powerful and might require a more powerful power supply than is in the computer currently. For example, many computers come with 450 W or 600 W PSUs. A user may decide to upgrade the video card but not bother to engineer the power that will be required. I have seen this happen several times.

Incorrect answers: Video cards need to be compatible with the motherboard—and not necessarily with the CPU. If the monitor could not display the higher resolution, the operating system would still boot, but you would probably see garbled information on the screen. Because a video card comes with its own RAM, the computer's RAM usually does not need to be upgraded.

65. Answer: B

Explanation: Of the listed answers, the best option is to use a wireless charging pad for the mobile device. The device can be charged before each event and can work as a good portable solution.

Incorrect answers: A built-in battery case usually has to connect to the device's USB port (or Lightning port), which—if there is no passthrough capability—might stop the user from working with flash drives. (It's also better—from a monetary standpoint—to use something that is already available as opposed to purchasing something new.) It doesn't matter how many charging cords you have; if AC wall outlets are not accessible, you will have to charge during the event in another way. Putting the device into airplane mode would stop it from accessing the Internet, but Internet access is a requirement in this scenario.

66. Answer: C

Explanation: To configure the BIOS/UEFI to boot from the network, you have to enable the Preboot Execution Environment (PXE) network adapter. To allow the computer to be brought out of sleep mode by another system on the network, you need to configure Wake-on-LAN (WOL) in the BIOS/UEFI. (The system doing the "waking up" would need to send a magic packet across the network to do so.)

Incorrect answers: WAP stands for wireless access point; WPA3 refers to the Wi-Fi Protected Access version 3 encryption used on a WAP. WDS, which stands for Windows Deployment Services, is used in Windows Server to deploy installations of Windows to remote computers. A magic packet is a special packet sent to a computer to wake it up, but it is configured in Windows. The Ghost application is used to create or install images of operating systems. Unattend.xml is the answer file created for unattended installations of Windows over a network.

67. Answers: C and E

Explanation: The printer could simply be out of paper, or the spooler could be malfunctioning. If the printer is out of paper, fill all trays and suggest that the user check the trays every couple days or so. If the spooler is not functioning, you should restart the spooler service in the Services console window or in the Command Prompt with the **net stop spooler** and **net start spooler** commands.

Incorrect answers: If the printer were low on toner, you would get weak print or completely blank pages. If the network cable were unplugged, you wouldn't be able to ping the printer. Printers don't always use gateway addresses, but if this one did, it wouldn't affect your ability to connect to it (as long as it was on the LAN). The gateway address is used so that the printer can communicate with computers beyond the LAN.

68. **Answer: D**

Explanation: Voice over IP (VoIP) is a streaming telephony application. Streaming applications such as VoIP and online games can benefit from QoS. QoS stands for quality of service, which is the capability to provide different priorities to different applications (or computers). It guarantees network bandwidth for real-time streaming of media applications such as VoIP. But always check whether the customer's Internet connection has the required bandwidth. For example, a typical 4K video stream requires 25 Mbps.

Incorrect answers: The SSID is the name or identifier of a wireless network. Instant messaging and email are not streaming applications; therefore, they would not benefit from the use of QoS.

69. **Answer: A**

Explanation: If a power failure occurs, try power cycling the PC. In this scenario, it could be that power went out for five minutes. When power returned, the monitor was still on (thus, the LED) but the computer remained off (thus, nothing on the display). Really, in this case, you are just turning *on* the computer.

Incorrect answers: Peripherals should have no bearing on this scenario unless they also plug in. If you power cycle the PC and there is still nothing on the display, try disconnecting the peripherals from the PC, disconnecting the AC power (if the PC has that), and rebooting the PC. If the monitor has an LED light, you know it is getting power, so the UPS does not need to be power cycled. However, if there was a five-minute power loss and the UPS didn't keep the PC running, you should check the UPS battery. Turning the breaker switches for the circuit on and off is always fun but would simply cut power to the AC outlets temporarily.

70. **Answers: A, C, E, and G**

Explanation: Check the power LED on the laptop first and see what it is doing. It could be that the user simply wasn't pressing the power button. If the LED blinks slowly once in a while, the laptop might be in a sleep state. Then check the power light on the AC adapter. Make sure the AC adapter is getting power; if it is, check whether it is the right adapter. Check whether the system is in hibernate mode by pressing and holding the power button. Finally, the power button might be faulty, so make sure it isn't loose. If no AC adapter is available, you should also check whether the battery is connected properly and charged. Make sure the user keeps the AC adapter on hand at all times.

Incorrect answers: Audio, the inverter, and the function keys usually do not cause booting failure. They should not affect whether you can turn on the laptop.

71. Answer: A

Explanation: You should update the BIOS/UEFI. If it hasn't been updated in a while, it probably won't recognize newer memory modules. Flash the BIOS!

Incorrect answers: Most of today's motherboards don't have jumper settings for RAM. In fact, the only jumper you often find is the BIOS configuration jumper, which needs to be configured only if a person forgot a password. The BIOS will have a problem recognizing the RAM far before the OS starts up; no OS updates are required to make RAM recognizable to the system. If the computer needed a new CMOS battery, you would know because the time in the BIOS would reset to an earlier date.

72. Answer: B

Explanation: You would mark SATA drive 1 as active. If you cannot access Disk Management, you have to do it by booting the system with WinRE (System Recovery Options); accessing the Command Prompt; executing the **diskpart** command; and typing the commands **select disk 1**, **select partition 1**, and **active**. A RAID 1 array is a mirroring array with two drives. The second drive keeps an exact copy of the first drive in real time. If drive 1 doesn't take over automatically when drive 0 fails, you have to set it to active. Remember that a partition with an operating system must be set to active; otherwise, the computer will not be able to boot to the partition.

> **NOTE**
>
> Ultimately, you would want to replace drive 0 and re-create the mirror.

Incorrect answers: Replacing drive 1 is not necessary because that drive did not fail. Replacing drive 0 is inevitable if you want to re-create the mirror but not necessary if you just want to get the system to boot for now. Replacing the array's controller is most likely not necessary. You should try replacing the drive first. It is possible (though unlikely) that the drive and the controller failed at the same time, but you should always start with the most likely culprit (and never change out more than one device at a time).

73. Answer: C

Explanation: Check the IEC cable first if you sense that there is a power issue. That is the power cable for the computer; make sure it is connected to the computer and to the AC outlet.

Incorrect answers: Afterward, if the cable is not the issue, you could check the AC wall outlet. Use a receptacle tester or your trusty multimeter to make sure the AC outlet is wired properly and supplying the correct voltage. If that is fine, you can check the power supply and the 24-pin power connector. Check the circuit breaker only if the power has been cut to an area of the building and only if you have access to the electrical panels.

74. Answer: C

Explanation: The video card should be your first stop on the upgrade express train. When images do not display properly, a subpar video card is typically the issue. A CAD/CAM workstation requires a powerful video card.

Incorrect answers: The CPU also plays a role in this scenario (though not as much as the video card does), especially when rendering images, so that is the second thing you should check. Use third-party benchmarking tools or view WinSAT (in Windows) details to find out what has the lowest score and go from there. The video card is most likely the lowest. See the following note for more information about WinSAT. CAD/CAM workstations often require video cards that can cost $1000 or more. Always read the directions carefully and use proper ESD prevention techniques prior to installing a card—especially one that expensive. RAM is important, but it is not as important to the CAD/CAM workstation as the video card (especially based on the question's scenario). Generally, as long as the computer has enough RAM to run Windows and the AutoCAD software, it should be okay. The storage drive isn't much of a factor while the CAD software is running, but for storing and accessing files, an SSD (or M.2) drive is recommended.

NOTE

To run WinSAT on Windows, open PowerShell (as an admin) and run the command **winsat prepop**. Warning: It's best to run this with no other applications open, and you need to be ready for the test to take several minutes. You can watch what is being tested in real time, but to see the actual results, you must type **Get-WmiObject -Class Win32_WinSAT**. This will pull data from an XML file—created during the previous procedure—and display those results. Following is an example of the results after running this test on a Core i5 laptop with an SSD and upgraded RAM:

```
CPUScore:        8.6
D3DScore:        9.9
DiskScore:       8.2
GraphicsScore:   6.5
MemoryScore:     8.6
```

Note that the graphics score is the lowest, which is common with laptops, though the disk score could be low as well if the laptop uses a magnetic-based drive.

This example just scratches the surface of the **WinSAT** command. Be sure to update PowerShell for best results.

---

75. Answer: D

Explanation: A firewall is used to implement security for the computer network; for example, a firewall might include access control lists (ACLs) that allow or deny incoming and outgoing traffic.

Incorrect answers: A managed switch connects computers and servers on the network and can be configured from a remote workstation (usually by logging in to the switch via a browser). A repeater is a physical device that amplifies a network signal so that it can travel farther. The gateway device is usually a router; it acts as a doorway to the Internet or other networks for the computer on the LAN.

76. **Answer: A**

    Explanation: This is an example of software as a service (SaaS). Google, Microsoft, Apple, and other companies offer such services to end users and business users.

    Incorrect answers: Infrastructure as a service (IaaS) offers computer networking, storage, load balancing, routing, and VM hosting. Platform as a service (PaaS) provides various software solutions to organizations, especially the capability to develop and test applications. DaaS can stand for either data as a service or desktop as a service. Data as a service is similar to SaaS in that products are provided on demand, but it is more data oriented as opposed to app oriented. In desktop as a service, a cloud provider hosts the back end of a virtual desktop; this is also known as virtual desktop infrastructure (VDI).

77. **Answer: B**

    Explanation: The technician should clean the pickup rollers. Dirty or oily rollers could cause a paper jam directly behind or above the paper tray.

    Incorrect answers: The feeder rollers would cause a jam further in the printer. A fuser issue would cause a jam up toward the end of the printing path. The drum (or toner cartridge) will usually not cause a paper jam, but in rare cases, simply replacing the toner cartridge can help.

78. **Answer: C**

    Explanation: If the wireless printer is losing connections when multiple users are on the network, the reason is probably that there aren't enough automatically assigned IP addresses to go around. You should configure the printer to use a static IP address instead of receiving one dynamically from the router. This address will be permanent and should fix the problem. Often, companies insist that printers (as well as routers, switches, and servers) always get static addresses to avoid problems of this sort.

    Incorrect answers: Increasing the IP lease times might work—or it might not. When multiple users attempt to get on the wireless network, someone is going to lose out; it might be a person at a laptop, or it might be the printer or another device. Therefore, increasing the IP lease times is not a permanent solution. Another access point might increase your wireless coverage, but it will do nothing for your IP issue. The whole problem here is that the printer was configured for DHCP; it was obtaining its IP address automatically from the DHCP server within the router. When it is changed to static, it doesn't have to compete for the five dynamically assigned IPs.

79. **Answer: A**

    Explanation: In this scenario, your organization is running a web server on the LAN. Your job is to make sure that all clients outside your network on the Internet that are attempting to access the web server can do so. You must configure port forwarding for this to work. The HTTPS requests, or whatever port the clients use to access the web server (perhaps 443, but not necessarily), should be forwarded to the IP address and port of the web server on your network.

Incorrect answers: Exceptions are meant to allow certain computers access into or out of the firewall, but this would give the external clients too much access. You should streamline this configuration so that the external traffic is all directed to your web server, and port forwarding is the best way to do this. NAT, which stands for Network Address Translation, is used to match up the private IP address numbers of your internal computers to the external public IP addresses they attempt to connect to; it protects the private IP identity of the internal computers. However, it's actually not the interior traffic you are concerned with. Instead, you are concerned with the external traffic trying to get into your network and visit your web server—and the web server *only*.

80. **Answer: C**

Explanation: The wireless access point is most likely the problem. Perhaps it was turned off or disabled or lost its connection to the network. This WAP failure causes the laptops to fail when attempting to connect to websites; furthermore, the laptops won't have any Internet connection whatsoever. There are a lot of reasons a client computer may not be able to connect to a WAP, but if several wireless clients cannot make the connection, you can usually assume that the problem is not at the client side and instead is at the central connecting device—in this case the WAP. Laptops often connect wirelessly because they are mobile devices, whereas PCs often connect in a wired fashion because they are stationary and don't necessarily need a wireless connection.

Incorrect answers: If the PCs can connect to the Internet fine (as the question states), you can probably rule out the router, cable modem, firewall, and UTM device—unless, of course, one of the devices was configured with some kind of rule stating that the laptops can't connect to websites. This is unlikely, but it is a possibility if the network has a firewall or UTM. UTM stands for unified threat management; UTM devices combine the functionality of firewalls, intrusion detection systems (IDSs), and proxy servers, among other things. UTMs and next-generation firewalls (NGFWs) are designed to integrate a variety of threat defenses into one device.

An IPv6 link-local address is an address that starts with fe80. It is not a device at all but instead is a software-based TCP/IP configuration.

An encryption mismatch is always possible when it comes to wireless connections. Perhaps the WAP is configured for WPA2 or WPA3 and AES, but a laptop is configured with WPA or TKIP or both. That mismatch would cause the laptop to fail to connect to the wireless network and, ultimately, the Internet.

However, for several laptops to fail due to encryption mismatches, they would all have to be configured improperly, which again is unlikely, and at which point someone would be held accountable for the mistake. Don't let this happen to you! Verify your configurations after you have made them; always test! Testing and troubleshooting are huge parts of the real IT world and the A+ exams, so be sure you study them and practice them intensely.

CHAPTER FIVE

Review of the Core 1 (220-1101)

Phew! That was a lot of questions. But if you're reading this, you survived. Great work!

Now that you have completed the practice exams, let's do a little review of the 220-1101 domains, talk about your next steps, and look at some test-taking tips.

Review of the Domains

Remember that the 220-1101 exam is divided into five domains, as shown in Table 5.1.

TABLE 5.1 Core 1 (220-1101) Domains

Domain	Percentage of Exam
1.0 Mobile Devices	15%
2.0 Networking	20%
3.0 Hardware	25%
4.0 Virtualization and Cloud Computing	11%
5.0 Hardware and Network Troubleshooting	29%
Total	100%

Hardware and troubleshooting make up the majority of questions on the exam, but don't forget about networking, mobile devices, and virtualization and cloud computing. Remember to practice all of the domains and objectives in a hands-on manner while you study the theory behind the concepts.

Many technicians are great with PC hardware, mobile devices, and networking. But for a tech who is weak in the troubleshooting area, the final exam score could be in jeopardy. Study all the concepts in each of the domains. Pay strict attention to troubleshooting concepts; this is where many techs are lacking in knowledge and experience.

Everyone who takes the exam gets a different group of questions. Because the exam is randomized, one person may see more questions on, say, printers than the next person. Or one person might see more questions on laptops. The exam differs from person to person. To reduce your risk of failing, be ready for any question from any domain and study all of the objectives.

In general, this exam deals with installation, configuration, and especially troubleshooting methods, and it is hardware based for the most part. The bulk of the software side of things is reserved for the 220-1102 exam, as is security.

Review What You Know

At this point, you should be pretty well versed in the topics covered on the 220-1101 exam. I still recommend going back through all of the questions and making sure there are no questions, answers, concepts, or explanations you are unclear about. If there are, additional study is probably necessary. If something really just doesn't make sense, is ambiguous or vague, or doesn't appear to be technically correct, feel free to contact me at my website (https://dprocomputer. com), and I will do my best to clarify. (Any errata is listed there as well.)

Here are a couple great ways to study further:

▶ **Take the exams in flash card mode:** Use a piece of paper to cover up the potential answers as you take the exams in this book. This approach helps make you think a bit harder and aids in committing everything to memory. There are also free flash card applications that you can download to your computer to help you organize your studies.

▶ **Download the A+ 220-1101 objectives:** You can get them from https:// www.comptia.org/certifications/a. Go through the objectives one by one and check each item that you are confident in. If you are unsure about any items in the objectives, study them hard. That's where the test will trip you up. There are approximately 12–15 pages of objectives per exam, and going through them will take a while. But this approach really helps close any gaps in your knowledge and gives you an extra boost for the exam.

▶ **Study the 220-1102 questions and then return to the 220-1101 practice exams:** This might sound a bit crazy, but I have found that if an A+ candidate has a strong grasp of *all* A+ topics, he or she is more likely to pass either one of the exams. My recommendation is for you to go through the 220-1102 practice exams, return to the 220-1101 exams for review, and then take the actual CompTIA A+ 220-1101 exam. It's a big extra step, but it has proven very effective with my students and readers.

▶ **Consider my other A+ products:** For example, consider my *CompTIA A+ Core 1 (220-1101) and Core 2 (220-1102) Exam Cram* or my *CompTIA A+ 220-1101 Complete Video Course.* You can find more information about these resources at my website: https://dprocomputer.com.

More Test-Taking Tips

The CompTIA A+ exams contain two types of questions: multiple choice and performance based. The majority of the questions are multiple-choice questions that ask you to select one or more correct answers. The performance-based questions are scenario-oriented questions that test your knowledge by asking you to click on items, click and drag or navigate through a system, and type commands. Knowing the theory is not enough to pass the exam; you have to actually prove your technical ability in a hands-on way.

The majority of multiple-choice questions have four multiple-choice answers, but some have more. These answers are usually connected within the same concept. For example, a question about video connectors might provide four answers—DVI, HDMI, DisplayPort, and VGA—all of which are video ports. Some of the questions are not as synergistic; they might have a group of answers that seem at odds with each other. For example, a question about computer networking protocols might provide four answers: DHCP, DNS, Cat 6, and T568B. While DHCP and DNS are protocols within the TCP/IP suite, Cat 6 and T568B are cabling standards. Be ready for questions whose answers span multiple categories of technology.

Regardless of the type of question, there is often one answer that is just totally wrong. Learn to identify a wrong answer; once you have, you will automatically improve your chances of getting the correct answer, even if you have to guess.

No single question is more important than another. Approach each question with the same dedication, even if you are not interested in the topic or don't like how the question is worded. (Remember that the CompTIA exams are designed and double-checked by a panel of experts.) However, keep in mind that you can mark questions, skip them, and return to them later. If a question doesn't make any sense at all to you, try using that technique—especially for the performance-based questions. Don't let any one question unsettle you: Skip it, mark it, and come back to it later.

When you take the exam, remember to slowly read through the questions and all the answers. Don't rush through. Here are some more smart methods you can use when presented with difficult questions:

▶ Use the process of elimination.

▶ Be logical in the face of adversity.

▶ Follow your gut instinct.

▶ Don't let one question beat you.

▶ If all else fails, guess.

I expand on these points in Chapter 11, "Wrap-up."

If you finish the exam early, use the time allotted to you to review all of your answers. Chances are you will have time left over at the end, and you want to use it wisely. Make sure that everything you have marked has a proper answer that makes sense to you. But try not to overthink! Give the exam your best shot and be confident in your answers.

Taking the Real Exam

Do not register for the actual exam until you are fully prepared. When you are ready, schedule the exam to commence within a day or two so that you don't forget what you have learned.

Registration can be done online. Register at Pearson VUE (https:// home.pearsonvue.com). The site accepts payment by major credit card for the exam fee. First-timers need to create an account with Pearson VUE. Exams can be taken at a Pearson VUE testing site or from home.

Here are some good general practices for taking the real exam:

▶ Pick a good time for the exam.

▶ Don't overstudy the day before the exam.

▶ Get a good night's rest.

- ▶ Eat a decent breakfast.

- ▶ Show up early.

- ▶ Bring earplugs.

- ▶ Brainstorm before starting the exam.

- ▶ Take small breaks while taking the exam.

- ▶ Be confident.

I embellish on these concepts in Chapter 11.

Well, that's it for the 220-1101 portion of this book. Good luck on your exam!

CHAPTER SIX

Introduction to the 220-1102 Exam

The CompTIA A+ Core 2 (220-1102) exam covers operating systems such as Windows, Linux, and macOS; computer and network security; mobile device operating systems such as Android and iOS; software troubleshooting; and operational procedures. The largest percentage of the exam focuses on operating systems—mainly, the installation, configuration, and troubleshooting of Windows—but you will also see many questions on the other topics.

In this chapter, I briefly discuss how the exam is categorized, give you some test-taking tips, and prepare you to take the three 220-1102 practice exams that follow.

Exam Breakdown

The CompTIA A+ 220-1102 exam is divided by domain. Each domain makes up a certain percentage of the test. The four domains of the A+ 220-1102 exam and their respective percentages are listed in Table 6.1.

TABLE 6.1 220-1102 Domains

Domain	Percentage of Exam
1.0 Operating Systems	31%
2.0 Security	25%
3.0 Software Troubleshooting	22%
4.0 Operational Procedures	22%
Total	100%

Chances are that when you take the real CompTIA exam, the questions will be based on these percentages. But you never know. The questions are chosen at random, so you have to be prepared for anything and study all of the objectives.

Each domain has several objectives. There are far too many to list in this book, but I recommend that you download a copy of the objectives for yourself. You can get them from CompTIA's A+ web page (https://www.comptia.org/certifications/a), and I link to them at my website (https://dprocomputer.com) as well.

Let's talk about each domain briefly.

Domain 1.0: Operating Systems (31%)

We've hardly talked about Windows up until this point. But now that we're here, you'll see lots of questions on Windows—I guarantee it.

This domain covers how Windows can be installed, how it is configured, and how it is used. It covers Windows settings, the Windows Control Panel, and a plethora of Windows tools. You'll have to be ready to network Windows computers together, too; be ready to set up workgroups, domains, networking connections, and plenty more. In addition, this domain gets into commands such as **ipconfig**, **netstat**, **shutdown**, and **robocopy**, which are issued in PowerShell or the Command Prompt. Then there's maintenance and backup of Windows. That's a lot already, and this is not a finite list. Know Windows well.

However, it's not all about Windows; Linux, macOS, iOS, Android, and Chrome OS are covered in this domain as well. So, the objectives are in depth. There's a lot of information to cram into one domain, but remember that this domain does not cover Windows troubleshooting; that topic is left for Domain 3.0.

Domain 2.0: Security (25%)

Security takes on a bigger role every year in the IT world. The CompTIA A+ 220-1102 exam reflects this growth. This domain deals with common security threats, physical and digital prevention methods, how to secure the various operating systems listed in the first domain, how to dispose of storage drives properly, and how to secure a small office or home office (SOHO) network. Basically, careful consideration for security should be applied to anything technology oriented.

> **NOTE**
>
> Many test-takers have the most difficulty with this domain and the troubleshooting domain. Be ready.

Domain 3.0 Software Troubleshooting (22%)

Here it is: troubleshooting. It's the troubleshooting methodologies that make the ultimate computer tech. And it's those skills that will make or break you on this exam. So practice in a hands-on manner and break and fix those test systems!

Whenever you encounter a technical problem, try to approach it in a logical manner. The best way to do this is to use some kind of troubleshooting theory.

Remember the CompTIA six-step troubleshooting methodology from the 220-1101 exam? I'd like you to try to incorporate that six-step process into your line of thinking as you read through the practice exams and whenever you trouble-shoot a PC, mobile device, networking, or security issue:

Step 1.   Identify the problem.

Step 2.   Establish a theory of probable cause. (Question the obvious.)

Step 3.   Test the theory to determine the cause.

Step 4.   Establish a plan of action to resolve the problem and implement the solution.

Step 5.   Verify full system functionality and, if applicable, implement preventive measures.

Step 6.   Document the findings, actions, and outcomes.

This section could be considered the most difficult and, unfortunately in the IT field, the most insidious. Issues can look or act like one thing yet be another. Stay focused when dealing with troubleshooting questions. You'll know them when you see them; they include real-world scenarios and often end in a question such as "What should you do to fix the problem?" or "How can this be resolved?"

Know this domain inside and out, and you will be well on your way to passing the A+ 220-1102 exam, attaining your A+ certification, and becoming a true expert at troubleshooting.

Domain 4.0: Operational Procedures (22%)

The fourth domain of the 220-1102 exam deals with safety procedures, environmental concerns, documentation, incident response, prohibited content, communication, professionalism, basic scripting, and remote access. Many of these topics are the "intangibles" of the A+ exam. Although this domain is tied for the smallest percentage of the exam, these concepts could be considered some of the most important topics for the real world. This last domain helps develop a well-rounded technician. Apply the concepts in this domain to everything else you do.

Test-Taking Tips

Just as with the 220-1101 practice exams, I recommend that you take it slowly through these practice exams. Carefully read through each question. Read through *all* of the answers. Look at each answer and consider whether it is right or wrong. And if an answer is wrong, define why it is wrong. This approach will help you eliminate wrong answers in the search for the correct answer. When you select an answer, be confident in your decision.

Be ready for longer questions. The length of these questions is due to the complexity of some of the scenarios. You need to imagine yourself within each situation and think how you would approach the problem step by step. Be prepared to write things down as you look at a question. Doing so can help you organize your thoughts. It's allowed on the real exam as well.

> **NOTE**
>
> If you take an exam in person at a testing center, you should be given something to write on. Be sure that you receive it before you start your exam.

Finally, don't get stuck on any one question. You can always mark it and return to it later. I provide more tips as you progress through the book, and I summarize all test-taking tips at the end of this book.

Getting Ready for the Practice Tests

The practice tests in the following three chapters are based on the 220-1102 exam. Each test is followed by in-depth explanations. Be sure to read them carefully. Don't move on to another exam until you have become proficient at the first one. By that I mean you should be scoring 90% or higher. Be positive that you understand the concepts before moving on to another exam. This will make you an efficient test-taker and allow you to benefit the most from this book.

Consider timing yourself. Give yourself 90 minutes to complete each exam. Write down your answers on a piece of paper. When you are finished, if you still have time left, review your answers for accuracy.

Each exam is more difficult than the one before it. Don't get overconfident if you do well on the first exam; your skills will be tested more thoroughly as you progress. And don't get too concerned if you don't score 90% on the first try. This just means you need to study more and try the test again later. Keep studying and practicing!

After each exam is an answer key, followed by in-depth answers/explanations. Don't skip the explanations, even if you think you know the concept. I often add my two cents, which can add insight to the nature of the question as well as help you answer other similar questions correctly.

Ready yourself: Prepare your mind and then go ahead and begin the first 220-1102 practice exam!

7

220-1102 Practice Exam A

Welcome to the first 220-1102 practice exam. This is the easiest of the 220-1102 exams. The subsequent exams will get progressively harder.

Take this first exam slowly. The goal is to make sure you understand all of the concepts before moving on to the next test.

Write down your answers and check them against the Quick-Check Answer Key, which immediately follows the exam. After the answer key, you will find the explanations for all of the answers. Good luck!

Practice Questions

1. Which of the following are operating systems? (Select all that apply.)

   ❏ **A.** Windows 11

   ❏ **B.** iOS

   ❏ **C.** Disk Management

   ❏ **D.** Chrome OS

   ❏ **E.** Linux

   ❏ **F.** Microsoft Office

   ❏ **G.** macOS

   ❏ **H.** VMware Workstation

Quick Answer: **162**
Detailed Answer: **163**

2. Which of the following is the default file system used by Windows?

   ○ **A.** FAT32

   ○ **B.** ext4

   ○ **C.** NTFS

   ○ **D.** exFAT

Quick Answer: **162**
Detailed Answer: **163**

3. Where is the notification area located in Windows?

   ○ **A.** In the System Properties dialog box

   ○ **B.** In the System32 folder

   ○ **C.** On the taskbar

   ○ **D.** Within the Start menu

Quick Answer: **162**
Detailed Answer: **163**

4. Which of the following is the minimum amount of RAM needed to install a 64-bit version of Windows 10?

   ○ **A.** 512 MB

   ○ **B.** 1 GB

   ○ **C.** 2 GB

   ○ **D.** 2 TB

Quick Answer: **162**
Detailed Answer: **163**

5. In Windows, the MMC is blank by default. Which of the following should be added to the MMC to populate it with programs?

   ○ **A.** Applets

   ○ **B.** Files

   ○ **C.** Directories

   ○ **D.** Snap-ins

Quick Answer: **162**
Detailed Answer: **164**

6. One of the computers in your warehouse often requires the replacement of power supplies, CPUs, and other internal devices. Which tool can help prevent these types of hardware faults?

Quick Answer: **162**
Detailed Answer: **164**

- ○ **A.** Compressed air
- ○ **B.** Antistatic wrist straps
- ○ **C.** Rescue disk
- ○ **D.** Multimeter

7. Which specific tool enables you to create a partition in Windows?

Quick Answer: **162**
Detailed Answer: **164**

- ○ **A.** Disk Management
- ○ **B.** **format** command
- ○ **C.** Computer Management
- ○ **D.** Disk Cleanup

8. Which type of partition should an operating system be installed to?

Quick Answer: **162**
Detailed Answer: **164**

- ○ **A.** Dynamic partition
- ○ **B.** Extended partition
- ○ **C.** Primary partition
- ○ **D.** Logical drive

9. Which of the following tools enables you to find out how much memory a particular application is using?

Quick Answer: **162**
Detailed Answer: **165**

- ○ **A.** MSConfig
- ○ **B.** Task Manager
- ○ **C.** **chkdsk**
- ○ **D.** System Information

10. Which of the following features is used to both start and stop services? (Select the two best answers.)

Quick Answer: **162**
Detailed Answer: **165**

- ❏ **A.** Services.msc
- ❏ **B.** Task Manager
- ❏ **C.** Performance Monitor
- ❏ **D.** MMC
- ❏ **E.** MSConfig

11. Which of the following user account permissions is needed to install device drivers on Windows?

Quick Answer: **162**
Detailed Answer: **165**

- ○ **A.** Standard user
- ○ **B.** Guest
- ○ **C.** Administrator
- ○ **D.** Power user

12. Which of the following commands creates a new directory in the Windows Command Prompt?

Quick Answer: **162**
Detailed Answer: **165**

- ○ **A.** cd
- ○ **B.** md
- ○ **C.** rd
- ○ **D.** ls

13. Which of the following commands is entered at the Command Prompt to learn more about the **dir** command? (Select the two best answers.)

Quick Answer: **162**
Detailed Answer: **166**

- ❏ **A.** dir help
- ❏ **B.** help dir
- ❏ **C.** dir /?
- ❏ **D.** dir man

14. Which interface is used to launch the **ipconfig** command?

Quick Answer: **162**
Detailed Answer: **166**

- ○ **A.** Command Prompt
- ○ **B.** Control Panel
- ○ **C.** MMC
- ○ **D.** Task Manager

15. One of your customers cannot access any websites but can access the company FTP site and can access internal email within Outlook. Which of the following will fix the problem?

Quick Answer: **162**
Detailed Answer: **166**

- ○ **A.** Reconfigure the proxy settings.
- ○ **B.** Disable the firewall.
- ○ **C.** Deactivate and reactivate the network interface card.
- ○ **D.** Remove and reinstall the web browser.

16. Which of the following can be used to keep storage drives free of errors and ensure that Windows runs efficiently? (Select the two best answers.)

Quick Answer: **162**
Detailed Answer: **167**

- ❏ **A.** Disk Management
- ❏ **B.** Disk Defragmenter
- ❏ **C.** chkdsk
- ❏ **D.** System Restore
- ❏ **E.** Task Scheduler

17. A SOHO wireless network has been compromised by an attacker who brute-forced a PIN to gain wireless access. Once the attacker had access, he modified the DNS settings on the SOHO router, and malware was spread throughout the network. Which of the following most likely allowed the attack to occur? (Select the two best answers.)

Quick Answer: **162**
Detailed Answer: **167**

- ❏ **A.** TKIP
- ❏ **B.** Latest WPA version
- ❏ **C.** Default login
- ❏ **D.** Old firmware
- ❏ **E.** WPS
- ❏ **F.** Guest network enabled

18. Which log file contains information about Windows setup errors?

Quick Answer: **162**
Detailed Answer: **167**

- ○ **A.** setupact.log
- ○ **B.** setuperr.log
- ○ **C.** unattend.xml
- ○ **D.** diskmgmt.msc

19. You want to perform a network installation of Windows. Which of the following must be supported by the client computer?

Quick Answer: **162**
Detailed Answer: **167**

- ○ **A.** PCIe
- ○ **B.** PXE
- ○ **C.** BitLocker
- ○ **D.** Multiboot

20. A customer's Device Manager shows an arrow pointing down over one of the devices. What does this tell you?

Quick Answer: **162**
Detailed Answer: **168**

- ○ **A.** The device's driver has not been installed.
- ○ **B.** The device is not recognized.
- ○ **C.** The device is disabled.
- ○ **D.** The device is in the queue to be deleted.

21. Which of the following is *not* an advantage of NTFS over FAT32?

    ○ **A.** NTFS supports file encryption.

    ○ **B.** NTFS supports larger file sizes.

    ○ **C.** NTFS supports larger volumes.

    ○ **D.** NTFS supports more file formats.

Quick Answer: **162**
Detailed Answer: **168**

22. A coworker just installed a second storage drive in his Windows computer. However, he does not see the drive in File Exploror. What did he forget to do? (Select the three best answers.)

    ❏ **A.** Format the drive

    ❏ **B.** Partition the drive

    ❏ **C.** Run FDISK

    ❏ **D.** Initialize the drive

    ❏ **E.** Set up the drive in the UEFI/BIOS

Quick Answer: **162**
Detailed Answer: **168**

23. How would you create a restore point in Windows?

    ○ **A.** Run Disk Defragmenter from the MMC.

    ○ **B.** Run PowerShell.

    ○ **C.** Run the System Restore program from System Properties.

    ○ **D.** Run the Disk Cleanup program from System Properties.

Quick Answer: **162**
Detailed Answer: **168**

24. Which of the following tasks *cannot* be performed from the Printer Properties screen?

    ○ **A.** Modifying spool settings

    ○ **B.** Adding ports

    ○ **C.** Pausing printing

    ○ **D.** Enabling sharing

Quick Answer: **162**
Detailed Answer: **168**

25. You are setting up auditing on a Windows computer. If it's set up properly, which of the following logs should contain entries?

    ○ **A.** Application log

    ○ **B.** System log

    ○ **C.** Security log

    ○ **D.** Maintenance log

Quick Answer: **162**
Detailed Answer: **169**

26. You are working as a computer technician for a mid-sized company. A user calls you and tells you that ransomware has been detected on a PC. You verify that the system indeed has ransomware on it. Of the listed answers, what should you now do first?

    ○ **A.** Disconnect the PC from the network

    ○ **B.** Run an anti-malware scan

    ○ **C.** Educate the user

    ○ **D.** Back up the data on the PC

Quick Answer: **162**
Detailed Answer: **169**

27. Which component of Windows enables users to perform common tasks as nonadministrators and, when necessary, as administrators without having to switch users, log off, or use Run As?

    ○ **A.** UDP

    ○ **B.** UAC

    ○ **C.** USB

    ○ **D.** VNC

Quick Answer: **162**
Detailed Answer: **169**

28. Which of the following tasks can be performed to secure a WAP/router? (Select all that apply.)

    ❏ **A.** Changing the default SSID name

    ❏ **B.** Turning off SSID broadcasting

    ❏ **C.** Enabling DHCP

    ❏ **D.** Disabling WPS

Quick Answer: **162**
Detailed Answer: **170**

29. When you connect to a website to make a purchase by credit card, you want to make sure the website is secure. Which of the following statements best describes how to determine whether a site is secure? (Select the two best answers.)

    ❏ **A.** You should look for the padlock in the locked position toward the top of the screen.

    ❏ **B.** You should look for the padlock in the unlocked position toward the top or bottom of the screen.

    ❏ **C.** You should look for the protocol HTTP in the address or URL bar.

    ❏ **D.** You should look for the protocol HTTPS in the address or URL bar.

Quick Answer: **162**
Detailed Answer: **170**

30. Which type of software helps protect against viruses that are attached to email?

Quick Answer: **162**
Detailed Answer: **170**

- ◯ **A.** Firewall software
- ◯ **B.** Antivirus software
- ◯ **C.** Edge
- ◯ **D.** Hardware firewall

31. Which of the following is an example of social engineering?

Quick Answer: **162**
Detailed Answer: **171**

- ◯ **A.** Asking for a username and password over the phone
- ◯ **B.** Using someone else's unsecured wireless network
- ◯ **C.** Hacking into a router
- ◯ **D.** A virus

32. Where are software-based firewalls most commonly implemented?

Quick Answer: **162**
Detailed Answer: **171**

- ◯ **A.** On routers
- ◯ **B.** On servers
- ◯ **C.** On clients
- ◯ **D.** On switches

33. Making data appear as if it is coming from somewhere other than its original source is known as which of the following terms?

Quick Answer: **162**
Detailed Answer: **171**

- ◯ **A.** Impersonation
- ◯ **B.** Phishing
- ◯ **C.** Zero-day
- ◯ **D.** Spoofing

34. A fingerprint reader is known as which type of security technology?

Quick Answer: **162**
Detailed Answer: **171**

- ◯ **A.** Biometrics
- ◯ **B.** Smart card
- ◯ **C.** Barcode reader
- ◯ **D.** SSID

35. Which of the following is the most secure password?

Quick Answer: **162**
Detailed Answer: **172**

- ◯ **A.** marquisdesod
- ◯ **B.** Marqu1sDeS0d
- ◯ **C.** MarquisDeSod
- ◯ **D.** Marqu1s_De_S0d_ver_2

36. Which shortcut key combination immediately locks Windows?

- ○ **A.** Ctrl+Alt+Del
- ○ **B.** Windows+R
- ○ **C.** Windows+M
- ○ **D.** Windows+L

Quick Answer: **162**
Detailed Answer: **172**

37. Which of the following is the most secure file system in Windows?

- ○ **A.** ext4
- ○ **B.** exFAT
- ○ **C.** NTFS
- ○ **D.** FAT32

Quick Answer: **162**
Detailed Answer: **172**

38. Which of the following is available in Pro editions of Windows but not Home editions?

- ○ **A.** Windows Hello
- ○ **B.** Secure Boot
- ○ **C.** BitLocker Device Encryption
- ○ **D.** Windows Security

Quick Answer: **162**
Detailed Answer: **172**

39. Which of the following terms refers to the process of manipulating people into giving access to network resources?

- ○ **A.** Shoulder surfing
- ○ **B.** Social engineering
- ○ **C.** Phishing
- ○ **D.** Spear phishing

Quick Answer: **162**
Detailed Answer: **173**

40. A customer's Windows computer needs a new larger, faster storage drive. Another technician in your company installs the new drive and then formats the old drive before delivering it to you for disposal. How secure is the customer's data?

- ○ **A.** Confidential
- ○ **B.** Very insecure
- ○ **C.** Secure
- ○ **D.** Completely secured

Quick Answer: **162**
Detailed Answer: **173**

41. Which of the following offers hardware-based authentication?

- ○ **A.** NTFS
- ○ **B.** Smart card
- ○ **C.** Strong password
- ○ **D.** Encrypted password

Quick Answer: **162**
Detailed Answer: **173**

42. Which protocol encrypts transactions through a website?

- ○ **A.** HTTP
- ○ **B.** TLS
- ○ **C.** PuTTY
- ○ **D.** Kerberos

43. Which of the following is typically included in a local security policy?

- ○ **A.** RAID use
- ○ **B.** Password length
- ○ **C.** Router password
- ○ **D.** Use of a password to log in

44. A coworker downloads a game that ends up stealing information from the computer system. What is the term for this?

- ○ **A.** Cryptominer
- ○ **B.** Spam
- ○ **C.** Trojan
- ○ **D.** Spyware

45. Which of the following is an open source operating system?

- ○ **A.** Android
- ○ **B.** iOS
- ○ **C.** Windows
- ○ **D.** macOS

46. Where can you obtain applications for mobile devices? (Select the two best answers.)

- ❏ **A.** Spotlight
- ❏ **B.** App Store
- ❏ **C.** Google Play
- ❏ **D.** File Explorer

47. You need to locate a mobile device that was stolen. Which technology can aid in this?

- ○ **A.** GPS
- ○ **B.** Screen orientation
- ○ **C.** Passcode lock
- ○ **D.** Gmail

48. Which kinds of data are typically synchronized on a smartphone? (Select the two best answers.)

Quick Answer: **162**
Detailed Answer: **175**

- ❏ **A.** Contacts
- ❏ **B.** .ps1 scripts
- ❏ **C.** Email
- ❏ **D.** SQL databases

49. Which of the following is the second step of the A+ best practice methodology for resolving problems?

Quick Answer: **162**
Detailed Answer: **175**

- ◯ **A.** Identify the problem.
- ◯ **B.** Establish a probable cause.
- ◯ **C.** Test the theory.
- ◯ **D.** Document.

50. You successfully modified the registry on a customer's PC. Now the customer's system gets onto the Internet normally. Which of the following steps should be performed next?

Quick Answer: **162**
Detailed Answer: **175**

- ◯ **A.** Bill the customer.
- ◯ **B.** Move on to the next computer.
- ◯ **C.** Document your solution.
- ◯ **D.** Run Disk Defragmenter.

51. A user gets an error that says "Error log full." Where should you go to clear the error log?

Quick Answer: **162**
Detailed Answer: **175**

- ◯ **A.** Device Manager
- ◯ **B.** System Information
- ◯ **C.** Keychain Access
- ◯ **D.** Event Viewer

52. Which of the following tools checks protected system files?

Quick Answer: **162**
Detailed Answer: **175**

- ❏ **A.** chkdsk
- ❏ **B.** dir
- ❏ **C.** ver
- ❏ **D.** sfc

53. After installing a new storage drive on a Windows computer, a user tries to format the drive. Windows does not show the format option in Disk Management. What did the user forget to do first?

Quick Answer: **162**
Detailed Answer: **176**

- ○ **A.** Run **chkdsk**.
- ○ **B.** Partition the drive.
- ○ **C.** Defragment the drive.
- ○ **D.** Copy system files.

54. Which Windows System Recovery option attempts to automatically fix problems?

Quick Answer: **162**
Detailed Answer: **176**

- ○ **A.** System Restore
- ○ **B.** Startup Repair
- ○ **C.** File History
- ○ **D.** Command Prompt

55. You are working at your organization's help desk. A user contacts you because the battery in a company-provided smartphone lasts only a short period of time. Which of the following tasks should you do to increase the battery life in the smartphone? (Select the two best answers.)

Quick Answer: **162**
Detailed Answer: **176**

- ❑ **A.** Increase the time until the screen automatically dims.
- ❑ **B.** Set the smartphone's display to maximum brightness.
- ❑ **C.** Connect to the organization's Wi-Fi network automatically.
- ❑ **D.** Disable 802.11ac and instead use 4G mobile data exclusively.
- ❑ **E.** Close applications when tasks are completed.
- ❑ **F.** Increase email synchronization from every five minutes to every one minute.

56. A blue screen is most often caused by _____.

Quick Answer: **162**
Detailed Answer: **176**

- ○ **A.** driver failure
- ○ **B.** memory failure
- ○ **C.** storage drive failure
- ○ **D.** LED monitor failure

57. A technician is installing a program on a Windows computer, and the installation fails. Which of the following statements describes the next best step?

Quick Answer: **162**
Detailed Answer: **177**

- ○ **A.** Run the installer as an administrator.
- ○ **B.** Contact the program's manufacturer.
- ○ **C.** Reinstall Windows on the computer.
- ○ **D.** Upgrade to the latest version of Windows.

58. Which of the following statements best describes how to apply spray cleaner to a monitor?

Quick Answer: **162**
Detailed Answer: **177**

- ○ **A.** Spray the cleaner directly on the monitor screen.
- ○ **B.** Spray the cleaner on the top of the monitor and wipe it down.
- ○ **C.** Spray the cleaner evenly on the monitor.
- ○ **D.** Spray the cleaner on a clean, lint-free cloth first.

59. You and a coworker are running network cables above the drop ceiling. The coworker accidentally touches a live AC power line and is thrown off the ladder and onto the ground. He is dazed and can't stand. He is no longer near the AC power line. Which of the following statements best describes the first step you should take?

Quick Answer: **162**
Detailed Answer: **177**

- ○ **A.** Cut the power at the breaker.
- ○ **B.** Move the coworker farther down the hall.
- ○ **C.** Begin CPR.
- ○ **D.** Call 911.

60. An employee is completing a credit card payment by phone, but the payment system has a temporary outage. To avoid delaying the customer, the employee writes down the credit card number, expiration date, and CVV on a notepad, planning to enter it into the payment system later. What has the employee violated?

Quick Answer: **162**
Detailed Answer: **177**

- ○ **A.** PII
- ○ **B.** PHI
- ○ **C.** PCI
- ○ **D.** PGP

Quick Check

61. You are working on a very old printer, and it begins to smoke. Which of the following statements best describes the first step you should take?

Quick Answer: **162**
Detailed Answer: **178**

- ○ **A.** Turn off the printer.
- ○ **B.** Call 911.
- ○ **C.** Unplug the printer.
- ○ **D.** Call maintenance.
- ○ **E.** Tell the printer it is bad to smoke.

62. Which of the following statements best describes the recommended method for handling an empty toner cartridge?

Quick Answer: **162**
Detailed Answer: **178**

- ○ **A.** Throw it away.
- ○ **B.** Incinerate it.
- ○ **C.** Refill it.
- ○ **D.** Recycle it.

63. One of your technicians is on a service call and is dealing with a furious customer who has been shouting loudly. The technician tries but cannot calm down the customer. Which of the following statements best describes the next step the technician should take?

Quick Answer: **162**
Detailed Answer: **178**

- ○ **A.** He should let the customer continue to shout; sooner or later the customer will get tired and calm down.
- ○ **B.** He should call the supervisor and complain.
- ○ **C.** He should leave the customer site and document the incident.
- ○ **D.** He should shout back at the customer in an attempt to regain control of the situation.

64. While you are working at a customer site, a friend calls you on your cell phone. Which of the following statements best describes the recommended course of action?

Quick Answer: **162**
Detailed Answer: **178**

- ○ **A.** Ignore the call for now.
- ○ **B.** Go outside and take the call.
- ○ **C.** Answer the phone as quietly as possible.
- ○ **D.** Text your friend.

65. Which of the following tools is used when setting a computer to boot with the Selective Startup feature?

Quick Answer: **162**
Detailed Answer: **179**

- ○ **A.** Task Manager
- ○ **B.** Windows RE
- ○ **C.** Safe Mode
- ○ **D.** MSConfig

66. Which of the following file extensions is used when saving
PowerShell scripts?

Quick Answer: **162**
Detailed Answer: **179**

   ○ **A.** .js

   ○ **B.** .vbs

   ○ **C.** .ps1

   ○ **D.** .py

   ○ **E.** .sh

   ○ **F.** .bat

67. You have been given the task of installing a new storage drive on
a server for a customer. The customer will be supervising your
work. Which of the following questions should you ask the
customer first?

Quick Answer: **162**
Detailed Answer: **179**

   ○ **A.** "What is the administrator password?"

   ○ **B.** "Are there any current backups?"

   ○ **C.** "Do you want me to shut down the server?"

   ○ **D.** "Which version of Windows Server is this?"

68. You just upgraded the president's computer's video driver. Now
the Windows system will not boot. Which of the following steps
should be taken first?

Quick Answer: **162**
Detailed Answer: **179**

   ○ **A.** Access the Windows RE Command Prompt.

   ○ **B.** Boot into Safe Mode and roll back the driver.

   ○ **C.** Reinstall the operating system.

   ○ **D.** Tell the president that you will fix the computer
tomorrow.

69. Which tool is used to analyze and diagnose a video card, including
its DirectX version?

Quick Answer: **162**
Detailed Answer: **179**

   ○ **A.** Device Manager

   ○ **B.** DxDiag

   ○ **C.** Services.msc

   ○ **D.** Disk Management

70. Which of the following statements best describes a common risk
when installing Windows drivers that are unsigned?

Quick Answer: **162**
Detailed Answer: **180**

   ○ **A.** System stability may be compromised.

   ○ **B.** Files might be cross-linked.

   ○ **C.** The drive might become fragmented.

   ○ **D.** Physical damage to devices might occur.

71. Which of the following settings must be established when you
want to make a secure wireless connection? (Select all that apply.)

- ❏ **A.** The brand of access point
- ❏ **B.** The wireless standard used
- ❏ **C.** The encryption standard used
- ❏ **D.** The SSID of the access point

72. Which Windows utility is used to prepare a drive image for
duplication across the network?

- ○ **A.** Robocopy
- ○ **B.** Sysprep
- ○ **C.** Ghost
- ○ **D.** Clonezilla

73. In Windows, when does a computer dump the physical memory?

- ○ **A.** When the wrong processor is installed
- ○ **B.** When a device is missing drivers
- ○ **C.** When the computer is shut down improperly
- ○ **D.** When the computer detects a condition from which it
cannot recover

74. When a person takes control of a session between a server and a
client, it is known as which type of attack?

- ○ **A.** DDoS
- ○ **B.** Brute force
- ○ **C.** Session hijacking
- ○ **D.** Malicious software

75. Which of the following Linux commands should be used to change
the permissions on a file?

- ○ **A.** chmod
- ○ **B.** top
- ○ **C.** grep
- ○ **D.** cat

76. Which of the following should be performed during a storage drive replacement to best maintain data privacy?

   ○ **A.** Completely erase the old drive prior to disposal.

   ○ **B.** Format the new drive twice prior to installation.

   ○ **C.** Use only FAT32 file systems when formatting the new drives.

   ○ **D.** Install antivirus software on the computer before removing the old drive.

Quick Answer: **162**
Detailed Answer: **181**

77. Which tool is used to back up data on the C: drive in Windows?

   ○ **A.** Nano

   ○ **B.** BitLocker

   ○ **C.** Time Machine

   ○ **D.** File History

Quick Answer: **162**
Detailed Answer: **181**

78. Which of the following is the minimum processor requirement for Windows 10/11?

   ○ **A.** 32 GB

   ○ **B.** 1 GHz

   ○ **C.** 2 GHz

   ○ **D.** 2 GB

Quick Answer: **162**
Detailed Answer: **181**

79. You create an answer file to aid in installing Windows. Which type of installation are you performing? (Select the best answer.)

   ○ **A.** Drive image installation

   ○ **B.** USB installation

   ○ **C.** Multiboot installation

   ○ **D.** Unattended installation

Quick Answer: **162**
Detailed Answer: **181**

80. You are troubleshooting a networking issue on a Windows computer. Which of the following commands should you try first?

   ○ **A.** **ip a**

   ○ **B.** **ipconfig /all**

   ○ **C.** **net user**

   ○ **D.** **autofix**

Quick Answer: **162**
Detailed Answer: **181**

Quick-Check Answer Key

1.	A, B, D, E, and G
2.	C
3.	C
4.	C
5.	D
6.	A
7.	A
8.	C
9.	B
10.	A and B
11.	C
12.	B
13.	B and C
14.	A
15.	A
16.	B and C
17.	C and E
18.	B
19.	B
20.	C
21.	D
22.	A, B, and D
23.	C
24.	C
25.	C
26.	A
27.	B

28.	A, B, and D
29.	A and D
30.	B
31.	A
32.	C
33.	D
34.	A
35.	D
36.	D
37.	C
38.	C
39.	B
40.	B
41.	B
42.	B
43.	B
44.	C
45.	A
46.	B and C
47.	A
48.	A and C
49.	B
50.	C
51.	D
52.	D
53.	B
54.	B

55.	C and E
56.	A
57.	A
58.	D
59.	D
60.	C
61.	C
62.	D
63.	C
64.	A
65.	D
66.	C
67.	B
68.	B
69.	B
70.	A
71.	C and D
72.	B
73.	D
74.	C
75.	A
76.	A
77.	D
78.	B
79.	D
80.	B

Answers and Explanations

1. Answers: A, B, D, E, and G

Explanation: Windows 11, iOS, Chrome OS, Linux, and macOS are all types of operating systems. Those operating systems (especially Windows) are the core focus of the 220-1102 exam.

Incorrect Answers: Disk Management is a tool in Windows that is used to create and modify partitions, initialize new drives, create and modify volumes, and so on. Microsoft Office is a suite of applications used for the creation and editing of documents, spreadsheets, slides, and much more. VMware Workstation is a desktop-based tool used for creating and running virtual machines. Okay, that was an easy one... moving on!

2. Answer: C

Explanation: New Technology File System (NTFS) is the default file system that Windows uses.

Incorrect Answers: FAT32 is an older, less desirable file system than NTFS that offers less functionality and less security and accesses smaller partition sizes. ext4 is the default file system used by Linux. exFAT is another file system supported by Windows that works best with flash-based drives (such as USB thumb drives).

3. Answer: C

Explanation: The notification area is the area toward the bottom right of your screen within the taskbar. It contains the time and any applications (shown as icons) currently running in memory.

Incorrect Answers: The System Properties dialog box contains configuration tabs for the computer name and network, hardware, system restore, and more. You can access any of the tabs in that dialog box quickly by going to Run and typing **systempropertiescomputername.exe**, **systempropertiesadvanced.exe**, and so on or by typing **sysdm.cpl ,1** and **sysdm.cpl, 3**. The System32 folder resides within the Windows folder; it contains critical Windows system files, such as ntoskrnl.exe, as well as applications such as cmd.exe. The Start menu gives access to most programs and configurations in Windows.

4. Answer: C

Explanation: Windows 10 64-bit requires a minimum of 2 GB of RAM.

Incorrect Answers: The 32-bit version requires 1 GB. The same goes for Windows 8.1 (which has an end-of-life date of January 2023). Keep in mind that 32-bit versions of Windows are not being actively developed anymore. A minimum requirement for older versions of Windows was 512 MB. 2 TB is the maximum amount of RAM that Windows 10 Pro can *access*. In comparison, Windows 10 Pro for Workstations and Windows 10 Enterprise can access 6 TB of RAM. (As of the writing of this book, the same numbers hold true for Windows 11 editions.)

5. Answer: D

Explanation: The MMC (Microsoft Management Console) is a blank shell until you add snap-ins (such as Computer Management, Disk Management, the Task Scheduler, or the Performance Monitor) for functionality.

Incorrect Answers: Some people refer to each program in the Windows Control Panel as an *applet*; the term was made famous by Apple. You don't add actual files or directories (folders) to the MMC; you add other programs within Windows. The MMC acts as an index for your programs and remembers the last place you were working (if you save it).

6. Answer: A

Explanation: Compressed air, if used periodically inside a computer, can help prevent hardware faults from occurring. Most likely, the warehouse is not the cleanest, and the computer is sucking in dirt 24 hours a day. If you take the computer outside, remove the cover, and carefully blow out the dust bunnies with compressed air, you might increase the life span of the hardware components. Consider using a computer vacuum or wet/dry vacuum to suck up any debris but be careful not to touch any components in the computer with the vacuum nozzle. Other ways to help prevent this problem are to install a filter in front of the computer where air is drawn into the system and to enable hibernation of the computer during off-hours. During this time, the computer does not draw any air into the case, limiting the intake of dust, dirt, and other pollutants.

Incorrect Answers: Antistatic wrist straps are necessary when installing devices, and if they are not used, devices could become damaged, but the frequency of the issues in the question points to environmental conditions rather than ESD. A rescue disk (or rescue disc or repair disc) is used to repair an OS when a catastrophic stop error or other similar error occurs. It rebuilds the OS so that it can function again. Because in this scenario the problem is hardware related, a rescue disk does not help the situation. A multimeter is used to test hardware; it cannot prevent hardware faults.

7. Answer: A

Explanation: Disk Management is a tool found in Computer Management that allows for the creation, deletion, and formatting of partitions and logical drives. To view this application, use the Search tool (and search for Disk Management), utilize the Start menu, or go to Run and type **diskmgmt.msc**.

Incorrect Answers: The **format** command is a utility in the Windows Command Prompt that can be used to format partitions as NTFS or another file system type, but it does not *create* partitions. Disk Cleanup is a built-in Windows program that can remove temporary files and other data that you probably won't use.

8. Answer: C

Explanation: Primary partitions are the first partitions created on a drive. An OS should always be installed to a primary partition, but before you install the OS, you should set the primary partition to active. If you are installing to a new storage drive, Windows automatically sets the partition to active for you. An MBR-based storage drive can have a maximum of four primary partitions, each with its own drive letter.

Incorrect Answers: If you need to subdivide a storage drive further, you can use an extended partition, which is then broken up into logical drives. A GUID Partition Table (GPT)–based drive is not limited to this number; it can have up to 128 primary partitions. *Dynamic* refers to a dynamic drive; if you want to resize partitions, you have to convert the drive to dynamic in Disk Management. By the way, any drive in Windows that has a drive letter is known as a *volume*.

9. **Answer: B**

   Explanation: Task Manager enables you, via a click of the Processes tab, to view all currently running processes and see how much memory each of them is using. You can open Task Manager by right-clicking the taskbar and selecting it, by going to Run and typing **taskmgr**, by pressing Ctrl+Shift+Esc, or by pressing Ctrl+Alt+Del and selecting Task Manager.

   Incorrect Answers: MSConfig is a utility in Windows that allows you to enable and disable services and boot Windows in different modes. **chkdsk** is a Windows command-line utility that searches for errors and fixes them (with the **/F** or **/R** switches). The System Information tool gives a summary of hardware resources, components, and the software environment; you can open it by going to Run and typing **msinfo32**.

10. **Answers: A and B**

    Explanation: You can start, stop, and restart services within the Services window (by going to Run and typing **services.msc**). From there, right-click the service in question and configure it as you wish. Task Manager can also be used to start and stop services, as well as to analyze the performance of the CPU, RAM, and the networking connections. You can also start and stop services with the **net start** and **net stop** and **sc start** and **sc stop** commands, and exclusively in PowerShell, you can use the **start-service** and **stop-service** commands.

    Incorrect Answers: Performance Monitor analyzes a computer in much more depth than does Task Manager. The MMC is the Microsoft Management Console, which is the index that can store other console windows such as Computer Management. Among other things, MSConfig is used to enable/disable services but not to *start* them.

11. **Answer: C**

    Explanation: The administrator is the only account level that can install device drivers.

    Incorrect Answers: Standard user and Guest accounts cannot install drivers or programs. The Power Users group is an older group from the Windows XP days that was carried over to newer versions of Windows for application compatibility, but it has no real power in today's Windows.

12. **Answer: B**

    Explanation: md is short for make directory and is the command to use when creating directories in the Command Prompt. (The older version of the command is **mkdir**.)

Incorrect Answers: cd is the command to change the directory. **rd** is the command to remove a directory. **ls** is a Linux command that displays the contents of a directory, similar to the Windows **dir** command.

13. **Answers: B and C**

    Explanation: To learn more about any command in Windows, open the Command Prompt (or PowerShell), type the command and then **/?**, or type **help** and then type the command.

    Incorrect Answers: dir help would attempt to find the file named HELP within the current directory. **dir man** would most likely result in a "file not found" error. Man pages are help pages used in Linux and macOS.

14. **Answer: A**

    Explanation: Use the Command Prompt to launch the command **ipconfig**. **ipconfig** is a networking command that displays the configuration of a network adapter. You can open the Command Prompt in a variety of ways. You can open the default Command Prompt by going to Run and typing **cmd.exe**. However, many commands require you to open the Command Prompt as an administrator (in elevated mode). To run it as an administrator, locate it in Windows, right-click it, and select Run as Administrator. Or, you could type **cmd** in the search field and then press Ctrl+Shift+Enter. Remember, though, that it is recommended to use PowerShell whenever possible in Windows.

    Incorrect Answers: The other tools are used in the GUI and cannot run commands such as **ipconfig**. Use the Command Prompt or the PowerShell to run commands in Windows.

15. **Answer: A**

    Explanation: The best listed answer is to reconfigure the proxy settings for the customer. Chances are that the customer uses a proxy server for HTTP and HTTPS website connections. Without the properly configured proxy settings, the user might not be able to access the websites but would be able to access other networking services, such as FTP and email.

NOTE

Another thing to check is whether the user is working on the correct web browser. Perhaps Edge has the properly configured proxy settings, but the user is working in Firefox, and that is what is causing the problem.

Incorrect Answers: Disabling the firewall (if there is one) is an insecure solution and probably won't work anyway because a typical firewall is designed to block *inbound* connections but still allow *outbound* connections. Deactivating and reactivating the network interface card shouldn't make a difference; the user can still access *some* network functions. Uninstalling and reinstalling the web browser will likely result in the same issue because it will use the same configuration. The default configuration for web browsers is to have no proxy setting.

16. **Answers: B and C**

   Explanation: Disk Defragmenter keeps Windows running more efficiently by making files contiguous and reducing the amount of physical work the storage drive has to do. The **chkdsk** command checks the storage drive for errors.

   Incorrect Answers: Disk Management is used to partition and format drives. System Restore allows you to take a snapshot of the OS, which enables you to revert to older settings if something goes wrong. The Task Scheduler (previously Scheduled Tasks), as the name implies, enables you to set what time you want particular tasks to run.

17. **Answers: C and E**

   Explanation: The attack was most likely successful because the SOHO router was configured with a default login and WPS. A default login means that the SOHO router is using the original username (often "admin") and password (typically a stock password selected by the manufacturer of the device, which anyone can look up on the Internet). A default login makes it extremely easy for an attacker to log in to a device. Always be sure to change the password of a SOHO router right after installing it. WPS stands for Wi-Fi Protected Setup, and for a long time it was based on an eight-digit PIN code that is somewhat easy to brute force. Think about it: Eight digits means only 10,000,000 possible combinations, and a basic laptop could crack that pretty quickly. One example of a WPS brute-force attack is the Pixie-Dust attack. To protect against such attacks, disable WPS!

   Incorrect Answers: TKIP, which stands for Temporal Key Integrity Protocol, is an outdated encryption protocol that is not normally enabled by default on a SOHO router. You actually want the latest WPA version installed, as it will help protect AES-encrypted sessions. Old firmware is not necessarily deprecated, and while it can be a security vulnerability, it is not the most likely answer here. A guest network is used to separate users (and devices) that you do not want to have full access to the SOHO router. It would not give an attacker much posture for attack.

18. **Answer: B**

   Explanation: setuperr.log contains information about setup errors during the installation of Windows. Start with this log file when troubleshooting. A file size of 0 bytes indicates no errors during installation.

   Incorrect Answers: setupact.log contains the events that occurred during the installation. unattend.xml is the answer file used by Windows during unattended installations. **diskmgmt.msc** is a command that can be run from the Run prompt or the command line to open the Disk Management utility.

19. **Answer: B**

   Explanation: To perform a network installation, a network adapter in the target computer must be PXE compliant. Also, there must be some type of server acting as a repository for the Windows installation files.

   Incorrect Answers: PCIe is an expansion bus. The network adapter makes use of this expansion bus if it is an actual network interface card (NIC) or if it is embedded in the motherboard. BitLocker is a full drive encryption feature included with select editions of Windows. Multiboot technology means that the computer can boot to two or more operating systems.

20. **Answer: C**

    Explanation: The arrow pointing down tells you that the device is disabled in Windows. In many cases, you can easily enable it by right-clicking and selecting Enable.

    Incorrect Answers: If the driver had not been installed, the device would most likely be sitting in a category called Unknown Devices. If a device is not even recognized by Windows, it will not show up on the list or will show up under Unknown Devices. There is no queue to be deleted.

21. **Answer: D**

    Explanation: NTFS and FAT32 support the same number of file formats. This is actually the only listed similarity between the two.

    Incorrect Answers: NTFS supports file encryption in the form of Encrypting File System (EFS) and BitLocker, supports larger file sizes, and supports much larger volumes.

22. **Answers: A, B, and D**

    Explanation: For secondary drives, you must go to Disk Management and initialize, partition, and format those drives.

    Incorrect Answers: FDISK is an older DOS command. Today's computers' UEFI/BIOS should see the drive automatically, with no configuration needed. In special cases, a storage drive might require special drivers.

23. **Answer: C**

    Explanation: System Restore is the tool used to create restore points. You can find it with the Search utility or by going to Control Panel > All Control Panel Icons > System and then clicking the System Protection link. (Or you can go to Run and type **systempropertiesprotection.exe**.)

    Incorrect Answers: The Disk Defragmenter is used to fix storage drives that have become slow due to fragmentation. PowerShell is the main command-line/scripting tool in Windows. Disk Cleanup removes unwanted junk, such as temporary files, from a system.

24. **Answer: C**

    Explanation: To pause printing in general and pause individual documents, double-click on the printer in question and make modifications in the window that appears.

    Incorrect Answers: All other tasks listed can be modified from the Printer Properties screen.

25. **Answer: C**

Explanation: After auditing is turned on and specific resources are configured for auditing, you need to check the Event Viewer's Security log for the entries. These could be successful logons or misfired attempts at deleting files; there are literally hundreds of options.

Incorrect Answers: The Application log contains errors, warnings, and informational entries about applications. The System log deals with drivers, system files, and so on. A system maintenance log can be used to record routine maintenance procedures; such a log is not included in Windows.

26. **Answer: A**

Explanation: The first thing you should do in the event of potential malware is to disconnect the PC from the network. Physically disconnect any network cables and disable wireless access. This question is based on the seven-step procedure for malware removal in CompTIA A+ Objective 3.3 and is listed below:

1. Investigate and verify malware symptoms.

2. Quarantine the infected systems.

3. Disable System Restore in Windows.

4. Remediate infected systems.

    a. Update anti-malware software.

    b. Scanning and removal techniques (e.g., safe mode, preinstallation environment).

5. Schedule scans and run updates.

6. Enable System Restore and create a restore point in Windows.

7. Educate the end user.

Study this procedure! In the scenario, you had already verified the fact that there was ransomware on the computer. The next step is to quarantine the infected system, which we do by disconnecting the PC from the network.

Incorrect Answers: You definitely want to run an anti-malware scan—but you want to do so after the issue has been mitigated (as part of step 5). Educating the user is also important, but that is the last step. Backing up data probably won't be possible because ransomware, by design, locks files. Either way, you wouldn't want to back up data from an infected system.

27. **Answer: B**

Explanation: With User Account Control (UAC) enabled, users perform common tasks as nonadministrators and, when necessary, as administrators without having to switch users, log off, or use Run As. If a user is logged in as an administrator, a pop-up window will appear, verifying that the user has administrative privileges before action is taken; the user need only click Yes. If the user is not logged on as an administrator, clicking Yes will cause Windows to prompt the user for an administrative username and password.

Incorrect Answers: UDP, which stands for User Datagram Protocol, is a TCP/IP protocol used for streaming media and other connectionless sessions. USB stands for Universal Serial Bus and has little to do with this question except to serve to confuse the unwary with another acronym. VNC stands for Virtual Network Computing; it's a type of program that allows a person at a computer to remotely take control of another computer or device. Examples include RealVNC and TightVNC.

28. **Answers: A, B, and D**

    Explanation: A multifunction network device that acts as both a wireless access point (WAP) and a router may come with a standard default SSID name (that everyone knows). It is a good idea to change it, even if the router doesn't ask you to do so automatically. After devices have been associated with the wireless network, turn off SSID broadcasting so that no one else can find your WAP (using normal means). Disabling WPS (Wi-Fi Protected Setup) will prevent attempts at brute-force hacking the WPS PIN code. Other ways to secure the wireless access point include changing the password, incorporating strong encryption such as Wi-Fi Protected Access (latest version) with Advanced Encryption Standard (AES), and initiating MAC filtering, which only allows the computers with the MAC addresses you specify access to the wireless network. On a side note, disabling DHCP and instead using static IP addresses removes one of the types of packets that are broadcast from the WAP, making it more difficult to hack— but also less functional and useful.

    Incorrect Answers: Enabling DHCP will make it easier to connect to the SOHO router from clients but won't increase the security of the router.

29. **Answers: A and D**

    Explanation: Although it could possibly be spoofed, the padlock in the locked position gives you a certain level of assurance and tells you that the website is using a secure certificate to protect your session. This padlock could be in different locations, depending on the web browser used. Hypertext Transfer Protocol Secure (HTTPS) also defines that the session is using either the Secure Sockets Layer (SSL) protocol or the Transport Layer Security (TLS) protocol.

    Incorrect Answers: HTTP by itself is enough for regular web sessions when you read documents and so on, but HTTPS is required when you log in to a site, purchase items, or do online banking. HTTPS opens a secure channel on port 443 as opposed to the default, insecure HTTP port 80. To be sure that you have a secure session, you can analyze the certificate and verify it against the certificate authority.

30. **Answer: B**

    Explanation: Antivirus software (from vendors such as McAfee or Norton) updates automatically to protect you against the latest viruses, whether they are attached to emails or are lying in wait on removable media. You might also choose to use the built-in Microsoft Defender or Windows Security on newer versions of Windows.

    Incorrect Answers: Firewalls protect against intrusion but not viruses. They could be hardware based, such as the ones found in most SOHO multifunction network devices, or software based, such as Windows Defender Firewall. Edge and Chrome (as well as other web browsers) can be configured to make your system more secure (especially when dealing with web-based emails), but that is not the best answer listed.

31. **Answer: A**

Explanation: Social engineering is the practice of obtaining confidential information by manipulating people. Asking for a username and password over the phone is a type of phishing attack (known as vishing).

Incorrect Answers: Using someone else's network is just plain theft. Hacking into a router is just that: hacking. A virus is a program that spreads through computers and networks (if executed by the user); it might or might not cause damage to files and applications.

32. **Answer: C**

Explanation: Software-based firewalls, such as Windows Defender Firewall, normally run on client computers.

Incorrect Answers: It is possible for software-based firewalls to run on servers, especially if a server is acting as a network firewall, but servers might rely on a hardware-based network firewall or an IDS/IPS solution. Hardware-based firewalls are also found in multifunction network devices. Some people might refer to these devices as *routers*, but the router functionality is really just one of the roles of the multifunction network device—separate from the firewall role. Plus, higher-end routers for larger networks are usually not combined with firewall functionality. Switches don't generally employ software firewalls.

33. **Answer: D**

Explanation: With spoofing, a malicious user makes web pages, data, or email appear to be coming from somewhere else.

Incorrect Answers: Impersonation involves presenting oneself as another person, imitating that other person's characteristics. It is often a key element in what is known as pretexting—the invention of a scenario in the hopes that a key person will reveal confidential information. With phishing, a person fraudulently attempts to gain confidential information from unsuspecting users. Zero-day attacks exploit vulnerabilities that haven't even been discovered yet or that have been discovered but have not been disclosed through the proper channels so that security administrators can be aware of them.

34. **Answer: A**

Explanation: Biometrics is the study of recognizing human characteristics such as fingerprints. A fingerprint reader is an example of a biometric device.

Incorrect Answers: Smart cards are often the size of credit cards and store information that is transmitted to a reader. A barcode reader is a device that scans codes made up of different-width parallel lines, and an SSID is a form of device identification that is broadcast from a wireless access point.

35. Answer: D

Explanation: A password gets more secure as you increase its length and then add capital letters, numbers, and special characters. Note that Marqu1s_De_S0d_ver_2 has a capital M, a 1 in the place of an *I*, underscores, a capital *D*, a capital *S*, and a zero. Plus, it is lengthy; it has 20 characters. Many organizations implement policies that require a minimum of 16 characters.

Incorrect Answers: The rest of the passwords are either not as long or not as complex as the correct answer.

36. Answer. D

Explanation: Windows+L automatically and immediately locks the computer. Only the person who locked it or an administrator can unlock it (unless, of course, another user knows the password).

Incorrect Answers: Ctrl+Alt+Del brings up the Windows Security dialog box. From there, you can lock the computer, too—but with an extra step. Windows+R brings up the Run prompt, and Windows+M minimizes all open applications.

> **NOTE**
>
> Another fun shortcut is Windows+X, which brings up the Power User menu. You can also do this by right-clicking Start.

37. Answer: C

Explanation: NTFS is the Windows New Technology File System. It secures files and folders (and, in fact, the whole partition) much better than the older FAT32 system does. EFS, BitLocker, and NTFS permissions are just a few of the advantages of an NTFS partition.

Incorrect Answers: ext4 is used by Linux-based systems (and so is ext3). exFAT is another type of file system used often with USB thumb drives, SD cards, and other removable memory cards. FAT32 is the predecessor to NTFS and is not used often, but you might see it used with flash drives or older storage drives.

38. Answer: C

Explanation: Of the listed answers, the only one that is available in Pro editions of Windows is BitLocker Device Encryption.

Incorrect Answers: The other answers are available in both Home and Pro editions of Windows. Windows Hello allows a user to unlock a device either with facial recognition, fingerprint scanning, or a PIN. Secure Boot helps prevent malicious software from loading during the startup process—but it works properly only if the BIOS/UEFI is Secure Boot capable (and most computers today are). Windows Security, Microsoft Defender, and the older Defender Antivirus are Microsoft programs that protect against malware.

39. **Answer: B**

    Explanation: With social engineering, individuals try to get information from users fraudulently, through manipulation.

    Incorrect Answers: Shoulder surfing is a form of social engineering in which a person uses direct observation to find out a target's password, PIN, or other authentication information. Phishing is a type of social engineering; it is implemented via email or over the phone (in which case it is called vishing). In spear phishing, specific individuals or groups of individuals are targeted with streamlined phishing attacks.

40. **Answer: B**

    Explanation: The data is very insecure. Many tools can recover data from a drive after it is formatted. Some companies "low-level" format a drive, or sanitize the drive (as opposed to doing a standard format in Windows, for example), and keep it in storage indefinitely. An organization might go further and use data wiping software; in fact, this might be a policy for the organization. Check your organization's policies to be sure you are disposing of or recycling storage drives properly.

    Incorrect Answers: *Confidential* is a term used to classify data. For example, personally identifiable information (PII) should be kept confidential (which means only the appropriate personnel can access it). *Secure* is a relative term. Remember: Nothing is ever *completely secured*.

41. **Answer: B**

    Explanation: Smart cards are physical cards that you use as authentication tools. They are sometimes referred to as *tokens* and have built-in processors. Examples of smart cards include the Personal Identity Verification (PIV) card used by U.S. government employees and the Common Access Card (CAC) used by Department of Defense personnel.

    Incorrect Answers: All of the other answers are software related and are logical in their implementations.

42. **Answer: B**

    Explanation: Transport Layer Security (TLS) encrypts transactions through a website. TLS certificates are often accompanied by the protocol HTTPS. (Note that TLS certificates are sometimes referred to as SSL certificates. SSL stands for the older protocol Secure Sockets Layer.)

    Incorrect Answers: HTTP by itself is not secure. PuTTY is a tool used for secure text-based connections to hosts and does not involve a website. Kerberos is the protocol used on a Microsoft domain to encrypt passwords.

43. **Answer: B**

    Explanation: Common local security policies specify password length, duration, and complexity. Just the use of a password doesn't constitute a password policy. An example of a password policy is an organization's mandates that passwords be

15 characters in length with at least 1 capital letter, 1 number, and 1 special character. In Windows, you access Local Security Policy > Security Settings > Account Policies > Password Policy to make changes to password policy settings.

Incorrect Answers: Simply having a RAID array is not a security policy, though security policies often define how a RAID array will be used. Again, just having passwords (such as router passwords or other passwords used to log in) does not establish policy. Specifying how passwords are selected and enforced is a security policy.

44. **Answer: C**

Explanation: A Trojan is a disguised program that is used to gain access to a computer and either steal information or take control of the computer.

Incorrect Answers: A cryptominer is software (or hardware) that is used to "mine" for cryptocurrency. Cryptominers can be knowingly used by miners or installed maliciously on systems. Spam is the abuse of email and the bane of humanity. Spyware is software unwittingly downloaded from the Internet that tracks the actions of a user while surfing the web.

45. **Answer: A**

Explanation: Android is an open source OS. It is freely downloadable and can be modified by manufacturers of mobile devices to suit their specific hardware. Android is based on Linux, which is open source.

Incorrect Answers: Apple's iOS and macOS and Microsoft's operating systems are closed source (or proprietary); a company would have to pay a fee for every license of the OS—that is, if it were even available to them.

46. **Answers: B and C**

Explanation: Android users download applications (apps) from Google Play. Apple users download apps from the App Store or from within iTunes.

Incorrect Answers: The Spotlight tool is a utility in Apple's macOS that allows a user to search the computer and the Internet by typing in search phrases. File Explorer is the file management tool in Windows.

47. **Answer: A**

Explanation: The Global Positioning System (GPS) technology (or location services) can be instrumental in locating lost or stolen mobile devices. Many devices have GPS technology installed; others rely on geotracking or Wi-Fi hotspot location techniques. (You are being watched!)

Incorrect Answers: Screen orientation is the direction of screen display—vertical or horizontal (or upside down)—which typically depends on how you hold the device. It can be calibrated on Android devices with the G-Sensor calibration tool. A passcode lock is a set of numbers that must be entered to open a mobile device or take it out of sleep mode. Gmail is Google's web-based email service and is incorporated into the Android operating system.

48. **Answers: A and C**

    Explanation: Some of the things you might synchronize on a smartphone include contacts, email, programs, pictures, music, and videos.

    Incorrect Answers: Mobile devices would not normally synchronize .ps1 scripts or SQL databases. .ps1 scripts are generated by PowerShell in Windows. SQL databases, such as MySQL or SQL Server databases, are relational databases that can be used to efficiently filter through massive amounts of data.

49. **Answer: B**

    Explanation: The second step is to establish a theory of probable cause. You are looking for the obvious or most probable cause of the problem.

    Incorrect Answers: Establishing a theory of probable cause comes after identifying the problem and before testing your theory. Documentation is last. While the troubleshooting process is listed in the 220-1101 objectives, it's always important; you'll always be using it, regardless of what technology you are working with. You never know what you might see on the exam!

50. **Answer: C**

    Explanation: Documentation is the final step in the CompTIA A+ troubleshooting methodology. It helps you better understand and articulate exactly a problem (and its solution). If you see the same problem again in the future, you can consult your documentation for the solution. Plus, others on your team can do the same. In addition, companies typically have policies requiring documentation of all findings as part of a trouble ticket.

    Incorrect Answers: Generally, as a technician working for individual customers on the road, you would present a bill at the end of your technical visit (after everything else is complete). But for many technicians, billing is not a responsibility; someone else takes care of that task. Always document the solution before moving on to the next computer. Running programs such as the Disk Defragmenter (Optimize Drives) is something you would do during an earlier phase of troubleshooting.

51. **Answer: D**

    Explanation: The Event Viewer contains the error logs; they are finite in size. You could either clear the error log or increase the size of the log.

    Incorrect Answers: The other three applications do not contain error logs. Device Manager is used in Windows to configure devices such as the mouse and display. System Information is a Windows utility that provides information about the system but is not configurable. Keychain Access is a utility in macOS that is used to store passwords and other credentials.

52. **Answer: D**

    Explanation: System File Checker **(sfc)** checks protected system files and replaces incorrect versions.

Incorrect Answers: None of the other options check system files. **chkdsk** can check for and repair errors—but just on regular files. **dir** displays the contents of a directory (folder). **ver** is a command that shows the version of Windows. It works in the Command Prompt but not in PowerShell.

53. Answer: B

Explanation: You must partition the drive before formatting.

Incorrect Answers: You can copy files only after formatting is complete. **chkdsk** has little value on an unformatted drive because it checks files for errors and integrity. Defragmenting should not be necessary in this case because there are no files on the drive yet. The same goes for copying files: You can't copy what you don't have! Something else not mentioned here is that a second drive would have to be initialized in Windows before use.

54. Answer: B

Explanation: The best answer is Startup Repair. Startup Repair attempts to fix issues automatically. It is available in the Windows RE System Recovery options. You might also attempt a Reset This PC procedure in WinRE or from within Windows.

Incorrect Answers: Although System Restore can "fix" problems, it only does this by resetting the computer to an earlier point in time, and this is therefore not the best answer. File History is a file backup program for Windows but is not available within the System Recovery environment. The Command Prompt is available in Windows RE, but to use it, you would have to type specific commands to perform any actions.

55. Answers: C and E

Explanation: Of the listed answers, you should configure the smartphone to connect to the Wi-Fi network automatically and have the user close applications when tasks are completed. If the smartphone is not configured to connect to the Wi-Fi network automatically, it will default to the mobile Internet data connection (which is often slower than Wi-Fi). You don't want to rely on the user connecting to Wi-Fi every time, so make it automatic! Also, train the user on how to close apps when they are done with their tasks; it only requires a quick swipe!

Incorrect Answers: All of the other answers would decrease battery life. The longer it takes for the screen to automatically dim, the more battery power is used. The same goes for setting the display to maximum brightness—which is a common culprit in short battery life. If you disable 802.11ac, then you actually disabled 5 GHz, high-throughput Wi-Fi! Using mobile data requires more battery power because the cellular radio typically has to work harder than the Wi-Fi radio would (unless your office is directly next to a cellular tower). Increasing email synchronization uses more battery power as well, but it's not nearly as much of a drain as setting the display to maximum brightness.

56. Answer: A

Explanation: The most common reason for a BSOD (blue screen of death, otherwise known as a stop error) is driver failure.

Incorrect Answers: The second most common reason for a BSOD is memory-/processor-related errors. Storage drives and LED monitors themselves should not cause stop errors, but their drivers might.

57. Answer: A

Explanation: Run the installer as an administrator. Programs cannot be installed by standard users or guests. You must have administrative rights to install programs.

Incorrect Answers: You should try to resolve the problem yourself before contacting the manufacturer. In the end, the manufacturer might not be able to provide meaningful help so be ready to solve problems on your own. Upgrading to a new version of Windows and reinstalling Windows are a bit extreme. Always remember to install programs as an admin and, if necessary, run older programs in compatibility mode.

58. Answer: D

Explanation: Spray cleaner on a lint-free cloth first and then wipe the display gently. A lot of companies sell products that are half isopropyl alcohol and half water. You could also make this cleaner yourself. Again, remember to put the solution on a lint-free cloth first.

Incorrect Answers: Never spray any cleaner directly on a display. Try not to get any liquid in the cracks at the edge of the screen because it could get behind the display and possibly cause damage to circuitry (especially over time).

59. Answer: D

Explanation: Because the immediate danger has passed, call 911 right away.

Incorrect Answers: After calling 911, you would apply first aid and CPR as necessary. The next step would be to shut off the power at the electrical panel or call the building supervisor/facilities department to have the power shut off. However, it is important to be aware of and comply with company policies before taking certain actions. Be aware of company policies before accidents happen!

60. Answer: C

Explanation: Writing down a credit card number is a violation of a Payment Card Industry (PCI) standard—specifically, the Payment Card Industry Data Security Standard (PCI-DSS). PCI information needs to be entered into a proper PCI-compliant program and stored in a PCI-compliant database. That includes the CC number, expiration date, and the card security code (CSC). In the question, the CSC is referred to as CVV, which is short for card verification value and is a Visa term.

Incorrect Answers: Personally identifiable information (PII) is any data that can identify a person, such as name and Social Security number. Protected health information (PHI) is health and medical information linked to a person. PGP stands for Pretty Good Privacy, which is a computer program that encrypts data communication.

61. Answer: C

Explanation: Turning off the printer might not be enough. It might be seriously malfunctioning, and you need to pull the plug. Depending on your organization's policy, you might need to call the facilities department or a building supervisor and document the situation.

Incorrect Answers: Dialing 911 is not necessary unless a fire has started. Wait at least 15 minutes before opening the printer to see what caused the smoke. Printer power supplies can fail just like PC power supplies can. In fact, a laser printer power supply does more work because it needs to convert for high voltages in the 600 V range. If you have a maintenance contract with a printer company, and the printer is under warranty or contained in the service contract, you could call the maintenance company to fix the problem. Be ready to give a detailed account of exactly what happened. You could tell the printer that it is bad to smoke, but that would be belligerent and would probably show that you have been working too hard. All kidding aside, be ready to disconnect power at a moment's notice.

62. Answer: D

Explanation: Recycle toner cartridges according to your company's policies and procedures or according to municipality rules and regulations.

Incorrect Answers: Do not throw away or incinerate toner cartridges. Although it is possible to refill toner cartridges, that is not the recommended way to handle an empty cartridge because it is messy and time-consuming. Most companies simply purchase new toner cartridges.

63. Answer: C

Explanation: The technician should leave the customer site and document the incident. In rare cases, there is no way to calm down the customer, and you might have to leave the site if there is no other alternative.

Incorrect Answers: If the customer has been shouting for a while and the technician cannot calm down the customer, it's pointless to stay and wait. You don't want to call your supervisor and complain about the situation while you're at the customer's location; that would probably infuriate the customer further. Wait until you have left the customer's premises. Never shout back at the customer; this is not a battle for power, and you should never take a customer's anger personally. Be sure to document the incident in depth after leaving the customer's location. Definitely let your supervisor know what has happened—without complaining.

64. Answer: A

Explanation: While you're on the job site, limit phone calls to only emergencies or calls from your employer about other customers.

Incorrect Answers: Taking a personal phone call, texting, or using social media sites while working at a client site is considered unprofessional. Be professional when you're on the job.

65. Answer: D

Explanation: MSConfig enables you to modify the startup selection. You can boot the computer in different modes with MSConfig. You can also enable and disable services.

Incorrect Answers: The Task Manager gives you a snapshot of your system's performance and allows you to shut down applications (tasks) or processes, even if the application is hanging or frozen. Windows RE is the Windows Recovery Environment, a special repair environment that is used to fix issues in the operating system. From it, you can fix system file issues and repair the boot sector, along with GPT and MBR-related issues. Safe Mode is one of the options in the Startup Settings within WinRE. It starts the computer with a basic set of drivers so that you can troubleshoot why devices have failed. It is also instrumental when dealing with viruses.

66. Answer: C

Explanation: The .ps1 extension is used for PowerShell files and scripts.

Incorrect Answers: .js is for JavaScript, .vbs is for Visual Basic script, .py is for Python, .sh is for Linux shell scripts (such as Bash), and .bat is for batch files used for scripting in Windows.

67. Answer: B

Explanation: Making sure that a backup is available is the first order of business. Always check whether there are backups and physically inspect and verify the backups before changing out any drives.

Incorrect Answers: After the backup has been taken care of, you can have the customer give you the password to log in (or let the customer log in) and find out which version of Windows Server is running.

68. Answer: B

Explanation: By rolling back the driver (which is done in Device Manager) while in Safe Mode, you can go back in time to the old working video driver.

Incorrect Answers: The Windows Recovery Environment might help (for example, if you used Startup Settings > Safe Mode or System Restore), but the WinRE Command Prompt is not the best answer because it is a different tool. Reinstalling the OS would wipe the partition of the president's data (and probably wipe you of your job). Fix the computer tomorrow? Ludicrous...unless you don't value your job very much.

69. Answer: B

Explanation: The DxDiag utility is used to analyze a video card and its DirectX version and to check whether drivers are digitally signed. You can access it by going to Run and typing **dxdiag**.

Incorrect Answers: Device Manager is used to install drivers for devices—among other things—but is not used to view the DirectX version that is installed. Services.msc is the console window where you can start and stop and enable/disable services such as the Print Spooler. Disk Management (diskmgmt.msc) is used to modify storage drive partitions and formatting.

70. **Answer: A**

    Explanation: By installing a driver that is not signed by Microsoft, you are risking instability of the operating system.

    Incorrect Answers: The driver has no effect on files or drive fragmentation. It is extremely uncommon for a driver to cause physical damage to a device. Note that Windows 8 and newer versions have driver signature enforcement enabled by default, which makes it more difficult to install unsigned drivers.

71. **Answers: C and D**

    Explanation: To make a secure connection, you need to know the service set identifier (SSID) of the AP and the encryption being used (for example, WPA2 or WPA3). The SSID takes care of the "connection" portion, and the encryption takes care of the "secure" portion. After all computers are connected, consider disabling the SSID for increased security.

    Incorrect Answers: Knowing the wireless standard being used can help you verify whether your computer is compatible (802.11ax, ac, n, or g), but the brand of access point isn't really helpful.

72. **Answer: B**

    Explanation: Sysprep is a utility that is built in to Windows for image deployment over the network.

    Incorrect Answers: Ghost and Clonezilla are third-party offerings. Robocopy copies entire directories (in the same physical order, too). Sysprep preps a system to be moved as an image file as opposed to moving directories of information.

73. **Answer: D**

    Explanation: If the computer fails and cannot recover, you usually see some type of critical or stop error. At this point, you must restart the computer to get back into the operating system (unless it is configured to do so automatically, which is the default setting in Windows). The reason for the physical dump of memory is for later debugging. The physical dump writes the contents of memory (when the computer failed) to a file on the storage drive.

    Incorrect Answers: Missing drivers do not cause this error, but a failed driver might. If the wrong processor is installed, you can probably not get the system to boot at all. Shutting down the computer improperly just means that the computer recognizes this upon the next reboot and might attempt to automatically fix errors if any occurred.

74. **Answer: C**

    Explanation: Session hijacking occurs when an unwanted mediator takes control of the session between a client and a server (for example, an FTP or HTTP session). An example of this would be an on-path attack—also known as a man-in-the-middle (MITM) attack.

Incorrect Answers: DDoS stands for distributed denial-of-service attack, an attack perpetuated by hundreds or thousands of computers in an effort to take down a single server; the computers involved in this type of attack, individually known as zombies, are often unknowingly part of a botnet. A brute-force attack is an attempt to crack an encryption code or password. Malicious software is any compromising code or software that can damage a computer's files; examples include viruses, spyware, worms, rootkits, ransomware, and Trojans.

75. Answer: A

Explanation: chmod is used to change the permissions of a file. It stands for "change mode" and applies to permissions.

Incorrect Answers: top is a process analysis utility in Linux. **grep** is a filtering utility used when searching for particular strings of information within files. **cat** is used to display the contents of a file within the terminal.

76. Answer: A

Explanation: The drive should be completely erased with bit-level erasure software. If it is to be disposed of or is to leave the building, it should also be shredded or degaussed (or both).

Incorrect Answers: Formatting is not enough because data remanence (residue) is left on the drive, and smart people with some smart software can use the remanence to reconstruct files. It is a waste of time to install AV software on a drive *before* removing it. However, AV software should be loaded up when the new drive is installed.

77. Answer: D

Explanation: The Windows File History utility (accessible in Setting and the Control Panel) enables a user to back up files or an entire PC.

Incorrect Answers: Nano is a text editor that is built into most Linux distributions. BitLocker is Microsoft's full drive encryption software. Time Machine is the backup program that is built into macOS.

78. Answer: B

Explanation: As of the writing of this book, Windows 10 and 11 require a *minimum* processor frequency of 1 GHz (with two or more cores).

Incorrect Answers: Windows 10 64-bit requires 32 GB of drive space. (Windows 11 requires 64 GB.) As of the writing of this book, 2 GHz is not a valid answer for Windows. The minimum RAM requirement for 64-bit versions of Windows 10 is 2 GB. (Windows 11 requires 4 GB of RAM.)

79. Answer: D

Explanation: An unattended installation of Windows requires an answer file. This file is normally named unattend.xml. Unattended installations can be done locally or as part of a network installation, using Windows Deployment Services (WDS) in Windows Server.

Incorrect Answers: Drive image installations use third-party programs such as Ghost or work with a System Restore image created within Windows. Local installation from USB is possible if you copy the Windows .iso file to the USB flash drive (if the drive is big enough) and obtain the USB/DVD download tool from the Microsoft website. A multiboot installation means that more than one operating system is being installed to the same drive. One or both of these could possibly be unattended installations. Remember that with multiboot installations, each OS should inhabit its own primary partition.

80. **Answer: B**

Explanation: Use the **ipconfig /all** command in Windows. It provides lots of information about the network interface card and the TCP/IP configuration.

Incorrect Answers: **ip a** is similar to **ipconfig /all** but it is used in Linux. (**ip a** is short for **ip address show**.) **net user** is a Windows command that displays all user accounts on the computer. While **autofix** isn't a valid command, there are plenty of commands in Windows that will attempt to fix problems for you, such as **sfc**, **chkdsk**, and many more! I highly recommend practicing in PowerShell and the Command Prompt. Know your command line!

Great Job So Far!

If you scored 90% or higher on this first 220-1102 practice exam, move on to the next one. If you did not, I strongly encourage you to study the material again and retake the practice exam until you get 90% or higher. Either way, you are doing excellent work so far. Keep at it!

CHAPTER EIGHT

220-1102 Practice Exam B

The previous 220-1102 exam is the introductory practice exam for Core 2. This next test takes the challenge to the next level and can be considered an intermediate practice test. I've included some more difficult questions in this exam.

The main goal of this practice exam is to make sure you understand all of the concepts before moving on to the next test. If you haven't taken a break already, I suggest taking one between exams. If you just completed the first exam, give yourself a half hour or so before you begin this one. If you didn't score 90% or higher on Exam A, go back and study; then retake Exam A until you pass with a score of 90% or higher.

Write down your answers and check them against the answer key, which immediately follows the exam. After the answer key, you will find the explanations for all of the answers. Good luck!

Practice Questions

1. Which of the following statements best describes how to restart the Print Spooler service? (Select the two best answers.)

Quick Answer: **203**
Detailed Answer: **204**

   ❏ **A.** Enter **net stop spooler** and then **net start spooler** at the command line.

   ❏ **B.** Enter **net stop print spooler** and then **net start print spooler** at the command line.

   ❏ **C.** Go to Run > services.msc and restart the Print Spooler service.

   ❏ **D.** Go to Computer Management > System Tools > Event Viewer and restart the Print Spooler service.

2. Where is registry hive data stored?

Quick Answer: **203**
Detailed Answer: **204**

   ○ **A.** \%systemroot%\Windows

   ○ **B.** \%systemroot%\Windows\System32\Config

   ○ **C.** \%systemroot%\System32

   ○ **D.** \%systemroot%\System32\Config

3. You are troubleshooting a user's Android smartphone. You need to enable USB debugging. Which of the following do you need to enable first?

Quick Answer: **203**
Detailed Answer: **204**

   ○ **A.** Screen sharing

   ○ **B.** APK downloads

   ○ **C.** Developer Mode

   ○ **D.** Phone rooting

4. Tom has an older laptop with a magnetic-based disk drive. He has been trying to speed up the computer by doing the following:

Quick Answer: **203**
Detailed Answer: **204**

   ▶ Upgrading the memory

   ▶ Removing old applications

   Unfortunately, the memory upgrade doesn't seem to be having any effect, and removing the old applications actually makes the laptop even slower. Which of the following should you do?

   ○ **A.** Defragment the drive

   ○ **B.** Rebuild the user profile

   ○ **C.** End tasks in the Task Manager

   ○ **D.** Update the laptop

5. You are using WSUS and testing new updates on PCs. What is this an example of?

Quick Answer: **203**
Detailed Answer: **205**

- ○ **A.** Host-based firewall
- ○ **B.** Application baselining
- ○ **C.** Patch management
- ○ **D.** Virtualization

6. Which versions of Windows does *not* allow for joining domains?

Quick Answer: **203**
Detailed Answer: **205**

- ○ **A.** Home
- ○ **B.** Pro
- ○ **C.** Pro for Workstations
- ○ **D.** Enterprise

7. One of your customers reports that there is a large amount of spam in her email inbox. Which of the following statements describes the best course of action?

Quick Answer: **203**
Detailed Answer: **205**

- ○ **A.** Advise her to create a new email account.
- ○ **B.** Advise her to add the spam senders to the junk email sender list.
- ○ **C.** Advise her to find a new ISP.
- ○ **D.** Advise her to reply to all spam and opt out of future emails.

8. In Windows, where can you configure devices like the display and storage drives to turn off after a certain amount of time?

Quick Answer: **203**
Detailed Answer: **206**

- ○ **A.** Power Plans
- ○ **B.** Display Properties
- ○ **C.** Computer Management
- ○ **D.** Task Manager

9. Which of the following procedures best describes how to find out which type of connection a printer is using?

Quick Answer: **203**
Detailed Answer: **206**

- ○ **A.** Right-click the printer, select Properties, and click the Sharing tab.
- ○ **B.** Right-click the printer, select Properties, and click the Advanced tab.
- ○ **C.** Right-click the printer, select Properties, and click the Separator Page button.
- ○ **D.** Right-click the printer, select Properties, and click the Ports tab.

10. Your customer is having problems printing from an application. You attempt to send a test page to the printer. Which of the following statements best describes why a test page should be used to troubleshoot the issue?

   ○ **A.** It allows you to see the quality of the printer output.

   ○ **B.** The output of the test page allows you to initiate diagnostic routines on the printer.

   ○ **C.** It verifies the connectivity and illuminates possible application problems.

   ○ **D.** It clears the print queue and reboots the printer memory.

11. One of your customers is asking for recommendations on how to prevent potential data and hardware loss during a natural disaster. Of the following, what should you recommend? (Select the two best answers.)

   ❑ **A.** Cloud storage

   ❑ **B.** Data recovery

   ❑ **C.** Backup testing

   ❑ **D.** Waterproof smartphones

   ❑ **E.** Hot/warm site

   ❑ **F.** Local backups

12. Which of the following actions will *not* secure a functioning computer workstation?

   ○ **A.** Setting a strong password

   ○ **B.** Changing default usernames

   ○ **C.** Disabling the guest account

   ○ **D.** Sanitizing the storage drive

13. Which utility enables you to implement auditing on a single Windows computer?

   ○ **A.** Local Security Policy

   ○ **B.** Group Policy Editor

   ○ **C.** AD DS

   ○ **D.** Services.msc

14. Which of the following statements best describes the main function of a device driver?

Quick Answer: **203**
Detailed Answer: **207**

- ○ **A.** Modifies applications
- ○ **B.** Works with memory more efficiently
- ○ **C.** Improves device performance
- ○ **D.** Allows the OS to talk to the device

15. Where are restore points stored after they are created?

Quick Answer: **203**
Detailed Answer: **207**

- ○ **A.** The Recycler folder
- ○ **B.** The System32 folder
- ○ **C.** The %systemroot% folder
- ○ **D.** The System Volume Information folder

16. Which of the following is considered government-regulated data?

Quick Answer: **203**
Detailed Answer: **208**

- ○ **A.** DRM
- ○ **B.** EULA
- ○ **C.** PII
- ○ **D.** DMCA

17. Which of the following are types of social engineering? (Select the two best answers.)

Quick Answer: **203**
Detailed Answer: **208**

- ❏ **A.** Malware
- ❏ **B.** Shoulder surfing
- ❏ **C.** Tailgating
- ❏ **D.** Rootkits

18. Which of the following is the service that controls the printing of documents on a Windows computer?

Quick Answer: **203**
Detailed Answer: **208**

- ○ **A.** Printer
- ○ **B.** Print server
- ○ **C.** Print pooling
- ○ **D.** Print Spooler

19. Which of the following is the best way to ensure that a storage drive is secure for disposal?

Quick Answer: **203**
Detailed Answer: **208**

- ○ **A.** Magnetically erase the drive.
- ○ **B.** Format the drive.
- ○ **C.** Run **bootrec /fixboot**.
- ○ **D.** Convert the drive to NTFS.

20. A month ago, you set up a wireless access point/router for a small business that is a customer of yours. Now, the customer calls and complains that Internet access is getting slower and slower. As you look at the WAP/router, you notice that it was reset at some point and is now set for open access. You suspect that neighboring companies are using the service connection. Which of the following statements best describes how you can restrict access to your customer's wireless connection? (Select the two best answers.)

   ❏   **A.** Configure the wireless access point to use the latest version of WPA.

   ❏   **B.** Configure MS-CHAPv2 on the WAP/router.

   ❏   **C.** Disable SSID broadcasting.

   ❏   **D.** Move the WAP/router to another corner of the office.

21. A first-level help desk support technician receives a call from a customer and works with the customer for several minutes to resolve the call, but the technician is unsuccessful. Which of the following steps should the technician perform next?

   ○   **A.** The technician should explain to the customer that he will receive a callback when someone more qualified is available.

   ○   **B.** The technician should escalate the call to another technician.

   ○   **C.** The technician should explain to the customer that the problem cannot be resolved and end the call.

   ○   **D.** The technician should continue working with the customer until the problem is resolved.

22. A customer complains that there is nothing showing on the display of his brand-new laptop. Which of the following should you attempt first on the computer?

   ○   **A.** You should replace the inverter.

   ○   **B.** You should reinstall the video drivers.

   ○   **C.** You should boot into Safe Mode.

   ○   **D.** You should check whether the laptop is in Standby or Hibernate mode.

23. A user boots a computer in the morning and notices that icons are much larger than they were the night before. The user tries changing the video resolution and rebooting the computer, but the icons still do not look correct. You ask the user questions and find out that the display read "finishing updates" when the computer was first booted in the morning. What should you do next to fix the problem?

Quick Answer: **203**
Detailed Answer: **209**

    ○ **A.** Roll back the video driver

    ○ **B.** Reboot the computer

    ○ **C.** Reload the operating system

    ○ **D.** Press F2 to access the BIOS/UEFI

24. A person working at a Linux computer types the command **apt-get update**. When the person presses Enter, Linux displays several messages, the most prominent one being "Permission denied." What should the user have typed *before* the command?

Quick Answer: **203**
Detailed Answer: **209**

    ○ **A. nano**

    ○ **B. chmod**

    ○ **C. sudo**

    ○ **D. grep**

25. Megan's laptop runs perfectly when she is at work, but when she takes it on the road, it cannot get on the Internet. Internally, the company uses static IP addresses for all computers. What should you do to fix the problem?

Quick Answer: **203**
Detailed Answer: **210**

    ○ **A.** Tell Megan to get a wireless cellular card and service.

    ○ **B.** Tell Megan to use DHCP.

    ○ **C.** Tell Megan to configure the Alternate Configuration tab of TCP/IP properties.

    ○ **D.** Configure a static IP address in the Alternate Configuration tab of the user's TCP/IP properties and enable DHCP in the General tab.

26. Which power-saving mode enables the best power savings while still allowing the session to be reactivated later?

Quick Answer: **203**
Detailed Answer: **210**

    ○ **A.** Standby

    ○ **B.** Suspend

    ○ **C.** Hibernate

    ○ **D.** Shutdown

27. John's computer has two storage drives, each 1 TB. The first one, the system drive, is formatted as NTFS. The second one, the data drive, is formatted as FAT32. Which of the following statements are true? (Select the two best answers.)

- ❏ **A.** Files on the system drive can be secured.

- ❏ **B.** Larger logical drives can be made on the data drive.

- ❏ **C.** The cluster size is larger, and storage is more efficient on the system drive.

- ❏ **D.** The cluster size is smaller, and storage is more efficient on the system drive.

28. When using the command line, a switch _____.

- ○ **A.** enables a command to work across any operating system

- ○ **B.** is used in application icons

- ○ **C.** changes the core behavior of a command, forcing the command to perform unrelated actions

- ○ **D.** alters the actions of a command, such as widening or narrowing the function of the command

29. You need to view any application errors that have occurred today. Which tool should you use?

- ○ **A.** Event Viewer

- ○ **B.** Local Security Policy

- ○ **C.** MSConfig

- ○ **D.** **sfc /scannow**

30. Which of the following commands can help you modify the startup environment?

- ○ **A.** **msconfig**

- ○ **B.** **ipconfig**

- ○ **C.** Boot Config Editor

- ○ **D.** Registry Editor

31. Which of the following log files references third-party software error messages?

- ○ **A.** Security log

- ○ **B.** System log

- ○ **C.** Application log

- ○ **D.** Setuperr.log

32. Which of the following provides the lowest level of wireless security protection?

Quick Answer: **203**
Detailed Answer: **211**

- ○ **A.** Disabling the SSID broadcast
- ○ **B.** Using RADIUS
- ○ **C.** Using the latest version of WPA
- ○ **D.** Enabling WEP on the wireless access point

33. A customer uses an unencrypted wireless network. One of the users has shared a folder for access by any computer. The customer complains that files sometimes appear and disappear from the shared folder. Which of the following statements best describes how to fix the problem? (Select the two best answers.)

Quick Answer: **203**
Detailed Answer: **211**

- ❏ **A.** Enable encryption on the router and the clients.
- ❏ **B.** Encrypt the drive that has the share by using EFS (Encrypting File System).
- ❏ **C.** Increase the level of security on the NTFS folder by changing the permissions.
- ❏ **D.** Change the share-level permissions on the shared folder.

34. A customer is having difficulties with his storage drive, and the system won't boot. You discover that the operating system has to be reloaded. Which of the following would be the best way to explain this to the customer?

Quick Answer: **203**
Detailed Answer: **212**

- ○ **A.** "I need to rebuild the computer."
- ○ **B.** "I need to format the drive and reload the software."
- ○ **C.** "I need to run a **bootrec /fixboot** on the computer."
- ○ **D.** "I need to restore the system; data loss might occur."

35. Users in your accounting department are prompted to provide usernames and passwords to access the payroll system. Which type of authentication method is being requested in this scenario?

Quick Answer: **203**
Detailed Answer: **212**

- ○ **A.** MFA
- ○ **B.** Single factor
- ○ **C.** TACACS+
- ○ **D.** RADIUS

36. Which of the following commands makes a duplicate of a file?

Quick Answer: **203**
Detailed Answer: **212**

- ○ **A.** **move**
- ○ **B.** **copy**
- ○ **C.** **dir**
- ○ **D.** **ls**

37. Which tool in Windows enables a user to easily see how much memory a particular process uses?

Quick Answer: **203**
Detailed Answer: **212**

- ○ **A.** System Information Tool
- ○ **B.** Registry
- ○ **C.** Task Manager
- ○ **D.** Performance Monitor

38. Windows was installed on a computer with two storage drives: a C. drive and a D: drive. Windows is installed to C:, and it works normally. The user of this computer complains that his applications are drive intensive and that they slow down the computer. Which of the following statements best describes how to resolve the problem?

Quick Answer: **203**
Detailed Answer: **212**

- ○ **A.** Move the paging file to the D: drive.
- ○ **B.** Reinstall Windows on the D: drive rather than on the C: drive.
- ○ **C.** Defragment the D: drive.
- ○ **D.** Decrease the size of the paging file.

39. Which of the following tools should be used to protect a computer from electrostatic discharge (ESD) while you are working inside it?

Quick Answer: **203**
Detailed Answer: **213**

- ○ **A.** Multimeter
- ○ **B.** Crimper
- ○ **C.** Antistatic wrist strap
- ○ **D.** PSU tester

40. You are running some cable from an office to a computer located in a warehouse. As you are working in the warehouse, a 55-gallon drum falls from a pallet and spills what smells like ammonia. Which of the following statements best describes the first step you should take in your efforts to resolve this problem?

Quick Answer: **203**
Detailed Answer: **213**

- ○ **A.** Call 911.
- ○ **B.** Call the building supervisor.
- ○ **C.** Get out of the area.
- ○ **D.** Save the computer.

41. While you are upgrading a customer's server storage drives, you notice looped network cables lying all over the server room floor. Which of the following statements best describes how to resolve this issue?

- ○ **A.** Ignore the problem.
- ○ **B.** Tell the customer about safer alternatives.
- ○ **C.** Call the building supervisor.
- ○ **D.** Notify the administrator.

42. Which of the following statements best describes the recommended solution for a lithium-ion battery that won't hold a charge any longer?

- ○ **A.** Throw it in the trash.
- ○ **B.** Return it to the battery manufacturer.
- ○ **C.** Contact the local municipality and ask about their disposal methods.
- ○ **D.** Open the battery and remove the deposits.

43. Which of the following statements is *not* assertive communication?

- ○ **A.** "I certainly know how you feel; losing data is a terrible thing."
- ○ **B.** "Could you explain again exactly what you would like done?"
- ○ **C.** "Do your employees always cause issues like these on computers?"
- ○ **D.** "What can I do to help you?"

44. A customer has a malfunctioning PC, and as you are about to begin repairing it, the customer proceeds to tell you about the problems with the server. Which of the following statements best describes how to respond to the customer?

- ○ **A.** "Wait until I finish with the PC."
- ○ **B.** "I'm sorry, but I don't know how to fix servers."
- ○ **C.** "Is the server problem related to the PC problem?"
- ○ **D.** "I have to call my supervisor."

45. Which of the following could be described as the chronological paper trail of evidence?

- ○ **A.** First response
- ○ **B.** Chain of custody
- ○ **C.** Setting and meeting expectations
- ○ **D.** Data preservation

46. Which of the following statements best describes what *not* to do
    when moving servers and server racks?

    ○ **A.** Remove jewelry.

    ○ **B.** Move a 70-pound wire rack by yourself.

    ○ **C.** Disconnect power to the servers before moving them.

    ○ **D.** Bend at the knees and lift with your legs.

Quick Answer: **203**
Detailed Answer: **214**

47. Active communication includes which of the following?

    ○ **A.** Filtering out unneccssary information

    ○ **B.** Declaring that the customer doesn't know what he or
    she is doing

    ○ **C.** Clarifying the customer's statements

    ○ **D.** Mouthing off

Quick Answer: **203**
Detailed Answer: **214**

48. One of your vendors needs to access a server in your data center
    for maintenance of a software package. The security policy for
    your organization restricts the use of port 3389. However, com-
    mand-line protocols are allowed. Which of the following would be
    the most secure solution?

    ○ **A.** FTP

    ○ **B.** SSH

    ○ **C.** RDP

    ○ **D.** SCP

Quick Answer: **203**
Detailed Answer: **215**

49. Which of the following statements best describes the first course
    of action in removing malware?

    ○ **A.** Identify malware symptoms.

    ○ **B.** Quarantine infected systems.

    ○ **C.** Disable System Restore.

    ○ **D.** Remediate infected systems.

    ○ **E.** Schedule scans and run updates.

    ○ **F.** Enable System Restore.

    ○ **G.** Educate the end user.

Quick Answer: **203**
Detailed Answer: **215**

50. You are working on a Windows computer that is performing slowly. Which of the following commands should you use to resolve the problem? (Select the two best answers.)

    ❏ **A.** format

    ❏ **B.** dism

    ❏ **C.** ipconfig

    ❏ **D.** chkdsk

    ❏ **E.** dir

    ❏ **F.** diskpart

Quick Answer: **203**
Detailed Answer: **215**

51. A customer working in a scientific lab reports that an optical drive in a PC is no longer responding. Which of the following is the first question you should ask the customer?

    ○ **A.** "What has changed since the optical drive worked properly?"

    ○ **B.** "Did you log in with your administrator account?"

    ○ **C.** "What have you modified since the optical drive worked?"

    ○ **D.** "Have you been to any inappropriate websites?"

    ○ **E.** "Why are you still using an optical drive? No one uses those anymore!"

Quick Answer: **203**
Detailed Answer: **216**

52. A coworker is traveling to Europe and is bringing her desktop computer. She asks you what concerns there might be. Which of the following statements best describes how to respond to the customer? (Select the two best answers.)

    ❏ **A.** Advise her that the computer is not usable in other countries.

    ❏ **B.** Advise her to check for a compatible power adapter for that country.

    ❏ **C.** Advise her to use a line conditioner for the correct voltage.

    ❏ **D.** Advise her to check the voltage selector on the power supply.

Quick Answer: **203**
Detailed Answer: **216**

53. After you remove malware/spyware from a customer's PC for the third time, which of the following steps should be taken next?

    ○ **A.** Tell the customer you can't fix the system again.

    ○ **B.** Do nothing; the customer pays every time.

    ○ **C.** Show the customer how to avoid the problem.

    ○ **D.** Change the customer's user permissions.

Quick Answer: **203**
Detailed Answer: **216**

54. You are asked to fix a problem with a customer's Active Directory Domain Services domain controller that is outside the scope of your knowledge. Which of the following statements best describes the recommended course of action?

- ○ **A.** Learn on the job by trying to fix the problem.
- ○ **B.** Tell the customer that the problem should be reported to another technician.
- ○ **C.** Assure the customer that the problem will be fixed very soon.
- ○ **D.** Help the customer find the appropriate channels to fix the problem.

55. When you are working on a PC, which of the following should you do to prevent electrical shock? (Select the three best answers.)

- ❏ **A.** Remove metallic jewelry.
- ❏ **B.** Press the "kill switch" on the back of the PSU.
- ❏ **C.** Wear an antistatic strap.
- ❏ **D.** Disconnect the power cord.
- ❏ **E.** Use proper cable management.
- ❏ **F.** Keep components in an antistatic bag.

56. You are troubleshooting a Windows Server computer that you have little knowledge about. The message on the screen says that there is a "DHCP partner down" error. No other technicians are available to help you, and your manager wants the server fixed ASAP, or you are fired. Which of the following statements best describe the recommended course of action? (Select the two best answers.)

- ❏ **A.** Identify the problem.
- ❏ **B.** Escalate the problem.
- ❏ **C.** Establish a plan of action.
- ❏ **D.** Call tech support.
- ❏ **E.** Verify full system functionality.
- ❏ **F.** Test the theory to determine cause.

57. Which of the following protects confidential information from being disclosed publicly?

- ○ **A.** Classification
- ○ **B.** Social engineering
- ○ **C.** HTTP
- ○ **D.** Drive wipe

58. You are working on an infected computer that is currently turned off. You are concerned that the boot sector is affected and that there is the potential for malware spread. What should you do to scan the boot sector?

   - ○ **A.** Boot to WinRE.
   - ○ **B.** Boot into Safe Mode.
   - ○ **C.** Mount the drive using a forensic platform.
   - ○ **D.** Boot the drive in another computer.

59. Which of the following Windows tools typically enables you to *configure* a SOHO router?

   - ○ **A.** Web browser
   - ○ **B.** Device Manager
   - ○ **C.** MSConfig
   - ○ **D.** File Explorer

60. What might you need to supply during a local clean installation of Windows Pro edition if newer hardware is not seen correctly?

   - ○ **A.** Windows Enterprise edition media
   - ○ **B.** Image deployment
   - ○ **C.** Installing from a recovery partition or disc
   - ○ **D.** Third-party drivers
   - ○ **E.** Additional partitions

61. A coworker maps a network drive for a user, but after a system reboot, the drive is not seen in File Explorer. Which of the following steps should be taken first to ensure that the drive remains mapped?

   - ○ **A.** Check Reconnect at Sign-in when mapping the drive.
   - ○ **B.** Select the drive letter needed to connect each time the coworker logs on.
   - ○ **C.** Check the folder connection when mapping the drive.
   - ○ **D.** Use the **net use** command instead.

62. Based on the physical hardware address of the client's network device, which of the following is commonly used to restrict access to a network?

   - ○ **A.** WPA key
   - ○ **B.** DHCP settings
   - ○ **C.** MAC filtering
   - ○ **D.** SSID broadcast

63. A print job fails to leave the print queue. Which of the following services may need to be restarted?

- ○ **A.** Print driver
- ○ **B.** Print Spooler
- ○ **C.** Network adapter
- ○ **D.** Printer

64. After a network application is installed on a computer running Windows, the application does not communicate with the server. Which of the following actions should be taken first?

- ○ **A.** Use Samba for connectivity.
- ○ **B.** Reinstall the latest security update.
- ○ **C.** Add the port number and name of the service to the exceptions list in Windows Defender Firewall.
- ○ **D.** Add the port number to the network firewall.

65. You work for a Fortune 500 company. Several mobile device users report issues connecting to the WLAN in the warehouse area of the building. However, those mobile users can connect to the Internet via 5G service. You test for wireless connectivity with your laptop in the lobby of the building and can connect with no problem. While you are doing your tests, you receive automated messages from a network sniffing program, telling you that devices are failing due to a power outage. Which of the following is most likely causing the wireless connectivity issue?

- ○ **A.** SSID broadcasting has been turned off.
- ○ **B.** The warehouse environment is unclean, and the network devices located there are getting clogged with dust and dirt.
- ○ **C.** The WAP in the warehouse is down.
- ○ **D.** The DHCP scope for the WLAN is full.
- ○ **E.** The system locked out all wireless users.

66. One of your Windows users is trying to install a local printer and is unsuccessful, based on the permissions for the user account. Which of the following types best describes this user account?

- ○ **A.** Power user
- ○ **B.** Administrator
- ○ **C.** Guest
- ○ **D.** Domain Admin

67. When accessing an NTFS shared resource, which of the following are required? (Select the two best answers.)

Quick Answer: **203**
Detailed Answer: **221**

    ❏ **A.** An active certificate

    ❏ **B.** Correct user permissions

    ❏ **C.** Local user access

    ❏ **D.** Correct share permissions

68. You are contracted to recover data from a laptop. In which two locations might you find valuable irreplaceable data? (Select the two best answers.)

Quick Answer: **203**
Detailed Answer: **221**

    ❏ **A.** Ntoskrnl.exe

    ❏ **B.** Windows folder

    ❏ **C.** Pictures

    ❏ **D.** Email

    ❏ **E.** System32 folder

69. Which utility enables auditing at the local level?

Quick Answer: **203**
Detailed Answer: **221**

    ○ **A.** OU Group Policy

    ○ **B.** Local Security Policy

    ○ **C.** Active Directory Policy

    ○ **D.** Site Policy

70. A customer has forgotten his password and can no longer access his company email address. Which of the following statements best describes the recommended course of action?

Quick Answer: **203**
Detailed Answer: **221**

    ○ **A.** Tell him to remember his password.

    ○ **B.** Ask him for information confirming his identity.

    ○ **C.** Tell him that the password will be reset in several minutes.

    ○ **D.** Tell him that he shouldn't forget his password.

71. Which of the following can help locate a lost or stolen mobile device?

Quick Answer: **203**
Detailed Answer: **222**

    ○ **A.** Passcode

    ○ **B.** Auto-erase

    ○ **C.** GPS

    ○ **D.** Encryption

72. Which of the following can be disabled to help prevent access to a wireless network?

Quick Answer: **203**
Detailed Answer: **222**

    ◯   **A.**   MAC filtering

    ◯   **B.**   SSID broadcast

    ◯   **C.**   WPA passphrase

    ◯   **D.**   WPA key

73. A user just connected to a corporate VPN. Now, the user's workstation is no longer able to browse websites. You discover that it is possible to use a different web browser on the same computer to reach websites correctly. Other users are able to connect to websites through the VPN. Which of the following should you do next?

Quick Answer: **203**
Detailed Answer: **222**

    ◯   **A.**   Flush the DNS cache

    ◯   **B.**   Scan the user's workstation for malware

    ◯   **C.**   Disconnect from and then reconnect to the VPN

    ◯   **D.**   Use an enterprise-level sandbox

    ◯   **E.**   Verify the browser's proxy configuration

    ◯   **F.**   Tell the user to use the alternate web browser

74. In Windows, which utility enables you to select and copy characters from any font?

Quick Answer: **203**
Detailed Answer: **222**

    ◯   **A.**   Language Bar

    ◯   **B.**   Sticky Keys

    ◯   **C.**   Control Panel > Fonts

    ◯   **D.**   Character Map

75. Which of the following can be described as removing the limitations of Apple iOS?

Quick Answer: **203**
Detailed Answer: **223**

    ◯   **A.**   Rooting

    ◯   **B.**   Jailbreaking

    ◯   **C.**   VirusBarrier

    ◯   **D.**   Super-admin powers

76. A customer's personal settings are not saving properly. You suspect that the user's local Windows profile is corrupt. You attempt
to check the size of the ntuser.dat file, but it does not appear in the
user's profile directory. Which of the following utilities should you
use to view the file?

- ○ **A.** Sync Center
- ○ **B.** Display Settings
- ○ **C.** User Accounts
- ○ **D.** Folder Options

Quick Answer: **203**
Detailed Answer: **223**

77. Which of the following provides language support for representing
characters and is built into Windows?

- ○ **A.** Unicode
- ○ **B.** EBCDIC
- ○ **C.** ASCII
- ○ **D.** ITU-T
- ○ **E.** .ps1

Quick Answer: **203**
Detailed Answer: **223**

78. Which of the following is the best source of information about
malicious software detected on a computer?

- ○ **A.** Operating system documentation
- ○ **B.** Anti-malware software website
- ○ **C.** Readme.txt file included with the anti-spyware software
  installation
- ○ **D.** The user of a previously infected computer

Quick Answer: **203**
Detailed Answer: **224**

79. You are working for a company as a roaming PC tech and have
been assigned work by a network administrator. The admin notifies
you that the company is experiencing a DDoS attack. Half a dozen
internal Windows PCs are the source of the traffic. The admin
gives you the Windows computer names and tells you that they
must be scanned and cleaned immediately. Which of the following
effects to the PCs should you as a PC technician focus on fixing?
(Select the two best answers.)

- ❏ **A.** Zombies
- ❏ **B.** Spyware
- ❏ **C.** Ransomware
- ❏ **D.** Virus
- ❏ **E.** Botnet

Quick Answer: **203**
Detailed Answer: **224**

Quick Check

Quick Answer: **203**
Detailed Answer: **224**

80. You are troubleshooting a networking problem with Windows, and you can't seem to fix it using the typical Windows GUI-based troubleshooting tools or PowerShell. You have identified the problem and established a theory of probable cause. (In fact, you are on your fourth theory.) Which tool should be used to troubleshoot the problem, and in what stage of the troubleshooting process should you do the troubleshooting?

    ○ **A.** **regsvr32**; Conduct external or internal research based on symptoms.

    ○ **B.** **gpupdate**; Perform backups before making any changes.

    ○ **C.** USMT; Verify full system functionality.

    ○ **D.** **regedit**; Test the theory to determine cause.

    ○ **E.** Boot Camp; Document findings, actions, and outcomes.

Quick-Check Answer Key

1. A and C	**28.** D	**55.** B, C, and D
2. D	**29.** A	**56.** A and D
3. C	**30.** A	**57.** A
4. A	**31.** C	**58.** C
5. C	**32.** A	**59.** A
6. A	**33.** A and C	**60.** D
7. B	**34.** D	**61.** A
8. A	**35.** B	**62.** C
9. D	**36.** B	**63.** B
10. C	**37.** C	**64.** C
11. A and E	**38.** A	**65.** C
12. D	**39.** C	**66.** C
13. A	**40.** C	**67.** B and D
14. D	**41.** B	**68.** C and D
15. D	**42.** C	**69.** B
16. C	**43.** C	**70.** B
17. B and C	**44.** C	**71.** C
18. D	**45.** B	**72.** B
19. A	**46.** B	**73.** E
20. A and C	**47.** C	**74.** D
21. B	**48.** B	**75.** B
22. D	**49.** A	**76.** D
23. A	**50.** B and D	**77.** A
24. C	**51.** A	**78.** B
25. D	**52.** B and D	**79.** A and D
26. C	**53.** C	**80.** D
27. A and D	**54.** D	

Answers and Explanations

1. Answers: A and C

Explanation: At the command line, this service is simply known as Spooler. Type **net stop spooler** and **net start spooler** to restart the service. Or you could go to Run > services.msc to restart the service. (Or, in Computer Management, you can find the Print Spooler service in Services and Applications > Services.) From there, you can start, stop, pause, resume, or restart services and also set their startup type to Automatic, Manual, or Disabled.

Incorrect answers: When stopping a service in the Command Prompt (or PowerShell), remember to use the command-line name, not the name used in the GUI. In this case, the command-line name is spooler, whereas the GUI-based name is Print Spooler. The Event Viewer is used to view and analyze log files.

2. Answer: D

Explanation: Remember that %systemroot% is a variable. It takes the place of whatever folder contains the operating system. This is usually the path \Windows. For example, if you were to run a default installation of Windows, the path to the registry hives would be C:\Windows\System32\Config. The main hives are SAM, SECURITY, SOFTWARE, SYSTEM, and DEFAULT. You can access and configure them by opening the Registry Editor (Run > regedit.exe) and opening the HKEY_LOCAL_MACHINE subtree. Other hive information is stored in the user profile folders.

Incorrect answers: The other locations are incorrect. The Windows folder is %systemroot%, so the paths that include \%systemroot%\Windows don't make any sense. The System32 folder houses all of the 64-bit protected system files (and many applications) for Windows.

3. Answer: C

Explanation: On Android devices, you would need to enable Developer Mode, also known as Developer Options. How this is done can vary from one device to the next, but a typical process is to go to Settings > About and then tap the Build Number option repeatedly (often seven times). At that point, you will see Developer Options listed within Settings. Inside Developer Options, you will find settings such as USB Debugging that can be enabled.

Incorrect answers: Screen sharing can be accomplished with third-party tools or with the Android Debug Bridge (ADB), which works only if you have Developer Mode enabled. Android Package (APK) is the default file format used by Android. Rooting the phone goes beyond Developer Mode and gives the user (and apps) 100% administrative access. This also opens the device to a myriad of attacks and so is considered insecure and avoided by most organizations.

4. Answer: A

Explanation: You should attempt to defragment the drive. Because it is a magnetic-based disk drive—a hard disk drive (HDD)—it will become fragmented over time.

Fragmentation is common with older laptops that do not use solid-state drives. The more applications that are installed and uninstalled, the more a drive becomes fragmented. To make the files contiguous, use the Windows Disk Defragmenter (Optimize Drives) utility. Note that if a drive has less than 15% free space, you may need to run the command-line utility with the -f option: **defrag.exe -f**.

Incorrect answers: Rebuilding the user profile may be necessary if the profile is large. This can be indicated by slow logon times. Ending tasks in the Task Manager might help temporarily if there are any tasks that need to be terminated, but they might restart on the next reboot of the laptop. Also, the number of unnecessary tasks is probably limited because the user has already removed unnecessary programs (which is one of the best ways to increase the speed of the operating system). Updating the laptop is always a good idea (especially for security reasons) but probably won't improve the laptop's performance.

5. **Answer: C**

   Explanation: Patch management is the patching of many systems from a central location. It includes the planning, testing, implementing, and auditing stages. There are various software packages you can use to perform patch management. Windows Server Update Services (WSUS) is an example of Microsoft patch management software. Other Microsoft examples include the Configuration Manager (which is part of Microsoft Endpoint Manager), and there are plenty of third-party offerings as well.

   Incorrect answers: A host-based firewall is a software firewall that is loaded on a computer to stop attackers from intruding on a network. Application baselining is the performance measurements of an application over time. Virtualization occurs when an operating system is installed to a single file on a computer. Often, it runs virtually on top of another OS.

6. **Answer: A**

   Explanation: Windows Home edition does not allow for the joining of domains.

   Incorrect answers: The rest of the listed answers (Pro, Pro for Workstations, and Enterprise) all allow for joining domains. Essentially, you should recommend Home edition for home use, and one of the others for business use.

7. **Answer: B**

   Explanation: You should recommend that the user add the senders to the junk email sender list. Doing so blocks those senders' email addresses. (Alternatively, the entire domain can be blocked.) However, this option could take a lot of time; another option is to increase the level of security on the spam filter within the email program. Any further spam can then be sent to the junk email sender list.

   Incorrect answers: Users need their email accounts, and creating a new one can result in a lot of work for the user. Finding a new ISP is overreacting a bit; plus, the user has no idea if one ISP will be better at stopping spam than another. Never tell a user to reply to spam. Spam emails should be sent to the spam folder and never replied to as replying is a security risk and, at the very least, would lead to more spam messages.

8. **Answer: A**

   Explanation: To turn off devices after a specified period of time in Windows, access Control Panel > Power Options. Then click Change Plan Settings for the appropriate power plan. (This can also be accessed by searching within Settings.)

   Incorrect answers: Display Properties allows you to modify things such as screen resolution. Computer Management is a commonly used console window in Windows; it includes the Event Viewer, Disk Management, and Services. The Task Manager is used to analyze system resources and end tasks (among other things).

9. **Answer: D**

   Explanation: On the Ports tab, you can find how the printer is connected to the computer. It might be via a USB, COM, LPT, or TCP/IP port. You might get to this tab by selecting Properties or Printer Properties, depending on the printer.

   Incorrect answers: The Sharing tab allows you to share a locally connected (or remotely controlled) printer on the network. The Advanced tab has options such as print spooling and printer pooling. The Separator page button allows you to configure a page that is inserted after every print job.

10. **Answer: C**

    Explanation: The test page verifies connectivity and gives you insight about possible application problems at the computer that is attempting to print.

    Incorrect answers: In this case, you aren't worried about the quality of the printer output; it is the computer and the application that you are troubleshooting. You use test pages to make sure the computer can print properly to the printer, not to initiate diagnostic routines. Those would be initiated from the built-in display and menu on the printer or in Windows by right-clicking the printer, selecting Printer properties, and then selecting Print Test Page. Printing a test page does not clear the print queue or reset printer memory. You would have to do that at the printer and/or at the computer controlling the printer.

11. **Answers: A and E**

    Explanation: Of the listed answers, you should recommend cloud storage and a hot or warm site. The cloud storage acts as offsite storage of data, away from the customer's building. The hot or warm site acts as a secondary office that is ready to go (or close to ready to go) if the main office is compromised. Depending on the company's budget, it might not be able to afford a hot site, but a warm site can work well if there is an efficient disaster recovery plan in place, and if the cloud-based data is quickly accessible.

    Incorrect answers: *Data recovery* is rather vague. Also, the customer doesn't want to have to recover data; they want the data to be safe. Backup testing is always important, regardless of where the data will be stored; however, the question isn't about backing up data; it's about how data will be stored. Waterproof smartphones might work in a flood or a hurricane, but it's difficult to waterproof things like PCs, servers, networking equipment, and so on. Local backups will not help in the event of a disaster; the customer needs offsite storage of data.

12. **Answer: D**

   Explanation: Sanitizing the storage drive does not secure a computer workstation. It does, however, prevent anyone from accessing data on the drive; however, it also ensures that the computer workstation won't be functional anymore. A data sanitization method is the specific way in which a data destruction program or file shredder overwrites the data on a drive or another storage device.

   Incorrect answers: Setting strong passwords, changing default usernames, and disabling the guest account are all ways of securing a computer workstation.

13. **Answer: A**

   Explanation: Because there is only one computer, you can implement auditing only locally. This is done with the Local Security Policy. (This policy is not available in all editions of Windows.)

   Incorrect answers: The Group Policy Editor and Active Directory Domain Services (AD DS) are used by Windows Servers in a domain environment. Some versions of Windows have the Local Group Policy Editor, where auditing can also be turned on. If you type **services.msc** at the Run prompt, services.msc will open the Services console window; you can turn services on and off and modify their startup type from this window.

14. **Answer: D**

   Explanation: A device driver provides a connection between the operating system and a device. It is a program that makes the interaction between the two run efficiently. It simplifies programming by using high-level application code. The best device drivers come from the manufacturers of devices. They are the ones who developed the device, so it stands to reason that their code would be the most thoroughly tested and debugged.

   Incorrect answers: A device driver does not modify applications, but an updated driver could indirectly affect how an application behaves. Some device drivers use memory better than others; it all depends on how well they are coded. A device driver may or may not improve device performance; that depends on several factors, including whether it is an update and how the update is designed to change how the device functions.

15. **Answer: D**

   Explanation: After a restore point is made, it is stored in the System Volume Information folder. To view this folder, you must log on as an administrator, show hidden files and folders, and assign permissions to the account that wants to view that folder. The System Volume Information folder is located in the root of the volume that the restore point was created for.

   Incorrect answers: The Recycler folder is the place where deleted information is stored temporarily (until the Recycle Bin is emptied). The System32 folder houses many of the 64-bit system files for the operating system. The %systemroot% folder is, by default, C:\Windows.

16. **Answer: C**

    Explanation: PII stands for personally identifiable information. PII is regulated by many laws, such as the Privacy Act of 1974 and several others, including GDPR and PCI-DSS.

    Incorrect answers: DRM stands for digital rights management, which is a way of protecting data from illegal copying and distribution. A EULA, which stands for end-user licensing agreement, is an agreement used for software such as Windows and Office. The DMCA, which stands for Digital Millennium Copyright Act, provides laws dealing with digital information and ownership.

17. **Answers: B and C**

    Explanation: Shoulder surfing and tailgating are both types of social engineering. A shoulder surfer attempts to view information on a person's desk or display without the person's knowledge. With tailgating, a person attempts to gain access to a secure area by following closely on the heels of another employee, usually without that person's knowledge.

    Incorrect answers: A rootkit is a program that is designed to gain administrator-level access to a computer. It is a type of malicious software (or malware).

18. **Answer: D**

    Explanation: The Print Spooler controls the queue and the printing of documents.

    Incorrect answers: A printer is a physical printing device; Microsoft also refers to the print driver software as the printer. A print server is a device that controls one or more printers; it is usually connected to a network. With print pooling, two or more printers are grouped together so that a user's document will print faster: If one printer is occupied, the other takes over.

19. **Answer: A**

    Explanation: Magnetically erase the drive; for example, degauss the drive. Degaussing a drive is an excellent way to remove all traces of data—but only if the drive is electromagnetic! Of course, physical destruction (shredding, pulverizing) is better; degaussing might be used on top of physical destruction.

    Incorrect answers: Formatting the drive is not enough due to the data residue that is left behind. Running **bootrec /fixboot** rewrites the boot sector of the drive, but the data remains. Converting the drive from FAT32 to NTFS (with the **convert** command) keeps the data intact.

20. **Answers: A and C**

    Explanation: If the WAP/router was reset, any security settings that you originally set up are most likely gone. If you backed up the settings previously, you could restore them. Either way, some type of encryption protocol (preferably WPA3/WPA2) is necessary. The passphrase or network key generated by the WAP/router needs to be installed on each client before it can be recognized on the network. This passphrase/key should be kept secret, of course. After all the clients have been associated with the WAP/router, disable SSID broadcasting so that no one else can "see" the router (without more advanced software).

    Incorrect answers: MS-CHAPv2 is used with remote connections such as VPNs. Moving the WAP/router probably won't work if this is a small business. Today's SOHO routers have powerful radios with a lot of range. Chances are that moving the router to one corner of the office won't have any effect.

21. **Answer: B**

Explanation: The tech should escalate the call to another technician. This is exactly why help desks are configured in groups and levels: Level 1, Level 2, Level 3, and possibly beyond. Don't try to be a superhuman. In technology, there is almost always someone who knows more than you about a specific subject. First, route the call to the next-level tech and then let the customer know that you are doing so.

Incorrect answers: Good help desks are set up in such a way that someone is always available. Every problem can be resolved. Finding the solution is just a matter of knowledge and persistence. (Remember this when you take the real exams.) Don't try to fix the problem, regardless of the time needed. Your time—and the customer's time—is very valuable. Escalate so that you, your organization, and the customer can approach and solve the problem efficiently.

22. **Answer: D**

Explanation: The computer might need a special keystroke, a press of the power button, or just a little more time to come out of Hibernate mode. Remember: Check simple, quick solutions first because they are usually the culprits.

Incorrect answers: Booting into Safe Mode and reinstalling video drivers can be time-consuming, but, if necessary, you can attempt these steps in that order—after checking the power state. Replacing the inverter is not a likely answer with a brand-new laptop; a laptop may not even have an inverter.

23. **Answer: A**

Explanation: You should roll back the driver to its original state. You will need to boot into Safe Mode to do this. Chances are that the operating system update installed a new video driver—and it is not working properly with the system.

Incorrect answers: The computer was already rebooted, and another reboot will probably not help. However, this can be a good troubleshooting technique, helping you to see what the computer does while booting. Reloading the operating system is usually a last resort to problems because it is time-consuming, and there is a risk of data loss. F2 is a common key to use when entering the BIOS/UEFI. While there are video settings in the BIOS, it is improbable that the issue is being caused by the BIOS.

24. **Answer: C**

Explanation: The person should have typed **sudo** first before the **apt-get update** command. In this scenario, the person is working as a typical user but is trying to run a command that requires administrative privileges. The user account would need to be a member of the sudo group and would have to preface any administrative command with **sudo**. By the way, **apt-get update** is a command that can be run on Debian-based systems to attempt to ascertain if any updates are available for the operating system. Other similar Linux update commands include **apt update** and **dnf update**.

Incorrect answers: **nano** is a text editor in Linux. **chmod** is used to change permissions on files and directories in Linux. **grep** is a filtering tool.

25. Answer: D

Explanation: The issue is that Megan needs to obtain an IP address through DHCP when on the road. But setting the network adapter to obtain an IP address automatically is not enough. To connect to the internal company network, the Alternate Configuration tab must be configured as a user-configured static IP address. This solution enables Megan to connect to networks while on the road by obtaining IP addresses automatically and allows her to connect to the internal company network with the static IP address.

Incorrect answers. Megan shouldn't do anything. As a technician, you should fix the problem, so the other options, where Megan is doing her own troubleshooting, are incorrect.

26. Answer: C

Explanation: Hibernate mode saves all the contents of RAM (as hiberfil.sys in the root of C:) and then shuts down the system so that it is using virtually no power. To reactivate the system, you must press the power button. At that point, the entire session is loaded from RAM, and you can continue on with the session.

Incorrect answers: Standby (Sleep in Windows) and Suspend modes turn off the storage drive and display and throttle down the CPU and RAM, but they still use power. Although these power modes use less power than the computer being powered on, altogether they end up using much more power than Hibernate mode does. Shutdown is great for power savings, but the session is lost when the computer is shut down.

27. Answers: A and D

Explanation: NTFS can use NTFS file-level security, whereas FAT32 cannot. NTFS clusters are smaller than FAT32 clusters. NTFS partitions are therefore more efficient (when installed correctly) than FAT32 partitions.

Incorrect answers: NTFS can create larger partitions (or logical drives) than FAT32 in general, so larger logical drives would exist on an NTFS partition, not on a FAT32 partition. Also, logical drives are based on the older MBR partitioning scheme and are not necessary on most of today's computers that use a GPT partitioning scheme.

28. Answer: D

Explanation: A switch (or option) alters the action of a command but not by forcing it to perform unrelated actions.

Incorrect answers: A switch works only at the current time within the operating system you are currently using, so "to work across any operating system" doesn't make sense in this scenario. Switches are not used in application icons; they are used within commands. For example, **dir /p** would display directory contents page by page.

29. Answer: A

Explanation: The Event Viewer contains the log files of all the errors that occur on the machine. In this case, you would go to the Application log. Another common log is the System log, which shows errors concerning the OS and drivers.

Incorrect answers: In the Local Security Policy, you can set up auditing and create password policies for the computer. MSConfig enables you to boot the computer in different modes and enable or disable services and applications. **sfc /scannow** is a command run in the Command Prompt (by an administrator only) that scans the integrity of the protected system files and repairs them, if possible.

30. Answer: A

Explanation: The **msconfig** command (and MSConfig utility) enables you to modify the startup environment via the General and Boot tabs.

Incorrect answers: **ipconfig** displays all network adapters' settings. The Boot Config Editor, BCDEdit, is used to modify the Boot Configuration Data (BCD) store. You might need to modify the BCD if you are trying to dual-boot a computer. The Registry Editor allows you to make changes to Windows by accessing various hives of information and individual entries. Although the BCDEdit and Registry Editor utilities might be able to modify some startup features, they are not "commands" and are used for more advanced and less frequently used modifications than **msconfig**.

31. Answer: C

Explanation: The Application log in the Event Viewer displays errors concerning Windows applications as well as third-party applications.

Incorrect answers: The Security log shows auditing events. The System log shows events concerning system files, drivers, and operating system functionality. Setuperr. log is a log file that is created during the installation of Windows. If it is created, it is stored in %windir%\Panther and is not within the Event Viewer.

32. Answer: A

Explanation: Disabling the SSID broadcast is a security precaution, but it only keeps out the average user. Any attacker with two bits of knowledge can scan for other things the wireless access point broadcasts.

Incorrect answers: Using WEP is more secure than not using any encryption; it's better to have WEP than to have an open network with the SSID disabled. RADIUS is an external method of authenticating users; it often requires a Windows Server machine. The latest version of WPA is very secure; if you can enable one security option, make it WPA3—or WPA2, if WPA3 is not available.

33. Answers: A and C

Explanation: Use the latest version of WPA encryption on the router (and clients) to deny wardrivers and other stragglers access to the customer's network and, ultimately, any shared folders on the network. Increase the level of NTFS security by changing the permissions in the Security tab of the shared folder.

Incorrect answers: EFS isn't necessary if you set up encryption on the wireless access point, but if you are dealing in confidential information, you should consider using EFS as well. Here's the deal: Share-level permissions are rarely modified. NTFS permissions are more configurable, so that is where the bulk of your time configuring permissions will go.

34. Answer: D

Explanation: Always explain specifically and exactly what you must do and what the ramifications are. Verify that the customer agrees to the proposed work (in writing).

Incorrect answers: Try to avoid being vague ("I need to rebuild the computer") and, conversely, avoid technical acronyms and jargon. Always make sure the customer is fully aware of the situation.

35. Answer: B

Explanation: Single-factor authentication is being used here. In this case, the only factor of authentication is something the users know—usernames and passwords.

Incorrect answers: MFA, which stands for multifactor authentication, combines two or more types of authentication methods—for example, a password and a fingerprint. MFA is recommended over single-factor authentication. TACACS+ and RADIUS are authentication protocols, not authentication methods, and are often involved with single sign-on (SSO), federated identity management (FIM), and MFA authentication schemes. Regardless, the scenario says that the users are logging in to a payroll system, which is a separate entity from any authentication servers.

36. Answer: B

Explanation: **copy** is used to make a duplicate of a file in another location.

Incorrect answers: **move** enables you to shift a file to another location. **dir** gives you the contents of a specific folder. **copy**, **move**, and **dir** are Windows commands. **ls** lists the directory contents on a Linux-based system (as does **dir** in many Linux distributions).

37. Answer: C

Explanation: The Task Manager enables a user to see the amount of memory and the percentage of processing power a particular process uses in real time. This can be done on the Processes tab.

Incorrect answers: System Information gives you information about the hardware and software of the computer, but it is static (text only) and doesn't change in real time. The Registry stores all of the settings of Windows and is modified with the Registry Editor. Performance Monitor can graph the performance of the different components in the computer and, if configured properly, can do the same thing as the Task Manager in this scenario—but not as easily.

38. Answer: A

Explanation: By moving the paging file (or swap file, aka virtual memory) to the D: drive, you are freeing up C: to deal with those drive-intensive programs.

Incorrect answers: Reinstalling Windows is a huge process that you should avoid at all costs, especially when unnecessary, as it would be in this example. Defragging the C: drive would help if that is where the OS and applications are, but defragging the D: drive will not speed up the applications. Decreasing the pagefile size never helps. However, increasing the size of this file, moving it, and adding RAM are all ways to make applications run faster.

39. **Answer: C**

Explanation: Use an antistatic wrist strap when working inside a computer to protect against electrostatic discharge (ESD). Other ways to prevent ESD include using an anti-static mat, touching the chassis of the case (self-grounding), and using antistatic bags.

Incorrect answers: A multimeter is used to run various electrical tests. A crimper is used to connect plugs and other connectors to the ends of a cable—for example, crimping RJ45 plugs on to the ends of a twisted-pair cable. A PSU tester is used to test the voltage of a power supply unit and other electrical connections inside a computer.

40. **Answer: C**

Explanation: If something is immediately hazardous to you, you must leave the area right away.

Incorrect answers: After leaving the area of a hazard, you can call 911, the building supervisor/facilities department, or your manager, depending on the severity of the situation. Computers and all other technology are less important than human life. Remember that. Plus, if backup systems have been implemented properly, you have nothing to lose if a computer is damaged. If the situation is not an emergency, be sure to reference the material safety data sheet (MSDS) for the substance you encounter.

41. **Answer: B**

Explanation: You need to explain to the customer that there is a safer way. Cable management is very important when it comes to the safety of employees. Trip hazards such as incorrectly routed network cables can have devastating effects on a person.

Incorrect answers: Don't ignore the problem. It is not your place to notify the building supervisor or administrator because this is not your company. However, you might opt to tell your manager about the event. A wise consulting company wants to protect its employees and wants to know of potential hazards at customer locations.

42. **Answer: C**

Explanation: Every municipality has its own way of recycling batteries. They might be collected by the town or county yearly, or perhaps there are other recycling programs that are sponsored by recycling companies. Call the municipality to find out exactly what to do.

Incorrect answers: You should definitely recycle batteries and not throw them in the trash. Manufacturers probably won't be interested in batteries that don't charge any longer. It is more likely that you will recycle them. Be safe: Never open a battery!

43. **Answer: C**

Explanation: Asking a customer if employees always cause issues is just plain rude; this type of communication should be avoided.

Incorrect answers: The other three statements are positive and helpful—or at least consoling. Avoid being judgmental of a customer.

44. **Answer: C**

   Explanation: Ask if the server problem is related to the PC problem. Try to understand the customer before making any judgments about the problem. Make sure it isn't a bigger problem than you realize before making repairs that could be futile. If you find out that it is a separate problem, ask the customer which issue should be resolved first.

   Incorrect answers: You never know if problems are interrelated, so always listen to the customer and be patient before starting any work. If necessary—and if it is a separate problem—you can escalate the server issue to another technician, but you should state that you will do so. Statements about what you know and don't know are rarely necessary. You might have to ultimately call your supervisor about the server issue. But as an A+ technician, you might have the server knowledge required. It depends on the problem. Find out the entire scope of the issues at hand and whether or not the problems are related before beginning any work.

45. **Answer: B**

   Explanation: Chain of custody is a chronological paper trail of evidence that may or may not be used in court.

   Incorrect answers: First response describes the steps a person takes when first responding to a computer with prohibited content or illegal activity: It includes identifying what exactly is happening, reporting through proper channels, and preserving data and devices. Setting and meeting expectations deal with customer service; this is something you should do before you start a job for a customer. Data (and device) preservation is a part of first response; a person who first arrives at the scene of a computer incident will be in charge of preserving data and devices in their current state.

46. **Answer: B**

   Explanation: Don't attempt to move heavy objects by yourself. Ask someone to help you.

   Incorrect answers: Removing jewelry, disconnecting power, and bending at the knees and lifting with the legs are all good safety measures.

47. **Answer: C**

   Explanation: One example of active communication is clarifying a customer's statements. For instance, if you are unsure exactly what the customer wants, clarify the information or repeat it back to the customer to ensure that everyone is on the same page.

   Incorrect answers: Never declare that the customer doesn't know what he is doing. Doing so is a surefire way to lose the customer and possibly your job. It should go without saying: Mouthing off could be the worst thing you could do. Save that for the drive home on the freeway. (I'm just kidding!) Be professional at all times when working with customers—and perhaps while driving as well.

48. **Answer: B**

    Explanation: The best answer is to have the vendor use Secure Shell (SSH). This allows for a command line–based connection to the server. For example, **ssh vendor@10.0.2.143** would connect the username *vendor* to the server with the IP address 10.0.2.143. There's more to it, but I think you get the idea. SSH provides for encrypted communications between a client and a server; it is an industry standard. However, it is command line only (by default). Get to know SSH—for the exam and for the IT field.

    Incorrect answers: File Transfer Protocol (FTP) allows a person to upload and download files to and from an FTP server. It does not allow for maintenance of specific software packages that are installed on the server. Also, it is not very secure. Better alternatives include SFTP (which uses SSH) and FTPS. Remote Desktop Protocol (RDP) is a GUI-based tool used to remotely control Windows systems. It is not command line based. Key point: RDP uses port 3389 (by default), which has been restricted by the organization's security policy. Secure Copy (SCP) is another utility that uses SSH for communications. However, it is only used to copy files to remote hosts; it is not used for maintenance.

49. **Answer: A**

    Explanation: The first step in the malware removal best practices procedure is to identify malware symptoms.

    Incorrect answers: The other steps in the malware removal best practices procedure are (2) quarantine infected systems; (3) disable System Restore; (4) remediate infected systems; (5) schedule scans and run updates; (6) enable System Restore; and (7) educate the end user.

50. **Answers: B and D**

    Explanation: The best listed answers are **dism** and **chkdsk**. For a computer that is running slowly, try using the **chkdsk** (check disk) and **sfc** (System File Checker) commands. Then, if those run into problems, try using the **dism** (Deployment Image Servicing and Management) command. **chkdsk** and **sfc** can repair problems with the drive and with system files. **dism** can repair problems with the system image (from which **sfc** will draw information).

NOTE

While **dism** is not specifically listed in the A+ objectives, it is a good tool to know. Remember that the A+ objectives may not cover 100% of what will be on the exam!

    Incorrect answers: format is used to ready a partition for files. **ipconfig** is used to view network IP configuration data on a Windows system. **dir** lists the files and folders within a current folder (directory). **diskpart** is used to make modifications to the partitions on a storage drive; it is the command-line equivalent of Disk Management. Know the command line!

51. Answer: A

Explanation: You should first ask if anything has changed since the optical drive worked properly.

Incorrect answers: Don't blame the user by asking what "you" modified; it implies that you think the user caused the issue. Always ask if anything has changed before asking any other questions. Try not to accuse a user of accessing inappropriate websites because doing so could be considered inflammatory and harassment. Think like a robot with the single purpose of fixing the problem but act like a professional and courteous human being. Also, optical drives are necessary in some environments. Think before you speak; chances are there is a good reason a person in a scientific lab is using an older—but viable—technology.

52. Answers: B and D

Explanation: Your coworker might need an adapter; otherwise, the plug may not fit in some countries' outlets. Some power supplies have selectors for the United States and Europe (115 and 230 volts). If the wrong voltage is selected, the power supply will not work, and the computer will not boot; setting the voltage incorrectly can also be a safety concern. Newer power supplies might auto-sense the voltage. If a power supply doesn't have one of those red switches, check the documentation to see if it can switch the voltage automatically.

Incorrect answers: A computer most certainly can be used in other countries, as long as it is configured properly and you have the right adapter. Line conditioners simply clean the power for a specific voltage. If your circuit has dirty power (for example, if it is fluctuating between 113 and 130 volts), a line conditioner will keep it steady at 120 volts.

53. Answer: C

Explanation: Teach the user how to avoid this problem by recommending safe computing practices (even if you have taught the customer before). The customer will then be more likely to come back to you with other computer problems. 'Nuff said.

Incorrect answers: Avoid saying "can't"; it's a negative expression that belittles your own ability, which is most likely greater than that. Embrace the teaching method. Over time, it means that you will encounter the same problem less often, and the customer will ultimately thank you for your input. Changing user permissions might help if the person is an administrator. Better yet, you could urge the customer to use a standard user account by default.

54. Answer: D

Explanation: Make sure that the customer has a path toward a solution before dismissing the issue. This might end up being another technician or the entire team.

Incorrect answers: Do *not* try to fix the problem if the scope of work is outside your knowledge. Some PC technicians might not work on domain controllers because they are advanced Microsoft servers that are used in client/server networks. If possible, watch the technician who is ultimately assigned to the job while he or she is performing the work. However, you don't want to tell the customer to report the problem elsewhere; you should take the lead and find the appropriate channels and see the problem through, even if you aren't in charge of the technical fix. Never assure a customer that a problem will be fixed very soon. If you encounter more problems (and you most likely will if you do not know the technology), then your false promises will inevitably lead to a loss of customer respect—for you and for your organization.

55. Answers: B, C, and D

Explanation: You should wear an antistatic strap and either disconnect the power cord or press the "kill switch" on the back of the power supply unit (PSU). The power cord carries 120 volts at 15 amps—and such voltage and amperage entail obvious danger. The best way to work on a PC is to disconnect the power cord from the PSU. However, if the PC's PSU is equipped with an on/off switch (aka "kill switch"), you could turn that off instead. The recommended method is to do both! If for some reason a person failed to do either of these, the antistatic strap would still prevent electrical shock because a proper strap has an embedded 1 megaohm resistor that can absorb some of the electricity. It's important to use such a strap in any event because you never know what other electrical sources you might come into contact with and you want to protect the computers you're working on from ESD. You should also unplug everything else from a PC you are working on, especially network lines and older modem lines.

Incorrect answers: Metallic jewelry shouldn't cause electrical shock, but it's a good idea to remove jewelry anyway so it doesn't get snagged on a computer component. Proper cable management is always a good idea—inside and outside a computer. It's not going to prevent electrical shock, but cable management can improve airflow inside the computer and increase safety outside the computer. Keeping components inside an antistatic bag is a good idea—but only to protect the components. Remember to place an antistatic bag on an antistatic mat so that the components' (and the bag's) electrical potential is equalized, thus reducing the chance of ESD damage.

56. Answers: A and D

Explanation: You should attempt to identify the problem and call (or otherwise contact) Microsoft tech support. The message tells you that the DHCP partner is down. This means that there are two DHCP servers, one acting as a failover. As part of your identification of the problem, you should access the TechNet—for example, https://docs.microsoft.com/en-us/previous-versions/windows/it-pro/windows-server-2012-R2-and-2012/dn338985(v=ws.11). You will find out more about the problem and possibly learn that it isn't as bad as it might seem, and your manager might be overreacting slightly. (These things happen.) In reality, this message means that the partner DHCP server is down, but the one you are work-ing at locally is still functional and is responding to all DHCP requests. You should indeed fix the problem, of course, but now you can call Microsoft tech support in a methodical and calm way, armed with information about what you think the prob-lem is. When a company purchases a Windows Server operating system, it comes with tech support, either from Microsoft or from the company that built the server. Because your knowledge of Windows Server is limited, contacting tech support is a great way to not only fix the problem but also learn a thing or two from the people who work with the system all the time.

Incorrect answers: Escalating the problem is impossible because no other technicians are available to help you. The other answers refer to the CompTIA troubleshooting process, none of which you should attempt until you have called tech support. Now, if your knowledge of Windows Server is sufficient, you can attempt to solve the problem yourself. Though this might seem like a complex question, it really isn't. Trust in your knowledge of the fundamentals!

57. Answer: A

Explanation: The classification of data helps prevent confidential information from being publicly disclosed. Some organizations have a classification scheme for their data, such as normal, secret, and top secret. Policies are implemented to make top secret data the most secure on the network. By classifying data, you are determining who has access to it. This is generally done on a need-to-know basis.

Incorrect answers: Social engineering is the art of manipulating people into giving classified information. To protect a web-based connection (and data that passes through it), an organization would use HTTPS (and an encrypted certificate), not HTTP. Wiping a storage drive is a vague response. How is it being wiped? If it is being formatted, that is not enough to protect confidential information. You need to perform bit-level erasure with third-party software, degauss the drive, or destroy it to make sure that no one can access the data. Data is always stored somewhere on a server or NAS device, so properly disposing of a single drive doesn't protect any and all confidential information from being publicly disclosed.

58. Answer: C

Explanation: The best answer is to mount the drive using a forensic platform. There are several forensic imaging programs that can make an image of the drive, copy the drive, mount the drive, and so on. Using such a program is the best method.

Incorrect answers: You could also boot the drive in another computer that is simply a test computer (in an isolated environment), but that wouldn't give you the tools that a forensic platform has to offer—and if the boot sector is affected, you might want those tools. Also, you risk infecting the other system. WinRE and Safe Mode are tools used to troubleshoot Windows. Safe Mode can be used to attempt to scan a boot sector, but it isn't the best option. A forensic platform can scan the drive safely without the computer being booted at all. This way, there is less chance of the malware spreading any further.

59. Answer: A

Explanation: A web browser such as Edge, Firefox, or Chrome (or any other web browser) is normally used to configure a router.

Incorrect answers: In Device Manager, you enable and disable devices and install, update, and roll back drivers for devices. MSConfig is used to modify how a computer boots and to enable/disable programs and services. File Explorer is used to manipulate files in Windows.

60. Answer: D

Explanation: With a clean installation, the OS is installed to a blank partition. It could be a new storage drive or a drive or an individual partition that was wiped clean of data. Generally, a clean installation is attended to by the technician, who interacts step-by-step with the OS as it is installing. Newer hardware might not be seen correctly by some operating systems, so be ready to supply third-party drivers for hardware (such as storage drives, video, or RAID).

For example, if a system had a Serial Attached SCSI (SAS) drive or a RAID controller, you might need to supply the driver for that during the installation of Windows. It all depends on what Windows can recognize. But again, this is optional. If you have a typical SATA drive, Windows should most definitely recognize it automatically.

Incorrect answers: Enterprise edition is not necessary here. Windows Pro has essentially the same driver set and will either pick up on the new hardware or not. You are not performing image deployment here, nor are you installing from a recovery partition. The scenario states a "local clean installation," which means that a technician is sitting at the system doing the installation step-by-step. Once Windows knows which drive to install to, partitioning, formatting, and configuration of settings can commence—in that order. Additional partitions are not something a technician would "supply" so to speak. They are *configured* by the technician in whatever manner is necessary. It could be that the entire drive (C: drive, recovery partition, and EFI partition) will be automatically configured by Windows. Or perhaps a technician might opt to have additional partitions, but they are not absolutely necessary.

61. Answer: A

Explanation: Although Windows has the Reconnect at Sign-in checkbox selected by default, it could have been disabled.

Incorrect answers: You don't need to select the drive letter each time a connection is made; once you set up the mapped network drive, it uses that drive letter automatically each time. You should check the connection to the folder when mapping the drive, but based on the scenario, this worked fine when the drive was mapped; it was the reboot that caused the issue. If you choose to use the **net use** command, be sure to make persistent connections by adding **/persistent:yes** to the command syntax.

62. Answer: C

Explanation: MAC filtering is used to restrict computers from connecting to a network; it is based on the physical Media Access Control (MAC) address of the computer's network adapter. It works with wired or wireless connections.

Incorrect answers: WPA is used to encrypt the wireless session between a computer and a wireless access point (WAP); its key code is required to gain access to the network. DHCP settings simply allow a specific range of IP addresses and other IP data—such as gateway address and DNS server address—to be handed out to clients. The SSID broadcast is the name of the wireless network as broadcast out over radio waves by the WAP.

63. Answer: B

Explanation: The Print Spooler needs to be restarted on the computer that started the print job or the computer that controls the printer. This can be done in the Services console window or in the Command Prompt with the **net stop spooler** and **net start spooler** commands—or it can be done anywhere else that services can be started and stopped, such as in the Task Manager.

Incorrect answers: Print drivers are not services; they are not started, stopped, or restarted. Instead, they are either installed, uninstalled, updated, or rolled back. The network adapter and the printer are devices, not services.

NOTE

Okay, this is an easy question, but the real exam will have a couple easy ones thrown in as well. Don't think too hard when you actually do receive an easier question.

---

64. Answer: C

Explanation: Adding the port number and name of service to the Windows Defender Firewall exceptions list is the correct answer. But I'm going to pontificate more, as I usually do.

Incorrect answers: Samba is a tool used to connect Linux systems to Microsoft domains. Because the question only mentions Windows (and a "server"), it is unlikely that this is the problem. Uninstalling and reinstalling security updates does not help this particular situation. By default, any of today's Windows OS versions enable Windows Defender Firewall automatically and don't allow inbound connections from the server to the network application. Therefore, you need to make an "exception." In Windows, use Windows Defender Firewall with Advanced Security, either from Administrative Tools or by typing **wf.msc** at the Run prompt. If you decide to add a port, you need to know the port number of the application. For example, VNC applications might use port 5900 or port 5901 for incoming connections.

65. Answer: C

Explanation: The simple answer is that the wireless access point (WAP) is down, but the rest of the wireless access points are functioning normally. The WAP is most likely down because of a power outage in a portion of the warehouse. Perhaps a circuit tripped, or there was some "planned" maintenance that you weren't aware of.

Incorrect answers: It is unlikely that SSID broadcasting would be turned off; that would make it difficult for users to access the WAP. It is also unlikely that a Fortune 500 company would have an unclean warehouse. I mean, all warehouses get somewhat dirty, but in an enterprise company, they are cleaned often. Also, it is likely that the WAP is mounted to the ceiling or high on a wall, where it is unlikely to get dirty. The smallest class C DHCP scope can allow as many as 253 wireless connections (not including the WAP/router itself). It is unlikely that warehouse wireless connectivity would surpass this. If the entire wireless system locked out all wireless users, you would be receiving much more than several complaints about wireless connectivity issues.

66. **Answer: C**

   Explanation: The Guest account is the most likely answer here. This account has the fewest privileges of all Windows accounts. It cannot install printers or printer drivers. Standard users can also have issues with printers, depending on the version of Windows and the policies involved. But the Guest account has absolutely no administrative powers whatsoever.

   Incorrect answers: Power Users don't really have power anymore. They are included for backward compatibility with older versions of applications and how they interact with Windows. The Administrator account is the most powerful account on a local Windows system and has complete control over everything, unless there is a domain involved. Then you would want a Domain Administrator account.

67. **Answers: B and D**

   Explanation: The share-level permissions must first be set to enable access to the user. Then the NTFS file-level "user" permissions must also be set; the more restrictive of the two will take precedence. (Usually this is configured by making NTFS more restrictive.)

   Incorrect answers: Certificates are normally used in Internet or VPN sessions. *Local user access* is a somewhat vague answer but doesn't apply here; when a user connects to a shared resource, that person does so over the network to a remote computer.

68. **Answers: C and D**

   Explanation: Pictures and email are possibly valuable—and definitely irreplaceable if there is no backup.

   Incorrect answers: The rest of the answers mention things that can be restored or reinstalled from the operating system image or disc.

69. **Answer: B**

   Explanation: Of all the answers, the only one that deals with the local level is Local Security Policy.

   Incorrect answers: Organizational Unit (OU) Group Policy, Active Directory Policy, and Site Policy all require at least one domain controller on the network. You should know some domain-based policy terminology to compare the options in these policies to security options on the local computer. You can access the Local Security Policy from Administrative Tools or by typing **secpol.msc** at the Run prompt.

70. **Answer: B**

   Explanation: In many cases, passwords cannot be reset by the user or by the systems administrator. If that is the case here, you need to verify the identity of the person first. You might need to do so just as a matter of organizational policy.

   Incorrect answers: Telling the person not to do that or to simply remember the password is just rude. If the password can be reset and you are allowed to reset it, you should do so immediately.

71. **Answer: C**

    Explanation: GPS can help to locate a stolen or lost mobile device. Plenty of third-party programs allow a user to track a device, as long as it is on and has GPS installed and functioning. If the device is off, the program will display the last known good location.

    Incorrect answers: Passcodes are used to secure a device in the event that it is stolen or lost. Auto-erase is used to wipe the contents of a device that is lost or stolen. Encryption protects the data in the event that the user no longer has possession of it.

72. **Answer: B**

    Explanation: To aid in preventing access to a wireless network, disable the SSID. But only do this when all computers have been connected. If more computers need to be connected later, they will have to connect manually, or the SSID will have to be reenabled.

    Incorrect answers: Although disabling the SSID is an okay security method, it won't keep smart attackers out of your network. MAC filtering and WPA encryption (the latest version) do a much better job at that than disabling the SSID.

73. **Answer: E**

    Explanation: The best answer is to verify the web browser's proxy configuration. Chances are that the network is making use of a proxy server in conjunction with the VPN. Most likely, an incorrect proxy server name or IP address was entered into the settings. If another web browser (with no proxy configuration) is able to connect to websites, then you are most likely looking at a configuration issue in the original web browser.

    Incorrect answers: Flushing the DNS cache can help when DNS is not resolving properly, but it *does* work with the other web browser. You can flush the DNS cache in Windows with the **ipconfig /flushdns** command. There are a variety of ways to do this in Linux, including using the **systemd-resolve -flush-caches** command. It is unlikely that malware has affected the system. If, however, the user was redirected to other websites than intended, you should scan for malware. Disconnecting and reconnecting from and to the VPN is similar to rebooting a computer: It rarely works. An enterprise-level sandbox is a place where a developer can work on code in an isolated manner. Using the alternate browser is a temporary workaround, but it's not a good one because it defeats the security reasons for using a VPN and proxy server.

74. **Answer: D**

    Explanation: Character Map enables you to copy characters from any font type. To open it, search for "Character Map" or go to Run and type **charmap**.

    Incorrect answers: The Language Bar automatically appears when you use handwriting recognition or speech recognition. It can be configured within Region and Languages. Sticky Keys is a feature that helps users with physical disabilities; it can be turned on by rapidly pressing the Shift key five times and agreeing Yes. You can work with fonts by going to Settings > Personalization > Fonts or by accessing Control Panel > Fonts. From here you can add or remove text fonts.

75. Answer: B

Explanation: Jailbreaking is the process of removing the limitations of an Apple device's iOS. It enables a user to gain root access to the system and download previously unavailable applications, most likely unauthorized by Apple.

Incorrect answers: Rooting is similar to jailbreaking, but the term rooting is typically used with Android-based devices. It gives administrative capabilities to users of Android-based devices. Both jailbreaking and rooting are not recommended and may void device warranties. VirusBarrier was the first AV software designed for iOS; it was developed in response to a particularly nasty jailbreak. Super-admin powers is just a colorful term for what you get when you root or jailbreak a mobile device.

76. Answer: D

Explanation: Files such as ntuser.dat are protected system files and hidden by default. To view the file, you would have to go to Folder Options (either from File Explorer, Control Panel, or Settings) and unhide it and also allow the viewing of protected system files. A typical ntuser.dat file can be between 5 and 20 MB. If you see one that is much larger than that, then it could be corrupt and cause the system to perform poorly and erratically.

Incorrect answers: Sync Center is located within the Control Panel or can be found by using the search tool. It allows you to set up synchronization partnerships with external devices and enables you to manage offline files. Display Settings is where you go to modify things such as a monitor's resolution or color settings. User Accounts is where you would go to add or remove users. Be sure to know your Control Panel icons and Settings categories—for the exam and for the real world!

77. Answer: A

Explanation: Unicode is the code used to represent characters among multiple computers' language platforms. It is commonly used in Microsoft Word and other Office programs. For example, to show the logical equivalence symbol ($\equiv$), you would type **U+2261**, highlight that text, and then press the Alt+X shortcut on the keyboard, which changes the text into the symbol ($\equiv$).Unicode works regardless of the language a person is working in.

NOTE

The logical equivalence symbol should not show itself on the real exam! But you need to know the process.

Incorrect answers: ASCII and EBCDIC are different types of character encoding sets that work in the English language only. ITU-T deals with standards for telecommunications. .ps1 is the main file extension used for PowerShell scripts.

78. **Answer: B**

   Explanation: New malicious software (malware) is always being created. Because of this, the best place to find information about spyware, a virus, rootkit, ransomware, or other malware is at a place that can be updated often and easily: the anti-malware company's website.

   Incorrect answers: Operating system documentation usually does not include this kind of information. In addition, the OS documents and the anti-spyware readme.txt file will be outdated soon after they are written. Never trust what a user has to say about malware. The user is not the person who would remove it; a technician would.

79. **Answers: A and D**

   Explanation: The Windows PCs have probably been infected by a virus/worm and have been compromised and turned into zombies (bots). Trojans could also be involved in this scenario. The Windows PCs are probably part of a botnet that includes other computers as well. The botnet is orchestrated by a single computer that initiates the DDoS (distributed denial-of-service) attack. The infections that you as the technician will have to remove include the worm and the zombie program (or script). You might also be informed that the systems need to be isolated, wiped, and reimaged before they can be used again.

   Incorrect answers: Spyware is software installed on a computer to track the user/computer. Ransomware is malware that is used to encrypt the files on a user's computer. You as a PC technician won't be able to do much about the entire botnet.

80. **Answer: D**

   Explanation: Use the Registry Editor (regedit.exe) to try troubleshooting the problem if typical GUI-based and command-line methods have provided no resolution. The Registry Editor allows you to do any configuration necessary in Windows, and using it may be necessary for more complex troubleshooting problems. At this point, you are testing the theory to determine cause because you have already identified the problem and established a theory of probable cause. Remember your CompTIA A+ troubleshooting methodology from the 220-1101 objectives, which has the following steps:

   1. Identify the problem.
   2. Establish a theory of probable cause (question the obvious).
   3. Test the theory to determine the cause.
   4. Establish a plan of action to resolve the problem and implement the solution.
   5. Verify full system functionality and, if applicable, implement preventive measures.
   6. Document the findings, actions, and outcomes.

   Incorrect answers: **regsvr32** is used to register/unregister ActiveX controls and DLLs in the registry. **gpupdate** enables policy changes to take effect without the need for a logoff or restart. USMT is used to migrate user accounts. Boot Camp is a tool used in macOS to dual-boot Mac computers to Windows. It is the only answer listed that is not a Windows-based command.

You Are on Your Way!

That wraps up Exam B. Take a nice long break before moving on to the last 220-1102 exam in this book. (Well, not *too* long....)

If you scored 90% or higher on this 220-1102 practice exam, move on to the next one! If you did not, I strongly encourage you to study the material again and retake the first couple practice exams until you get 90% or higher on each of them. Keep going. You are doing awesome!

CHAPTER NINE

220-1102 Practice Exam C

Let's turn up the heat a bit more. The previous 220-1102 exam is an intermediate test. This third and final 220-1102 test could be considered an advanced practice test. A large percentage of the questions have a higher difficulty rating. Be ready for questions with longer, more in-depth scenarios and more complex answers.

If you haven't taken a break already, I suggest taking one between exams. If you just completed the second exam, give yourself a half hour or so before you begin this one. If you didn't score 90% or higher on exam B, study some more and then retake exam B until you pass with a 90% or higher score.

Write down your answers and check them against the Quick-Check Answer Key, which immediately follows the exam. After the answer key, you will find the explanations for all of the answers. Good luck!

Practice Questions

1. You work as a technician for an organization that has a custom web-based application that is used for the monitoring of networking devices. While using a web browser to access the application, you press F12, and within the js folder, you see the following code:

Quick Answer: **248**
Detailed Answer: **249**

```
$(function() {
// Attach collapsible behavior to select options(
function()
{
.    var selects = $('select[data-
toggle="collapse"]');
```

   Which of the following script types is this?

   ○ **A.** Python

   ○ **B.** PowerShell

   ○ **C.** Bash

   ○ **D.** JavaScript

   ○ **E.** Visual Basic Script

2. Viruses have been detected and removed on a customer's computer several times over the course of several weeks. Which of the following methods will best help prevent future occurrences?

Quick Answer: **248**
Detailed Answer: **249**

   ○ **A.** Delete temporary files, cookies, and browser history.

   ○ **B.** Defragment the hard drive.

   ○ **C.** Install antivirus software that uses manual updates.

   ○ **D.** Discuss safer web browsing habits with the customer.

3. Which of the following sends an invitation by email asking for help?

Quick Answer: **248**
Detailed Answer: **249**

   ○ **A.** Remote Desktop Connection

   ○ **B.** Service call

   ○ **C.** VNC

   ○ **D.** Remote Assistance

4. When you are performing a clean Windows installation, which of the following is the default location for the Windows system files?

Quick Answer: **248**
Detailed Answer: **250**

   ○ **A.** C:\Windows

   ○ **B.** C:\Windows\System32\Config

   ○ **C.** C:\Windows\System32

   ○ **D.** C:\System Files

5. You are required to set up a remote backup solution for music and photos stored on an Android tablet. The files cannot be stored at any company location. Which technology should be used?

- ○ **A.** iCloud
- ○ **B.** Google Cloud
- ○ **C.** Microsoft OneDrive
- ○ **D.** Local NAS device

6. You have been contracted to repair a computer at an organization that has strict rules about information leaving the premises. While troubleshooting the computer, you determine that the computer should be taken offsite to complete the repair. Which of the following should you do next?

- ○ **A.** Get authorization from your manager.
- ○ **B.** Delete proprietary information before leaving the building.
- ○ **C.** Check corporate policies for guidance.
- ○ **D.** Remove the HDD and send the computer for repair.

7. You need to copy and paste information from a web page, but you want to remove all formatting so that the information can be pasted cleanly into Word. Which program should be used as an intermediary?

- ○ **A.** CMD
- ○ **B.** Excel
- ○ **C.** Notepad
- ○ **D.** MMC

8. A computer is responding slowly, and the Windows Task Manager shows that spoolsv.exe is using 95% of system resources. Which of the following is most likely the cause of this problem?

- ○ **A.** Windows Update is running.
- ○ **B.** A virus infection has occurred.
- ○ **C.** Hyper-Threading has been disabled.
- ○ **D.** The printing subsystem is failing.

9. Which of the following describes the protocol IMAP?

   ○ **A.** A protocol that allows real-time messaging

   ○ **B.** An email protocol that allows users to selectively download messages

   ○ **C.** An email protocol that allows users to send but not receive messages

   ○ **D.** A protocol that authenticates users who are sending email

10. From which of the following locations could you disable a hardware component on a laptop in Windows?

   ○ **A.** Device Manager

   ○ **B.** Task Manager

   ○ **C.** File Explorer

   ○ **D.** Services console

11. A customer browses to a company's intranet page and receives an invalid certificate message. After analysis, you discover that the certificate has expired. You install a new certificate on the user's computer. However, the user still receives the same message when going to the intranet page. You try again with a different web browser, and it connects without error. You figure out that you need to make sure the old certificate is no longer used in the browser. Which of the following Internet Options settings should you use to ensure that the old certificate is removed?

   ○ **A.** Certificates

   ○ **B.** Advanced

   ○ **C.** Clear SSL State

   ○ **D.** Publishers

12. Users are reporting to you that a Windows feature asks them for confirmation before running certain applications or when making system changes. What is the name of this Windows feature, and where should you direct users to turn off the functionality?

   ○ **A.** Security Center; it can be turned off in the Services console window.

   ○ **B.** User Account Control; it can be turned off under Security in the Control Panel.

   ○ **C.** Windows Defender Firewall; it can be turned off under System Properties.

   ○ **D.** User Account Control; it can be turned off under User Accounts in the Control Panel.

13. You are a LAN administrator in charge of printers. Which of the following should you check first when a Windows user is trying to print a document and gets the error message "Print sub-system not available"?

   ○ **A.** The correct printer driver is installed.

   ○ **B.** The printer has been added.

   ○ **C.** The spooler service is running.

   ○ **D.** The printer has power from the jack.

Quick Answer: **248**
Detailed Answer: **252**

14. Your manager's Windows computer locks up after the graphical user interface starts to load. However, the computer will boot in Safe Mode. When you access the Event Viewer, you see an entry stating that a driver failed. Which of the following steps will help you further diagnose the problem?

   ○ **A.** Run **sigverif**.

   ○ **B.** Enable Boot Logging and then, in Safe Mode, analyze the ntbtlog.txt file.

   ○ **C.** Disable Driver Signature Enforcement.

   ○ **D.** Access Debugging Mode.

Quick Answer: **248**
Detailed Answer: **252**

15. Which of the following commands is used to fix errors on the system disk?

   ○ **A.** **robocopy**

   ○ **B.** **tracert /w**

   ○ **C.** **diskpart**

   ○ **D.** **chkdsk /F**

Quick Answer: **248**
Detailed Answer: **253**

16. You are troubleshooting a computer that has a web browser issue. The end user says that multiple browser pages open by themselves when she surfs the Internet. Also, you observe that the computer is running slowly. Which of the following actions should you perform first?

   ○ **A.** Install anti-malware software.

   ○ **B.** Update antivirus definitions.

   ○ **C.** Reboot the computer.

   ○ **D.** Enable a pop-up blocker.

Quick Answer: **248**
Detailed Answer: **253**

17. A new program is crashing and causing the computer to lock up. What is the best location to check for further information about the cause of the crash?

    ○ **A.** System log

    ○ **B.** Security log

    ○ **C.** Application log

    ○ **D.** Setup log

Quick Answer: **248**
Detailed Answer: **253**

18. You are tasked with disabling services from starting on a Windows PC. Which command should be run to bring up a window to make these changes?

    ○ **A. sfc**

    ○ **B. chkdsk**

    ○ **C. msconfig**

    ○ **D. gpupdate**

Quick Answer: **248**
Detailed Answer: **253**

19. You are tasked with creating a laptop naming convention that will make a customer's laptops easier to track and identify while in use. Which of the following naming conventions should you use?

    ○ **A.** Asset ID and MAC address

    ○ **B.** Location and RFID

    ○ **C.** Domain name, location, and asset ID

    ○ **D.** Domain name, location, and IP address

Quick Answer: **248**
Detailed Answer: **253**

20. One of your customers has a wireless network that is secured with WPA. The customer wants to improve data encryption so that the transmission of data has less chance of being compromised. Which of the following statements best describes the recommended course of action?

    ○ **A.** Reconfigure the network to use WPA3.

    ○ **B.** Use MAC address filtering.

    ○ **C.** Modify the WPA key every week.

    ○ **D.** Disable the SSID broadcast.

    ○ **E.** Install WEP.

Quick Answer: **248**
Detailed Answer: **254**

21. Which of the following commands is used to display hidden files?

    ○ **A.** dir /o
    ○ **B.** dir /a
    ○ **C.** dir /d
    ○ **D.** dir /?

Quick Answer: **248**
Detailed Answer: **254**

22. After you install a new video card, the PC loads Windows and continuously reboots. Which of the following statements best describes your first course of action?

    ○ **A.** Go into Safe Mode.
    ○ **B.** Run **chkdsk**.
    ○ **C.** Run the System Configuration utility.
    ○ **D.** Check the System log.

Quick Answer: **248**
Detailed Answer: **254**

23. Which of the following statements best describes how to prepare a mobile device to be protected in the event that it is stolen or lost? (Select the three best answers.)

    ❏ **A.** Disable Bluetooth.
    ❏ **B.** Configure remote backup.
    ❏ **C.** Enable Wi-Fi encryption.
    ❏ **D.** Enable GPS.
    ❏ **E.** Enable Wi-Fi tethering.
    ❏ **F.** Configure a pattern screenlock.

Quick Answer: **248**
Detailed Answer: **255**

24. Two accounting coworkers share the same file inside a folder. User A works on the file, makes changes, and saves the file. User B then works on the file, makes changes, and saves the file as well. The next time User A attempts to open the file, she receives an "access denied" error. Which of the following statements best describes the most likely cause of this error message?

    ○ **A.** The NTFS permissions were changed on the file to allow only execute.
    ○ **B.** The file was set with the system and hidden attributes.
    ○ **C.** The file was set to read-only by the accounts receivable administrator.
    ○ **D.** The file was moved before being modified and then moved back to the share.

Quick Answer: **248**
Detailed Answer: **255**

25. A customer calls you, reporting that a computer is experiencing the following problems:

Quick Answer: **248**
Detailed Answer: **255**

- ▶ Random slowness during the day
- ▶ Intermittent BSODs
- ▶ Random screensaver activation

Which Windows tool should you use to analyze the computer?

- ○ **A.** Task Manager
- ○ **B.** Event Viewer
- ○ **C.** Top
- ○ **D.** Performance Monitor

26. Which of the following are the best options for securing a data center? (Select the two best answers.)

Quick Answer: **248**
Detailed Answer: **256**

- ❏ **A.** Bollard
- ❏ **B.** Badge reader
- ❏ **C.** Cable lock
- ❏ **D.** USB-based hardware token
- ❏ **E.** Biometric lock
- ❏ **F.** Privacy shade

27. Which of the following is the best Windows utility to use if an administrator wants to perform administrative tasks that integrate scripts over a network?

Quick Answer: **248**
Detailed Answer: **256**

- ○ **A.** PowerShell
- ○ **B.** Command Prompt
- ○ **C.** Mission Control
- ○ **D.** Bash

28. You are working in the console of a Linux server. What command should you type to find out the type of file system used by the server's storage drives?

Quick Answer: **248**
Detailed Answer: **256**

- ○ **A.** **diskpart**
- ○ **B.** **rm**
- ○ **C.** **df -T**
- ○ **D.** **pwd**

29. Which of the following file systems is suited specifically for USB flash drives?

- ○ **A.** FAT32
- ○ **B.** exFAT
- ○ **C.** NTFS
- ○ **D.** ext4

Quick Answer: **248**
Detailed Answer: **256**

30. A program has been found to be collecting information such as the computer name and IP address and sending that information to a specific IP address on the Internet. Which kind of threat is this an example of?

- ○ **A.** Spyware
- ○ **B.** Virus
- ○ **C.** Rootkit
- ○ **D.** Spam

Quick Answer: **248**
Detailed Answer: **257**

31. You are required to stop the Windows Defender Firewall service. Which of the following best describes how to accomplish this? (Select the three best answers.)

- ❑ **A.** In Performance Monitor
- ❑ **B.** With the **net stop mpssvc** command
- ❑ **C.** Within MSConfig
- ❑ **D.** Within the Task Manager
- ❑ **E.** In System Information
- ❑ **F.** With gpedit.exe
- ❑ **G.** In services.msc

Quick Answer: **248**
Detailed Answer: **257**

32. You spill a chemical on your hands. It does not appear to be life threatening. Which of the following statements best describes the recommended course of action?

- ○ **A.** Call 911.
- ○ **B.** Call the building supervisor.
- ○ **C.** Consult the MSDS for the chemical.
- ○ **D.** Ignore it.

Quick Answer: **248**
Detailed Answer: **257**

33. Which command allows a user to change a file's permissions in Linux?

- ○ **A.** **chown**
- ○ **B.** **passwd**
- ○ **C.** **ls**
- ○ **D.** **chmod**

Quick Answer: **248**
Detailed Answer: **257**

34. While you are working on a computer at a customer's home, the customer informs you that he needs to leave for about 10 minutes and that his eight-year-old son can help you with anything, if you need it. Which of the following statements best describes the recommended course of action?

○ **A.** Tell the customer to get back home as soon as possible.

○ **B.** Tell the customer that you are not responsible for the child.

○ **C.** Tell the customer that an adult must be home while you work.

○ **D.** Tell the customer that the child must be removed.

35. You have encountered a previously unidentified customer issue. Being awesome, you fix the problem! Now, you are ready to close out the ticket. However, one thing remains. Which system should you access?

○ **A.** Bluetooth PAN

○ **B.** Knowledge base

○ **C.** Asset management system

○ **D.** IoT screened subnet

36. You have been asked to recommend an anti-malware program for a home user. However, the user does not want to pay for a license. Which of the following should you suggest?

○ **A.** Personal license

○ **B.** Corporate license

○ **C.** Open license

○ **D.** Enterprise license

37. A customer experiences a server crash. When you arrive, the manager is upset about this problem. Which of the following statements best describes the recommended course of action?

○ **A.** Stay calm and do the job as efficiently as possible.

○ **B.** Take the customer out for a cup of coffee.

○ **C.** Avoid the customer and get the job done quickly.

○ **D.** Refer the customer to your supervisor.

38. You complete a difficult repair of a laptop for a customer. The next day, the customer complains that the repair took too long and questions the steps you took to fix the problem. Which of the following should you do next?

   ◯ **A.** Record the customer's concerns and post them to your organization's social media page.

   ◯ **B.** Inform the customer that the job has been completed and refer the customer to your supervisor.

   ◯ **C.** Verbally defend each step you took and why it was necessary.

   ◯ **D.** Provide documentation of the repair to the customer.

39. As you are servicing a manager's PC at your company, you run across a list of names of employees who are supposedly about to be let go from the company. Some of these people are coworkers of yours. Which of the following statements best describes the recommended course of action?

   ◯ **A.** Shred the list.

   ◯ **B.** Act as if you never saw the list.

   ◯ **C.** In secret, tell everyone who was on the list.

   ◯ **D.** Yell at the manager for having that list out where it can be seen.

40. Which macOS graphical utility is most like the Windows "end task" feature?

   ◯ **A.** Time Machine

   ◯ **B.** Finder

   ◯ **C.** **kill 3035**

   ◯ **D.** Force quit

41. Which of the following statements best describes how to reduce the chance of ESD? (Select the three best answers.)

   ❑ **A.** Use an antistatic strap.

   ❑ **B.** Use an antistatic mat.

   ❑ **C.** Raise the temperature.

   ❑ **D.** Raise the humidity.

   ❑ **E.** Lower the humidity.

   ❑ **F.** Work in a carpeted area.

42. While you explain a technical concept to a customer, which of the following statements best describes the recommended course of action?

Quick Answer: **248**
Detailed Answer: **260**

- ○ **A.** Recommend a training class.
- ○ **B.** Sit next to the customer.
- ○ **C.** Use acronyms so that the customer feels comfortable about your knowledge.
- ○ **D.** Tell the customer to read the manual.

43. You are viewing the output of **ipconfig /all** on a Windows computer. You see the name *dpro42.com* toward the beginning of the results. Which type of network is this Windows computer most likely a part of?

Quick Answer: **248**
Detailed Answer: **260**

- ○ **A.** Workgroup
- ○ **B.** SAN
- ○ **C.** Domain
- ○ **D.** VPN

44. Which of the following should be used to clean a monitor's screen when you are not sure how to do so?

Quick Answer: **248**
Detailed Answer: **260**

- ○ **A.** Isopropyl alcohol
- ○ **B.** Mild detergent
- ○ **C.** Water
- ○ **D.** Boric acid

45. A customer tells you that he has difficulty remembering the dozen different sets of credentials for the various banks, online stores, and other websites that he logs into. Which of the following should you recommend to the customer?

Quick Answer: **248**
Detailed Answer: **260**

- ○ **A.** Trusted sources
- ○ **B.** Hashing
- ○ **C.** Password manager
- ○ **D.** Secure certificates

46. As part of risk management for your company, you have been tasked with backing up three physical servers on a daily basis. These backups will be stored to a NAS device on the LAN. Which of the following can you do to make sure the backup will work when needed?

   ○ **A.** Create alerts to let the administrators know when backups fail.

   ○ **B.** Set up scripts to automatically rerun failed backup jobs.

   ○ **C.** Store copies of the backups offsite at a data center.

   ○ **D.** Frequently restore the servers from the backup files and test them.

   ○ **E.** Configure the backups to restore to VMs for rapid recovery.

47. You have an Intel Core i7 system with a UEFI-enabled mother-board. Which of the following types of storage drive partitioning schemes should be selected when installing Windows?

   ○ **A.** MBR

   ○ **B.** FAT32

   ○ **C.** Dynamic drive

   ○ **D.** GPT

48. Which of the following statements best describes the recommended course of action to take prior to attempting to remediate infected Windows systems of malware?

   ○ **A.** Educate the end user.

   ○ **B.** Disable System Restore.

   ○ **C.** Schedule scans.

   ○ **D.** Update the anti-malware program.

49. A customer's mobile device cannot connect to Wi-Fi. According to the customer, it was working fine yesterday. Troubleshoot! Which of the following statements best describes the recommended course of action? (Select the three best answers.)

   ❑ **A.** Power cycle the device.

   ❑ **B.** Re-pair the device.

   ❑ **C.** Perform a hard reset.

   ❑ **D.** Forget the Wi-Fi network.

   ❑ **E.** Ensure that the correct SSID was entered.

   ❑ **F.** Change the IP address.

50. Which of the following utilities enables a Windows user to edit a file offline and then automatically update the changes when the user returns to the office?

Quick Answer: **248**
Detailed Answer: **262**

- ◯ **A.** Sync Center
- ◯ **B.** PowerShell
- ◯ **C.** Windows Defender Firewall
- ◯ **D.** Resource Monitor

51. A help desk phone support technician is finding it difficult to understand a customer due to a heavy accent. Which of the following statements best describes the first course of action the technician should take to help the customer resolve the problem?

Quick Answer: **248**
Detailed Answer: **262**

- ◯ **A.** Repeat the problem back to the customer.
- ◯ **B.** Have the customer call back at a later time.
- ◯ **C.** Ask the customer to not speak with an accent.
- ◯ **D.** Tell the customer that her accent is preventing the problem from being solved.

52. You are acquiring hardware devices and setting up a computer lab that will use virtual desktops. The lab computers need to connect automatically to the remote session upon boot and must be started remotely. Which of the following solutions must the hardware be able to support? (Select the two best answers.)

Quick Answer: **248**
Detailed Answer: **262**

- ❏ **A.** PXE
- ❏ **B.** Image deployment
- ❏ **C.** USB
- ❏ **D.** Multiboot
- ❏ **E.** Wake-on-LAN
- ❏ **F.** Unattended installation

53. Which of the following will occur if **%temp%** is executed from Run?

Quick Answer: **248**
Detailed Answer: **263**

- ◯ **A.** Applications located in the %temp% folder will be executed.
- ◯ **B.** The operating system's temporary folder will be opened.
- ◯ **C.** The current user's temporary folder will be opened.
- ◯ **D.** Applications will be deleted from the %temp% folder.

54. If you want to prevent a home user from being able to install software, to which group should you assign the home user? (Select the best answer.)

Quick Answer: **248**
Detailed Answer: **263**

- ○ **A.** Administrators
- ○ **B.** Power Users
- ○ **C.** Remote Desktop Users
- ○ **D.** Users

55. A Windows PC is not booting correctly. You need to locate bad sectors and recover information. Which command is best in this scenario?

Quick Answer: **248**
Detailed Answer: **263**

- ○ **A.** chkdsk C: /R
- ○ **B.** chkdsk C: /F
- ○ **C.** chkdsk C: /C
- ○ **D.** chkdsk C: /I

56. One of your coworkers has a smartphone that contains PII. Because the data is required for use and is valuable, the coworker cannot have the phone automatically wiped if it is lost or stolen. Which of the following is the best option for securing the device?

Quick Answer: **248**
Detailed Answer: **263**

- ○ **A.** Passcode
- ○ **B.** Swipe
- ○ **C.** PIN
- ○ **D.** Fingerprint

57. A user at your organization is working on an older shared computer and attempts to open the email application, which freezes when it is opened. The user calls you and tells you that the email application is not working. You remote into the computer, log in to it, and open the email application without issue. You ask the user to log back in, but the email application still freezes. You find out that other users of the shared computer do not have any issues with the email application. Which of the following should you do next to fix the problem?

Quick Answer: **248**
Detailed Answer: **264**

- ○ **A.** Rebuild the user's mail profile.
- ○ **B.** Apply software updates.
- ○ **C.** Add the user to the local administrators group.
- ○ **D.** Run a repair installation of the email application.

Quick Check

Quick Answer: **248**
Detailed Answer: **264**

58. A user who is part of a workgroup reports that she cannot print to a new printer. Everyone else in the workgroup can print to the new printer, and the user can still automatically send print jobs to the old printer. Which of the following statements describe how to remedy the problem? (Select the two best answers.)

- ❏ **A.** Add the new printer to the user's computer.
- ❏ **B.** Clear the print queue on the new printer.
- ❏ **C.** Change the user's password and permissions.
- ❏ **D.** Set the new printer as the default printer.

Quick Answer: **248**
Detailed Answer: **264**

59. Your organization has an Active Directory domain. One of the users, Bill, should not have read access to a folder named Accounting. The Accounting folder is shared on a network server, on a partition formatted as NTFS. Which of the following statements best describes how to stop Bill from having read access to the folder without impacting any other users on the network?

- ○ **A.** Remove Bill from all domain groups that have access to the Accounting folder.
- ○ **B.** Deny read access to the Accounting folder for Bill through local access security.
- ○ **C.** Deny read access to the Accounting folder for any group that Bill is a member of.
- ○ **D.** Deny read access to the Accounting folder for Bill through shared access security.

Quick Answer: **248**
Detailed Answer: **264**

60. Examine the following figure. Then answer the question that follows.

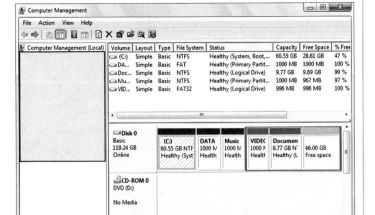

Which portion of Computer Management is displayed in the figure?

◯ **A.** Event Viewer

◯ **B.** Disk Management

◯ **C. gnome-disks**

◯ **D. diskpart**

61. Which of the following is the best Windows utility for backing up important system settings without requiring external storage?

◯ **A.** MSConfig

◯ **B.** Task Manager

◯ **C.** System Restore

◯ **D. robocopy**

Quick Answer: 248
Detailed Answer: 265

62. Your boss wants to encrypt a storage drive that will store critical data. Your boss needs to be able to drag and drop folders onto the volume and have them encrypted in real time. Which encryption technique should you suggest?

◯ **A.** BitLocker

◯ **B.** PKI

◯ **C.** TPM

◯ **D.** Kerberos

Quick Answer: 248
Detailed Answer: 265

63. Your boss asks you to troubleshoot a computer. Based on his observations, he thinks it might have been infected by some type of malware, but he is not sure. Which of the following statements best describes the first step you should take to remedy the problem?

◯ **A.** Run System Restore.

◯ **B.** Identify the malware.

◯ **C.** Roll back drivers.

◯ **D.** Research malware types.

Quick Answer: 248
Detailed Answer: 265

64. User A is part of the Users group on a Windows computer. User A attempts to access files at the following network path: \\server\ *fileshare*. The share called *fileshare* has the following share permissions:

Administrators: Full Control
Users: Read-Only
Guests: No Access

Quick Answer: 248
Detailed Answer: 265

However, the directory on the storage drive where the share is located has the following permissions:

Administrators: Full Control

Users: Change

Guests: No Access

Which level of access will the User A account have?

- ○ **A.** Read Only
- ○ **B.** Change
- ○ **C.** Full Control
- ○ **D.** No Access

65. Your boss wants to implement BitLocker on a second laptop for traveling purposes. Which of the following should be performed before implementing BitLocker?

- ○ **A.** Enable TPM in the BIOS/UEFI.
- ○ **B.** Disable UAC.
- ○ **C.** Defrag the hard drive.
- ○ **D.** Convert the file system to NTFS.

Quick Answer: **248**
Detailed Answer: **266**

66. You need to edit a protected .dll file on a Windows PC, but you cannot find the file you are looking for in the System32 folder. Which of the following Control Panel utilities should you configure?

- ○ **A.** Display
- ○ **B.** System
- ○ **C.** Indexing Options
- ○ **D.** File Explorer Options

Quick Answer: **248**
Detailed Answer: **266**

67. The CEO of your company clicked on a malicious email link. As a result, the system was hacked, and a year's worth of extremely confidential company data was stolen. Which of the following could have possibly prevented this from happening? (Select the two best answers.)

- ❏ **A.** AES
- ❏ **B.** firewall.cpl
- ❏ **C.** AUP
- ❏ **D.** User education regarding common threats

Quick Answer: **248**
Detailed Answer: **266**

68. You have been asked to load a copy of the company's purchased software on a personal computer. Which of the following statements best describes the first step you should take to remedy the problem?

    ○ **A.** Verify that the installation is allowed under the company's licensing agreements.

    ○ **B.** Notify the company's owner of the breach.

    ○ **C.** Advise the individual that downloading unlicensed software is illegal.

    ○ **D.** Leave the premises and call local law enforcement.

Quick Answer: **248**
Detailed Answer: **266**

69. Your friend is playing the latest first-person game on a PC, but the screen is pausing during game play. Your friend has a high-end graphics card and the maximum memory for the motherboard. Which of the following statements best describes how to remedy the problem?

    ○ **A.** Upgrade the drivers.

    ○ **B.** Reinstall the OS.

    ○ **C.** Replace the NVMe drive.

    ○ **D.** Reinstall the game.

Quick Answer: **248**
Detailed Answer: **267**

70. You have been asked to move data from one user's laptop to another user's laptop. Both laptops have EFS functioning. Which of the following statements best describes the first step you should take during this procedure?

    ○ **A.** Give the user of the second laptop administrator privileges.

    ○ **B.** Export the user's certificate.

    ○ **C.** Disable networking.

    ○ **D.** Convert the partition to FAT32.

Quick Answer: **248**
Detailed Answer: **267**

71. Which of the following statements is true?

    ○ **A.** Authentication can be something a user *knows*, such as a smart card.

    ○ **B.** Authentication can be something a user *is*, such as a fingerprint.

    ○ **C.** Authentication can be something a user *does*, such as a PIN or password.

    ○ **D.** Authentication can be something a user *has*, such as a signature.

Quick Answer: **248**
Detailed Answer: **267**

72. You are required to implement an organizational policy that states user passwords can't be used twice in a row. Which of the following policies should be configured?

Quick Answer: **248**
Detailed Answer: **267**

- ○ **A.** Minimum password length
- ○ **B.** Enforce password history
- ○ **C.** Minimum password age
- ○ **D.** Complexity requirements

73. You are working on a computer in which you just installed a new storage drive. The system already runs Windows. The new drive does not appear in File Explorer. Which of the following statements best describes the next step you should take to ensure that the drive will be recognized by the operating system?

Quick Answer: **248**
Detailed Answer: **268**

- ○ **A.** Reboot the computer.
- ○ **B.** Initialize and format the drive in Disk Management.
- ○ **C.** Configure the drive in the BIOS/UEFI.
- ○ **D.** Assign a drive letter to the drive in Disk Management.
- ○ **E.** Set the drive to active.

74. An external attacker is constantly trying to break into one of your customer's SOHO networks. Which of the following statements best describes the easiest, most practical way to protect the network from intrusion?

Quick Answer: **248**
Detailed Answer: **268**

- ○ **A.** Disable the SSID broadcast.
- ○ **B.** Install an antivirus server application.
- ○ **C.** Disconnect the Internet connection.
- ○ **D.** Install a firewall.
- ○ **E.** Install an IDS.

75. One of the administrators recently moved a large chunk of data from one server to another. Now, several users are reporting that they cannot access certain data shares and that they get an "access denied" error. The admin confirms that the users are in the proper security groups, but the users are still unable to access the shares. Which of the following are the most likely causes of the problem? (Select the two best answers.)

Quick Answer: **248**
Detailed Answer: **268**

- ❏ **A.** Denied permissions
- ❏ **B.** User account time of day restriction
- ❏ **C.** Mapped drives
- ❏ **D.** Administrative share permissions
- ❏ **E.** Disabled proxy settings

76. You are tasked with formatting an 8 TB external storage drive with a file system. The drive will be connected directly to a computer that dual boots to Windows and Linux. Which file system should you use?

   ○ **A.** exFAT

   ○ **B.** NFS

   ○ **C.** FAT32

   ○ **D.** ext4

77. You want to write a PowerShell script that will turn off a remote computer. Which of the following can you use to accomplish this? (Select the two best answers.)

   ❏ **A. stop-computer**

   ❏ **B. poweroff**

   ❏ **C. kill**

   ❏ **D. shutdown**

   ❏ **E. restart-computer**

78. Which switch to the **robocopy** command copies subdirectories but skips empty ones?

   ○ **A.** /E

   ○ **B.** /B

   ○ **C.** /S

   ○ **D.** /DCOPY:T

79. Which of the following are components of dealing with prohibited content? (Select the three best answers.)

   ❏ **A.** First response

   ❏ **B.** Maintaining a positive attitude

   ❏ **C.** Preserving data

   ❏ **D.** Creating a chain of custody

   ❏ **E.** Avoiding distraction

80. You are designing the environmental controls for a server room that contains several servers and other network devices. Which of the following statements best describes the role of an HVAC system in this environment? (Select the two best answers.)

   ❏ **A.** It shields equipment from EMI.

   ❏ **B.** It provides isolation in the event of a fire.

   ❏ **C.** It provides an appropriate ambient temperature.

   ❏ **D.** It maintains appropriate humidity levels.

   ❏ **E.** It vents fumes from the server room.

Quick-Check Answer Key

1. D	28. C	55. A
2. D	29. B	56. D
3. D	30. A	57. A
4. C	31. B, D, and G	58. A and D
5. B	32. C	59. D
6. C	33. D	60. B
7. C	34. C	61. C
8. D	35. B	62. A
9. B	36. C	63. B
10. A	37. A	64. A
11. A	38. D	65. A
12. D	39. B	66. D
13. C	40. D	67. C and D
14. B	41. A, B, and D	68. A
15. D	42. B	69. A
16. A	43. C	70. B
17. C	44. C	71. B
18. C	45. C	72. B
19. A	46. A	73. B
20. A	47. D	74. D
21. B	48. B	75. A and C
22. A	49. A, D, and E	76. C
23. B, D, and F	50. A	77. A and D
24. D	51. A	78. C
25. B	52. A and E	79. A, C, and D
26. B and E	53. C	80. C and D
27. A	54. D	

Answers and Explanations

1. Answer: D

Explanation: The snippet of code shown is an example of JavaScript. You can press F12 in a web browser to open the developer tools. Within this sidebar, the Sources section displays the code used by the web page, which often includes HTML, CSS, and JavaScript. For this question, you don't even need to look at the code because the question states that you are looking in the js folder, which is short for JavaScript. However, you could also tell by the code. For example, **$(function()** is from jQuery, a library that makes it easy to use JavaScript. Also, **var** is commonly used in JavaScript; it is a statement that declares a variable. In this example, a table or other data structure is "collapsible," which means it can be shrunk into a smaller space. So this question might seem complex, but it really isn't. Remember: The extension .js is normally associated with JavaScript.

Incorrect answers: .py is associated with Python, .ps1 is associated with PowerShell, .sh is associated with Bash and the Terminal (Linux/Unix), and .vbs is associated with Visual Basic Script (or VBScript).

2. Answer: D

Explanation: Because this situation happens often, you should educate the user on safer web browsing habits, such as being very careful when clicking on links brought up by search engines, not clicking on pop-up windows, and being conservative about the websites that are accessed. Also, the browser can be updated, add-ons can be installed to the web browser for increased protection, phishing filters can be enabled, and so on.

Incorrect answers: Deleting temporary files won't stop the user from visiting the same websites that probably caused the problem in the first place. Defragmenting the hard drive will help the drive and the OS perform better but won't help in the malware department. The computer should have an antivirus solution or, better yet, an anti-malware solution, and it should be set to update automatically every day.

3. Answer: D

Explanation: Connections can be made by sending Remote Assistance invitations by email. These invitations could ask for help or could offer help. This approach is often implemented in help desk scenarios in which a user invites a technician to take control of his computer so that it can be repaired. It's effectively a virtual service call. The technician doesn't need to come physically to the user's desk but instead connects remotely.

Incorrect answers: You can also take control of a computer without an invitation (if you are an administrator or a user with appropriate permissions); this can be done only if the computer to be controlled has the Remote Desktop feature turned on. Virtual network computing (VNC) is similar to Remote Desktop; it enables control of a computer remotely. Several third-party VNC companies offer free software. Microsoft doesn't refer to its software as VNC, though. Collectively, the Microsoft client software is referred to as Remote Desktop Services. (Originally, it was called Microsoft Terminal Services Client [MSTSC]. Mstsc.exe is the executable that can also be used in the Command Prompt.)

4. **Answer: C**

   Explanation: The default folder location for Windows system files is C:\Windows\System32—that is, if C: is the drive being installed to (which is the default). You might also see this referred to as X:\%windir%\System32 or simply \%windir%\System32. The X: is a variable meaning whichever volume is installed to. %windir% is a variable that refers to the main installation folder (usually Windows). %windir% is also expressed sometimes as %systemroot%.

   Incorrect answers: C:\Windows is the systemroot, where the OS is installed (although it also inhabits subfolders). C:\Windows\System32\Config is the folder where the registry hives are stored. There is no C:\System Files folder, unless you create it yourself.

5. **Answer: B**

   Explanation: You would use the Google Cloud solution so that files can be backed up to a location outside the company. This backup—or full synchronization—method is great for Android-based smartphones and tablets as well as Google Chromebooks. Several other third-party solutions are available as well.

   Incorrect answers: iCloud is the Apple solution for backup of files, apps, and so on. Microsoft OneDrive has the same types of features in a variety of solutions. Although there is some crossover between cloud platforms, generally Android users back up to Google Cloud. Using a company-based local network-attached storage (NAS) device would go against what you have been asked to do in the scenario. If the NAS were on the Internet or part of a cloud, however, that would be a different story.

6. **Answer: C**

   Explanation: You should check the company's policies and procedures first (or inquire with a compliance officer). If there is confidential or proprietary information that should not leave the premises (under normal circumstances), the company guidelines should define what to do in a repair situation.

   Incorrect answers: If the computer ultimately does have to leave the premises, you will probably have to obtain authorization and signatures from one or more people who work at the company; this goes beyond *your* manager, who works at your company, not the company you have been contracted to help. You should never delete any information from computers that you work on unless, of course, doing so is required as part of a storage drive scrub or drive replacement, and the data has been backed up. Removing the drive is not enough; there could be data elsewhere in the computer. Also, repairing a system without a drive can, in many cases, be difficult.

7. **Answer: C**

   Explanation: Use Notepad. This text-based editor applies virtually no formatting. Text and other information can be copied from a web page, pasted to a Notepad document, and then copied again and pasted into Word; all formatting is removed. Notepad (and third-party tools such as Notepad++) can also be used for scripting and web page development.

Incorrect answers: CMD (or, more specifically, cmd.exe) is the executable that opens the Microsoft Command Prompt. Excel is a program from Microsoft that enables you to create and modify spreadsheets. MMC, which stands for Microsoft Management Console, is a utility in Windows that enables you to work with several console windows within the same program; it saves the last place you were working.

8. **Answer: D**

   Explanation: The printing subsystem is most likely failing for one of a variety of reasons. The first solution is to terminate spoolsv.exe (which is the Print Spooler service) in the Task Manager or from the command line with the **taskkill** command. Then restart the computer. If that approach doesn't work, the system may have to be repaired, restored, or modified in the registry (which could be an in-depth process). It is also possible that a virus has compromised the system. There are viruses that are also called spoolsv.exe; a quick sweep of the system folders with AV software should uncover this…hopefully.

   Incorrect answers: If Windows Update is running, it should not take up nearly that many resources. FYI, the executable for Windows Update is wuauclt.exe. Hyper-Threading can be disabled in the BIOS/UEFI on some systems. This should have no effect on the system's ability to multitask, though, and multiple processes should be able to run simultaneously without a problem.

9. **Answer: B**

   Explanation: IMAP, which stands for Internet Message Access Protocol, allows an email client to access email on a remote mail server. Generally, the email client software leaves the messages on the server until the user specifically deletes them. So, the user can selectively download messages. This allows multiple users to manage the same mailbox.

   Incorrect answers: Real-time messaging can be accomplished by using instant messaging and chat programs. IMAP, like POP3, allows users to download or receive messages, but it does not send messages; a protocol such as SMTP would be used to send mail. IMAP, like POP3, authenticates the user, but again not for sending email— just when receiving email.

10. **Answer: A**

    Explanation: Use Device Manager to disable a component in Windows, regardless of whether it is a laptop or a PC. When you disable a device, a down arrow appears over the icon of the device, next to the name.

    Incorrect answers: Use the Task Manager to analyze basic system performance and stop processes. Use File Explorer to view folders, files, and other computers. Use the Services console (services.msc) to stop and start and modify the startup type of services.

11. **Answer: A**

    Explanation: You need the Certificates option. To get to this, go to Control Panel > Internet Options > Content tab. This is where you can remove old browser certificates. This holds true for the older Internet Explorer *and* Microsoft Edge (as of the writing of this book). You can also access Internet Options in Edge by typing **edge://settings** in the address bar and searching for "Manage certificates."

Incorrect answers: The Advanced tab has many options, such as for enabling TLS (1.2 or 1.3) and other security options. Clear SSL State is also in the Content tab of Internet Options. That removes any *cached* certificates. You can also remove cached certificates by closing the browser or restarting the computer, but these methods won't remove permanent certificates listed in the Certificates section. Publishers is also available in the Content tab; this is where trusted certificate publishers are listed.

12. **Answer: D**

    Explanation: User Account Control (UAC) is the portion of Windows that asks for confirmation of administrative rights before allowing a user to make system changes or run certain applications. It can be disabled in the User Accounts applet within the Control Panel by clicking the Change User Account Control Settings link. But beware: Only users who have administrative rights should even be permitted to turn off this setting. UAC can be further configured in the Group Policy Editor and in the Registry Editor. For more information about how UAC works, see https://docs.microsoft.com/en-us/windows/security/identity-protection/user-account-control/how-user-account-control-works.

    Incorrect answers: UAC is not turned off in the Security Center or with Windows Defender Firewall. It has separate functionality that is built into Control Panel > User Accounts. It cannot be turned off as a service in the Services console window (services.msc), though there is a related service called the Application Information service (using the service name *appinfo*), which deals with the usage of additional administrative privileges.

13. **Answer: C**

    Explanation: If a "print sub-system not available" or similar message appears, it most likely means the spooler has stalled. You can turn the spooler back on in the Services section of Computer Management or by issuing the command **net start spooler** in the Command Prompt.

    Incorrect answers: If the wrong printer driver was installed, either the user would get a message stating that the printer is not available or the document would print but the information would be garbled. If the printer was not added, the user would not be able to print any documents to any printers and therefore should not get an error message. If the printer was not getting power, the user would most likely get a message stating that the printer is not available.

14. **Answer: B**

    Explanation: Boot Logging can be enabled from the Windows Recovery Environment (WinRE) in Startup Settings. After this option is enabled, the system automatically creates a file called ntbtlog.txt. Afterward, you can access the system by booting into Safe Mode, once again from the Recovery Environment.

    Incorrect answers: sigverif is a program that can be run in Windows to verify whether drivers have been signed by Microsoft. Disabling Driver Signature Enforcement is another Startup Settings (WinRE) option; you might use it to help fix the issue but not to diagnose the problem. Debugging Mode is another option. In this scenario, you don't necessarily need to debug the system, but you should repair the individual driver that failed to load.

15. **Answer: D**

   Explanation: chkdsk /F allows you to fix errors on a disk. It does not fix all errors, but it checks for disk integrity, bad sectors, and similar issues.

   Incorrect answers: robocopy copies files and directory trees. **tracert /w** analyzes the path to another computer with a specific timeout per reply. **diskpart** is the command-line tool that enables you to make changes to the operating system's partition table.

16. **Answer: A**

   Explanation: The first thing you should do is install anti-malware software. It would be surprising if the computer doesn't have any, but it's a possibility.

   Incorrect answers: This could be a virus issue or another malware issue; you won't know until you investigate further. So, anti-malware is a better solution than just *anti-virus*. After installing the software, you should scan the system for malware, update that software, and then reboot the computer. Use the CompTIA A+ malware removal process to aid in this process. A pop-up blocker is good for ads but not necessarily for full pages that open by themselves. Plus, because the system is running slowly, the problem appears to be more than just pop-ups and is probably malware related.

17. **Answer: C**

   Explanation: The Application log is the location for all events concerning Windows applications and third-party programs.

   Incorrect answers: The System log contains information about drivers, system files, and stop errors but not application crashes. The Security log contains information regarding auditing events. The Setup log stores information on events that occurred during the installation of Windows.

18. **Answer: C**

   Explanation: msconfig is the only option listed with which you can disable services. The key in the question is the phrase "bring up a window." **msconfig** runs in a window, whereas the rest of the answers run as text at the command line. **msconfig** can also be used to modify how the system boots. (The Services console window can also be used to disable services, as well as start and stop them.)

   Incorrect answers: sfc is the System File Checker; it scans the integrity of protected system files and repairs problems, if necessary and if possible. Contrast this with **chkdsk**, which can locate and repair errors on the disk but not within system files. **gpupdate** can update user and computer policy settings on the local computer or on remote computers.

19. **Answer: A**

   Explanation: Use the asset ID and MAC address naming convention to help track and identify laptops while in use. An asset ID is an identification code that helps track computers or other assets in the organization. Many asset management systems use them. However, the system still needs to find the computer in this scenario. Because they are laptops and they could move from place to place, one good option is to locate the laptops by their MAC addresses. A MAC address is a physical address that is programmed into a chip on a network interface card; it is outside of, and not affected by, the operating system. Normally, the MAC address does not change, making it a good way to locate laptops that might move from place to place. The MAC address can be linked to the asset ID in the asset management system. This way, a technician can search for a particular computer by asset ID, and the system will cross-reference the MAC address and be able to find and report on that particular device. (Is this the only way to do this? No, but it is one way of making devices easier to track and identify.)

Incorrect answers: The problem with domain names and location information is that they are operating system based. They can change over time and do not necessarily provide actual *identity* of the system. IP addresses are also subject to change. If the systems are laptops, then they most likely obtain their IP addresses from a DHCP server, or more than one DHCP server if the laptops move from one location to another. If the DHCP server scope is modified, or if a new DHCP server is introduced to the network, or if the laptop moves to a new location, then the IP address of the system can change, making it more difficult to identify. Again, IP addresses are software based, whereas MAC addresses are hardware based. If at all possible, stick with hardware-based information for identification purposes.

20. **Answer: A**

Explanation: The best solution is to upgrade the wireless network from WPA to at least WPA2, and preferably WPA3.

Incorrect answers: MAC address filtering does not increase the level of data encryption, but it does filter out unwanted computers when they attempt to connect to the wireless access point. Modifying a wireless encryption key every week is not a good idea because all systems would have to reconnect to the wireless network, supplying that new key. In short, that is not efficient for the organization. Disabling the SSID broadcast deters new computers from making initial connections to the wireless access point. WEP is a deprecated wireless encryption protocol and should be updated to a newer and more powerful protocol if at all possible.

21. **Answer: B**

Explanation: dir /a can be used to display hidden files. Specifically, **dir /ah** can be used to show hidden files only.

Incorrect answers: dir /o deals with various sort orders of files (for example, alphabetical). **dir /d** sorts files by column in wide format, and **dir /?** displays the help file for the **dir** command.

22. **Answer: A**

Explanation: Try accessing Safe Mode first (by using WinRE) and see if the problem continues. It probably won't, and you will need to roll back the driver and locate, download, and install the correct one. Remember to get your drivers from the manufacturer's website and don't forget to download the correct driver for your particular operating system.

Incorrect answers: chkdsk checks the integrity of files and fixes them, if necessary. The System Configuration utility (MSConfig) is used to boot the computer in different ways. Although you normally could select Safe Boot here, it is not possible in this scenario because the system won't boot into Windows properly. You could check the System log while in Safe Mode, but it won't explain much except that the system shut down improperly and rebooted continuously.

23. Answers: B, D, and F

Explanation: First, you should configure some kind of remote backup. This way, if the device is compromised, you have the confidential data backed up outside of the device at another location. The other half of this solution (not mentioned in the answers) is remote wipe. If you are positive that the device is stolen or lost, and you know the data was backed up at some point, trigger a remote wipe to remove all data from the device. Also, enable GPS on the device so that it can be tracked if it is lost or stolen. In addition, configure a screenlock of some sort, whether it is a pattern that is drawn on the display, a PIN, or a password. A strong password is usually the best form of screenlock and the hardest to crack.

Incorrect answers: It doesn't make a difference how Bluetooth and Wi-Fi are configured: They won't help protect confidential data in the event of theft. Instead of having Wi-Fi encryption configured, a mobile device should be prepared with a file encryption or full drive encryption tool.

24. Answer: D

Explanation: Most likely User B moved the file to another location outside of the current partition, made the changes (which is possible since User B is the one who moved it), and then moved it back to the original location. Whenever a file is moved to another partition or volume, the file takes on the permissions of the parent folder. However, if the file had been moved *within* the volume, the permissions would have been retained. Tricky. Remember this: If the file is moved within the same volume, it retains permissions, so the permissions don't change. But if a file is moved to another volume, it takes on the permissions of the folder it is moved into. As for copying, the file's copy always takes on the permissions of the parent, regardless of where that copy is placed.

Incorrect answers: If NTFS permissions were changed to allow execute, User A should have been able to open the file. If the file was set with the hidden attribute, User A should not have been able to see the file. Accounts receivable might or might not set a file to read-only. However, User A should still be able to open the file, but in read-only mode.

25. Answer: B

Explanation: Use the Event Viewer in Windows to further analyze the issues described in the question—especially the one about intermittent BSODs.

Incorrect answers: The Task Manager is a great analysis program for monitoring processes and system resource usage, but it is not as useful for problems such as BSODs and random screensaver activation. Top is a process analysis tool in Linux. Performance Monitor is another analysis program; it is similar to Task Manager but can monitor every single "object" in the computer, so it is much more in-depth.

26. Answers: B and E

Explanation: The badge reader and biometric lock are the best of the listed answers (although all kinds of other security methods are possible). This scenario is an example of multifactor authentication (MFA). An RFID-based badge reader relies on something a person *has*, and the biometric lock system relies on something the user *is*. MFA systems are more secure because they *layer* security.

Incorrect answers: A bollard is a physical obstacle, often seen in parking lots; it is used to block cars from driving onto a sidewalk or into a building. Cable locks are a good idea for servers and other equipment in a server room or data center, but they don't secure a data center itself. A USB token is used for authentication to a computer, but not to the data center. Privacy (window) shades work well for blocking people from seeing what is inside a room, but they don't do much to actually secure the room. Plus, I haven't seen too many windows in the data centers and server rooms I have worked in!

27. Answer: A

Explanation: Windows PowerShell enables administrators to perform administrative tasks that integrate scripts and executables and can be run over a network. For even more power and flexibility, use Visual Studio Code (VSC) or the older PowerShell Integrated Scripting Environment (PowerShell ISE).

Incorrect answers: The Command Prompt is the basic version of a command line in Windows. It is not as functional as PowerShell. Mission Control is a macOS application that gives a bird's-eye view of all open windows. Bash is the default shell used by Linux/Unix. You work with it in a command-line tool. For example, in Ubuntu Linux, the default program for working in a Bash shell is the Terminal program.

28. Answer: C

Explanation: Use the **df -T** command to find out what file systems are used by each of the storage drive partitions. Note that the **-T** option is needed to see the file system types. The console is simply the name of the command line (terminal) in Linux if you are working on the server locally.

Incorrect answers: diskpart is a Windows tool for analyzing and configuring storage drives and partitions. **rm** in Linux will remove files or directories. **pwd** in Linux will show you the current directory path that you are working in.

29. Answer: B

Explanation: exFAT (also known as FAT64) is suited specifically for USB flash drives and many other mobile storage solutions. It is the successor to FAT32 and can format media that is larger than 32 GB with a single partition.

Incorrect answers: Older file systems such as FAT32 are very limited in terms of the partition size. NTFS can be a good solution for USB flash drives, but exFAT was developed specifically for USB flash drives and is a better solution with an operating system that supports it. ext4 is a commonly used file system in Linux-based systems.

30. Answer: A

Explanation: Spyware is a type of malicious software that is usually downloaded unwittingly by a user or is installed by third-party software. It collects information about the user and the user's computer without the user's consent.

Incorrect answers: A virus is code that runs on a computer without the user's knowledge; it infects a computer when the code is accessed and executed. A rootkit is software designed to gain administrator-level control over a computer system without being detected. Spam is the abuse of electronic messaging systems such as email.

31. Answers: B, D, and G

Explanation: You can stop a service in a variety of ways. One way is to go to the Services console window. You can do this by typing **services.msc** at the Run prompt. You can also stop services in the Task Manager by accessing the Services tab and right-clicking the service in question. But in the Task Manager, you have to know the executable name of the service. The name of the Windows Defender Firewall service is mpssvc. So, the third way (of the listed answers) is to use the **net stop mpssvc** command in PowerShell or the Command Prompt.

Incorrect answers: Performance Monitor, System Information, and gpedit.exe do not allow you to stop services. MSConfig (System Configuration Utility) can enable or disable services but not start or stop them.

32. Answer: C

Explanation: If the chemical spill is not life threatening, consult the material safety data sheet (MSDS) to determine the proper first aid (if any).

Incorrect answers: If it is an emergency, call 911. If you cannot get access to the MSDS, contact the facilities department of your organization or try your building supervisor. Never ignore a chemical spill. Take action before it becomes a problem.

33. Answer: D

Explanation: The **chmod** command allows a user to modify file and folder permissions at the Linux command line.

Incorrect answers: The **chown** command allows a user to change the ownership settings for a file. **passwd** enables a user to change the password at the command line. **ls** displays the contents of a directory in Linux. These commands can also be used in macOS.

34. Answer: C

Explanation: Whenever you're working in someone's home, make sure that an adult is available.

Incorrect answers: You cannot take on the responsibility for watching a child; there could be legal consequences for doing so. Plus, there is no point in discussing the matter. Most companies have policies that simply state the terms of your visit to a customer. It is not your responsibility to watch over children, nor should any service company agree to have its consultants do this. If the person insists on leaving, and you can pack up your things before that happens, do so, and then call your supervisor to inform him or her of the event.

35. Answer: B

Explanation: You should access the knowledge base (KB) so that you can document your findings. This is especially important because the problem has never been seen before (or at least documented in your organization). By entering your findings and solution into the KB, you help your team by providing information for anyone who needs to troubleshoot the same problem in the future.

Incorrect answers: A Bluetooth PAN is an ad hoc network of Bluetooth-enabled devices such as smartphones, headsets, printers, wireless access points, and so on. An asset management system is used to track and identify assets on a network, such as PCs, laptops, and other devices. Devices that are part of the Internet of Things (IoT) may or may not be part of a screened subnet. A screened subnet (or DMZ) is a good idea, though, especially for IoT devices in the home, as it creates a layer of separation between the IoT devices that usually communicate directly with the Internet and the more personal home devices. Another good option is to put these devices on the guest wireless network.

36. Answer: C

Explanation: An open license means that the software can be downloaded and used for free. It refers to open source software. An example of software with an open license is Linux. Know the difference between open source and closed source software!

Incorrect answers: Often, anti-malware suites offer advanced versions of the software for a fee. At that point, it would become a personal license. Corporate and enterprise licenses are not for home users; they are often bulk discount licenses for multiple users.

37. Answer: A

Explanation: Stay calm and do the job as efficiently as possible. There isn't much you can do when a customer is upset except fix the problem.

Incorrect answers: I'd be interested to see what would happen if a person asked the owner of the server out for a cup of coffee, but I'm pretty sure the reaction would be negative (at that particular moment at least). You don't want to avoid the customer, but you don't have to engage in anything except fixing the problem. You should refer the customer to your supervisor only if the person gets in the way of you doing your work. People being upset about tech…well, it's common, so be ready.

38. Answer: D

Explanation: You should provide written documentation to the customer to provide proof of everything that you performed and why.

Incorrect answers: Once again, stay calm. Don't let the complaint bother you. Remember that most customers (especially business customers) want things fixed immediately and don't really care about (and may not understand) what it takes to effectively troubleshoot a problem. Recording the customer's concerns is a good idea. Posting them to social media? Well, I think it goes without saying that that's a bad idea—and one that could possibly get you fired. Informing the customer that the job has been completed is redundant. You already completed the job and left the job site, so an answer like that is non-responsive; it doesn't provide the customer with anything valuable. In the end, you might need to refer the customer to a supervisor, but you should most definitely provide some kind of documentation first and answer any questions you can (within reason). Verbally defending what you did is not a good idea because there are no facts to back it up. Here's a saying for you that can extend to many other things in this world: Always provide proof of work!

39. Answer: B

Explanation: There isn't much you can do in a situation like this, especially if you already saw what was printed on the document. The best thing is to ignore it and act as if it never happened. It's not your place to take action based on a document that is lying around. Without intense scrutiny, it is hard to know exactly what a document is. The purported list might be real, but it might not be. It isn't your call to make. However, when working at a *customer* site, you should ask that all confidential materials be removed before you begin work. If something is left out in plain sight, you could let a manager know that there could be confidential data lying around.

Incorrect answers: Technicians must be security minded. Any documents owned by the company and printed by another user are not your property or your concern; they should not be handled or shredded. It could be a bad situation, but the right course of action is to not discuss it. As mentioned, the list could be real, or it could be a draft or a prank; either way, telling everyone about it could cost you your job. It is, however, something that you could bring up to a member of human resources, if necessary. Yelling is never a recommended course of action at the office. Save that for construction zones, demolition derbies, and heavy metal bands; or just avoid it altogether.

40. Answer: D

Explanation: The force quit option in Apple's macOS is most like the "end task" feature in the Windows Task Manager. It helps when an application is not functioning as intended and is either frozen or intermittently slows down the system.

Incorrect answers: Time Machine is the macOS backup utility, and it is similar to Windows File History and Windows System Restore. Finder is the macOS file and application exploration tool, and it is similar to the Windows File Explorer. In macOS and Linux systems, **kill 3035** is a command that terminates the process with the ID 3035. But that is done at the command line and not in a graphical utility.

41. Answers: A, B, and D

Explanation: To reduce the chance of electrostatic discharge (ESD), use an antistatic wrist strap and mat. If connected properly, they provide suitable self-grounding. Also, consider raising the humidity. The more humidity there is, the less friction and, ultimately, the less ESD there is.

Incorrect answers: Raising the temperature has no effect. Lowering the humidity increases the chance of ESD. Working in a carpeted area also increases the chance of ESD; try to work in a noncarpeted area. You should also touch the chassis of the computer before handling any components; this is a basic form of self-grounding. In addition, place components in antistatic bags when they are not in use.

42. **Answer: B**

    Explanation: Make the customer truly feel comfortable by sitting down next to the person and taking the time to explain the technical concept simply and concisely. The less jargon, the better.

    Incorrect answers: Recommending a training class is tantamount to dismissing the customer out of hand. Telling the customer to read the manual is just downright rude. I know, I say this often to you; however, you are a tech, so reading the manual is what you do. Tho ouctomor ic not cupposed to be super technically oriented. The acronym RTM should be kept within technical circles!

43. **Answer: C**

    Explanation: If you see the name *dpro42.com* toward the beginning of the results of an **ipconfig /all** command, the computer is most likely a part of the dpro42.com domain. This would be listed in the Primary DNS Suffix entry, which is usually directly after the Host Name entry. The .com is the giveaway. Some kind of DNS extension (such as .com or .net) is necessary with a domain.

    Incorrect answers: If the computer were simply part of a workgroup, the Primary DNS Suffix entry would be left blank (by default). A Windows computer won't usually be part of a storage area network (SAN). SANs are usually made up of NAS devices, RAID devices, and Fibre Channel connections. If the computer were connected to a VPN, you would see IP configuration details for a "Tunnel adapter" connection farther down in the **ipconfig /all** command output.

44. **Answer: C**

    Explanation: If you are not sure about what to clean a screen with, use water. Water will most likely not damage a screen.

    Incorrect answers: If the user manual for the monitor calls for it, you might see that you can use a half-and-half mixture of water and isopropyl alcohol. Do not use detergents on a screen; they are okay for the outside of a computer case but not for a display. And boric acid could be quite dangerous.

45. **Answer: C**

    Explanation: A password manager is a program that stores passwords in an encrypted format. It can be integrated into a web browser or can run independently. The important part is for the customer to set up and memorize a complex, lengthy password that allows access to the password manager program.

    Incorrect answers: The rest of the answers are all good ideas when surfing the web, but they don't help with the credentials memorization issue the customer is having. Trusted sources are websites that a web browser is allowed to download content from. Hashing is a way of verifying the validity of a file that is to be downloaded from the Internet. Secure certificates are used whenever a web browser connects to an HTTPS (TLS)-based site.

46. Answer: A

Explanation: The best option here is to create alerts to let any and all administrators know if a backup failure occurs. These alerts would either be created at the network-attached storage (NAS) device or at the individual servers to be backed up. If an admin receives an alert, that person will know to either rerun the backup or (more likely) fix the backup task and then run it. One of the issues here is that, without the alerts, you might not know if a backup fails.

Incorrect answers: Setting up scripts is a good idea for the backup processes themselves, but you first need to be alerted about an issue before you can script a rerun of the failed backup jobs. In this case, the backups are being stored to a NAS device locally (on the LAN), so they are not being stored offsite. You should always test a backup the first time it runs and periodically afterward; however, frequent restoration tests are very time-consuming, not to mention hardware intensive for the NAS device. Restoring to a VM is a good way to test, but it's not a good way to ensure rapid recovery, nor is it where the backups are supposed to be restored to; the question says "physical servers."

47. Answer: D

Explanation: If your system's motherboard is equipped with a UEFI BIOS, you should definitely take advantage of the GUID Partitioning Table (GPT). It is superior to the older MBR technology. GPT allows for up to 128 partitions, is not limited to the 2 TB maximum partition size of MBR, and it stores multiple copies of itself on the system.

Incorrect answers: As mentioned, MBR is inferior to GPT and should be avoided; however, you might service older systems that require it. FAT32 is not really a partitioning scheme but rather a type of file system—and an older one at that. NTFS or exFAT is preferable. A dynamic drive is a drive in Windows that has been upgraded from basic; it allows a user to change the size of the volumes on the drive.

48. Answer: B

Explanation: You should disable System Restore on a Windows system just before attempting to remediate the system of malware. This is step 3 of the CompTIA A+ best practices/procedure for malware removal. The entire procedure is as follows:

1. Investigate and verify malware symptoms.
2. Quarantine infected systems.
3. Disable System Restore in Windows.
4. Remediate infected systems.
    a. Update anti-malware software.
    b. Scan and removal techniques (safe mode, pre-installation environment).
5. Schedule scans and run updates.
6. Enable System Restore and create a restore point in Windows.
7. Educate the end user.

Incorrect answers: As you can see, the rest of the answers listed in the question occur after (or during) "remediate infected systems."

49. Answers: A, D, and E

Explanation: If a mobile device cannot connect to the network, you should attempt to power cycle the device, forget and reconnect to the Wi-Fi network, and ensure that the correct SSID was entered in the first place. Perhaps the number-one method would be to power cycle Wi-Fi (which is not listed in the answers).

Incorrect answers: Re-pairing has to do with Bluetooth, not Wi-Fi. Re-pairing means that you remove the paired Bluetooth device and then reconnect it. A hard reset wipes a device of its data and returns it to factory condition. This is a very last resort; there are plenty of other things you can try before that. Changing the IP address is possible but usually not necessary because most mobile devices obtain their IP addresses dynamically.

50. Answer: A

Explanation: Sync Center is a Windows feature that enables you to keep information synchronized between your computer and network servers. You can still access the files and modify them even if you don't have physical access to the server; in this case, they are modified "offline" and are synchronized automatically when you return to the network. Some mobile devices are also compatible with Sync Center. Sync Center can be configured within the Control Panel.

Incorrect answers: PowerShell is a command-line and scripting environment in Windows. Windows Defender Firewall is the built-in firewall tool in Windows; it provides protection to the operating system against external attacks. Resource Monitor is a Windows tool that allows you to analyze your system resources such as CPU, RAM, and network card in a condensed, easy-to-read fashion.

51. Answer: A

Explanation: The technician should repeat the problem back to the customer to make sure that everyone is talking about the same thing and that both parties understand each other. Always clarify.

Incorrect answers: Having the customer call back later is just delaying the problem. Asking a person with an accent to stop speaking with an accent is like telling a dog to stop wagging its tail: It is probably futile. A technician needs to be culturally sensitive. If you seriously cannot understand the customer even after attempting to listen several times and repeating the problem back, you will have to involve someone else who can help you or attempt to communicate with the person through email.

52. Answers: A and E

Explanation: The hardware for the lab computers should support Preboot eXecution Environment and have Wake-on-LAN capability. To run the virtual desktops, they need PXE to automatically boot to the network server. Wake-on-LAN (also known as WOL) should be enabled so that the lab computers can be started remotely and can wake up when pinged on the network.

Incorrect answers: Image deployment isn't needed because you are not installing an entire operating system on the lab computers; they will be running virtual desktops that will have to be preconfigured at a server. USB isn't required here; the lab computers will be getting their virtual desktops over the network (via fiber-optic, Ethernet, or wireless connections). You don't want a multiboot system here; that would mean that two operating systems are installed to the same drive of a lab computer. An unattended installation means that you are installing an operating system (such as Windows) to a system using an answer file to automate the installation. Again, you don't want an installation of an OS or an image deployment here; rather, you want to end up with virtual desktops on the lab computers.

53. Answer: C

Explanation: Entering **%temp%** at the Run prompt displays a folder with the current user's temporary files. For example, in Windows, this would show the path C:\Users\%username%\AppData\Local\Temp.

Incorrect answers: Nothing will be added, changed, or deleted. The folder will simply be displayed in a File Explorer window. The operating system's temporary folder is located at C:\Windows\Temp.

54. Answer: D

Explanation: A standard user cannot install software or make changes to the system without knowing an administrative login.

Incorrect answers: Administrators have full control over a system. Power users (way back in the Windows XP days) were able to install programs and device drivers and are found in newer versions of Windows only for backward compatibility with older applications. A Remote Desktop user can remote into another machine to control it from another location.

55. Answer: A

Explanation: **chkdsk /R** locates bad sectors and recovers the information from them.

Incorrect answers: **/F** fixes errors but doesn't locate bad sectors and recover the information from them. **/C** and **/I** skip certain checks of the volume (in this case, C:), which ultimately reduces the time it takes to check the volume.

56. Answer: D

Explanation: Of the listed answers, a fingerprint is the best option for securing the smartphone. If the smartphone is lost or stolen, another person would have a difficult time unlocking the device (though it would not be impossible). For a device that cannot be remotely wiped (for various reasons), the best alternative is the use of biometric authentication in combination with a strong password (for MFA) plus encryption.

Incorrect answers: Passcodes and PINs can be cracked, given enough time. Even a lengthy and complex password can be cracked eventually. "Swipe" simply means a user swipes on the screen to unlock it; no actual authentication is happening here, which means swiping is not a secure option.

57. **Answer: A**

Explanation: Of the listed answers, you should attempt to rebuild the user's mail profile. If the email program worked for you but doesn't work for the user, then chances are that the email application is fine, but the user profile needs to be repaired. It is likely that Microsoft Outlook is being used in this scenario. See the following link for information about rebuilding Outlook profiles for Outlook 2010 through 2016: https://support.microsoft.com/en-us/office/fix-your-outlook-email-connection-by-repairing-your-profile-4d5febf6-7623-486b-9a9f-d5cfc4264af3. Also, Microsoft 365 has fewer of these types of issues (though it can auto-rebuild profiles if needed). Consider recommending Microsoft 365 to the user.

Incorrect answers: Applying software updates is always a good idea, and it is probably done automatically by your security team. However, it shouldn't affect this scenario because other people are able to use the email application without issue. Never add a typical user to the administrators group. Remember the principle of least privilege! You could possibly attempt a repair installation of the email application—but you should do so only after you have tried rebuilding the user's profile. If you reinstall the email application, you risk having data issues with other user profiles. Again, the email application should be okay because other users are able to use it.

58. **Answers: A and D**

Explanation: If a user cannot print to a brand-new printer but everyone else can print to it, you should check whether the printer is installed on that user's computer and whether it is set as the default printer.

Incorrect answers: If the printer has not yet been installed, there will be no print queue to clear. However, if the printer has been installed, the next thing to check would be whether the print queue has failed. You could also check the print spooler. If the user can print to an older printer that is also shared by other users in the workgroup, you should not have to change the user's password or permissions.

59. **Answer: D**

Explanation: The best option in this scenario would be to deny read access to the Accounting folder for Bill through shared access security.

Incorrect answers: You would not use local access security because the folder is shared from a network server within your Active Directory domain. Also, if you remove Bill from all domain groups that have access to the Accounting folder, Bill will probably lose access to other folders as well. If you deny read access to the Accounting folder for any group that Bill is a member of, you will probably impact other users on the network negatively.

60. **Answer: B**

Explanation: The Disk Management component of Computer Management is displayed in the figure. You can tell because it shows each disk and the volumes within each disk.

Incorrect answers: The Event Viewer houses log information for the system, applications, and security auditing events. **gnome-disks** is a partitioning tool used with Linux. **diskpart** is the command-line tool used to create and modify partitions on the storage drive.

61. **Answer: C**

Explanation: System Restore is a feature that creates and saves data about the computer's system files and settings. It does this by creating restore points. You access it by going to the System Properties dialog box and clicking the System Protection tab. External storage is not necessary for these restore points; they are automatically stored in the system volume.

Incorrect answers: MSConfig is used to modify the way Windows boots and the services that are loaded at startup. The Task Manager is used to view system performance, enable/disable applications, stop services, and kill processes. **robocopy** is an advanced file copying tool that can be used to copy entire directory trees of data, but it doesn't copy settings.

62. **Answer: A**

Explanation: BitLocker is a type of whole-disk encryption (WDE). It encrypts all of the contents that are created on it or copied to it in real time. It requires a Trusted Platform Module (TPM) chip on the motherboard or an encrypted USB flash drive. Only select editions of Windows support BitLocker when used in this manner. Other lesser versions of Windows are compatible with BitLocker To Go for reading encrypted documents from USB flash drives.

Incorrect answers: PKI, which stands for public key infrastructure, is an entire system of technologies and users dealing with encryption. The TPM chip can be required for this scenario, but it is not the encryption itself. Kerberos is an authentication protocol.

63. **Answer: B**

Explanation: The first thing you should do is investigate and verify malware symptoms. (By the way, if the computer is on the network, disconnect it first.) Then, if there is malware present, you can research that malware and any possible cures by searching the Internet and accessing your AV provider's website.

Incorrect answers: Rolling back drivers should not be necessary, especially if you find it necessary to run a System Restore at some point. Remember your best practices procedure for malware removal!

64. **Answer: A**

Explanation: User A will end up having the Read-Only level of access to the share. Generally, a user gets the more restrictive level of access. The only thing that is different between the share's permissions and the parent directory's permissions is the level of control for the Users group. Normally, a share obtains its permissions from the parent folder—that is, unless that option is unchecked in the properties of the folder. Then the folder can be reconfigured for whatever permissions an admin wants to set for it. That must be what happened in this scenario.

Incorrect answers: Administrators get Full Control access to almost everything by default. Guests get No Access to just about everything by default. So the only possibilities for this question are Change and Read-Only. Again, in general, the typical Standard User account receives the more restrictive level of permissions.

65. Answer: A

Explanation: Before implementing the BitLocker solution in Windows, you should enable the Trusted Platform Module (TPM) chip in the BIOS/UEFI. This is the chip on the motherboard that includes the encryption code.

Incorrect answers: UAC, which stands for User Account Control, is a separate security option in Windows that checks whether users have administrative permissions before allowing them to carry out administrative tasks. Defragmenting the hard drive is not necessary, but it can't hurt to at least analyze the drive and see if it needs to be defragged. Defragging a drive that requires it can increase performance. BitLocker works on FAT10, FAT32, NTFS, and exFAT partitions, so you do not need to convert the file system.

66. Answer: D

Explanation: Use the File Explorer Options utility in the Control Panel of Windows. From there, you go to the View tab and then deselect the checkbox labeled Hide Protected Operating System Files (Recommended). You might also deselect the Hide Extensions for Known File Types checkbox to see which ones are .dll files. You can also access these settings from the File Explorer program by choosing View > Options > Change Folder and Search Options (in which case the dialog box will be named Folder Options). Or you can go to Run and type **control folders**.

Incorrect answers: The other Control Panel utilities do not apply here.

67. Answers: C and D

Explanation: This situation is more common than you might think. It seems as if no one is safe today from email threats and scams. We must be vigilant and make all users aware of the murky email waters ahead. Did the CEO attend user training and sign an AUP? Sometimes user education works; sometimes it doesn't. One way to make user education more effective is to have a technical trainer educate your users instead of doing it yourself. This can provide for a more engaging learning environment. During this training, you might opt to define the organization's acceptable use policy (AUP). This is a document that stipulates constraints and practices that a user must agree to before being granted access to a corporate network or the Internet.

Incorrect answers: Advanced Encryption Standard (AES) is the strongest form of wireless encryption commonly used with WPA2/WPA3. You can access Windows Defender Firewall by going to Run > firewall.cpl. However, neither AES nor Windows Defender Firewall will protect against clicking on malicious email links.

68. Answer: A

Explanation: You should first verify that the installation is allowed under the company's licensing agreement. It probably isn't, but you should check. Most organizations do not allow purchased software to be installed on an employee's home computer. If doing so is against organization policy, you should notify your supervisor. There are many types of licenses that you should be aware of, including end-user licensing agreements (EULA), digital rights management (DRM), commercial and enterprise licenses (such as client access licenses or CALs), open source versus closed source (that is, Android versus iOS), personal licenses, and so on. Again, be sure to follow and incorporate corporate end-user policies and security best practices when it comes to these types of licenses.

Incorrect answers: You would notify your supervisor/manager, not the company owner, unless it was a very small company. Verify whether the license is valid or allowed before advising any individuals. Calling law enforcement is premature because you have not yet verified the nature and validity of the license.

69. Answer: A

Explanation: If you see video issues such as pausing during game play, upgrade the video drivers. Make sure that you download the latest video driver from the manufacturer's website. Gamers cannot rely on Microsoft drivers.

Incorrect answers: Sometimes reinstalling a game is necessary, but it shouldn't be in this scenario. Replacing the NVMe drive can be expensive, and reinstalling the OS is time-consuming. Both are most likely drastic and unnecessary measures in this scenario.

70. Answer: B

Explanation: The first thing you should do is export the user's certificate from the first laptop to the second laptop. You can do this by clicking Start and typing **certmgr. msc** in the Search box; then locate and export the correct personal certificate. The Certificates console window can also be added to the MMC. Encrypting File System (EFS) is the standard single-file encryption method for Windows (in editions of Windows that support it).

Incorrect answers: Administrative privileges won't help immediately because the encryption will still be in effect, but an administrator can deal with the importing and exporting of certificates from one computer to another, and a typical user cannot. Networking need not be disabled, and you aren't sure which user is being referred to in the answers, but if the certificate has been exported, that user should be able to read the files. Partitions can be converted from FAT32 to NTFS but not vice versa.

71. Answer: B

Explanation: Authentication can be carried out by utilizing something a user is, such as a fingerprint; something a user knows, such as a password or PIN; something a user has, such as a smart card or token; and something a user does, such as writing a signature or speaking words.

Incorrect answers: A smart card is something the user *has* (a possession factor), not something the user knows. A PIN and a password are something the user *knows* (a knowledge factor), not something the user does. A signature is something the user *does*, not something the user has.

72. Answer: B

Explanation: This scenario is based on a Windows system. You should configure the enforce password history policy and set it to a number higher than zero. This way, when a user is prompted to change his or her password every 42 days (which is the default *maximum* password age), that user will not be able to use the same password. Password policies can be accessed in Windows within the Local Security Policy window > Security Settings > Account Policies > Password Policy.

Incorrect answers: Minimum password length is the policy that states the fewest characters a password must contain. Eight is a decent setting, but to be full-on secure, many organizations require at least 16 characters. There are several technical reasons for this, but the A+ exam does not go into that kind of depth. Minimum password age won't stop a user from reusing a password; it is usually set to zero by default. Complexity requirements policy, if enabled, forces a user to select a password that meets three of the following five categories: uppercase characters, lowercase characters, numbers, special characters (such as ! or #), and Unicode characters (not often implemented). Since 2017, the National Institute of Standards and Technology (NIST) has leaned toward lengthy passwords as opposed to complex passwords.

73. Answer: B

Explanation: When you add a second drive to a system that already has Windows installed, you will probably have to initialize the drive and format it in the Disk Management utility.

Incorrect answers: Rebooting the computer does not help the system see the drive. You can configure the drive in the BIOS/UEFI to a certain extent, but that won't help Windows see the drive. When you format the drive, Disk Management asks you to assign a drive letter. You don't need to set the drive to active because this drive does not have an OS to be booted to.

74. Answer: D

Explanation: The most practical way to prevent intrusion to the network is to install a firewall. In fact, if this is a SOHO network, chances are the network is controlled by a multifunction network device that already acts as a switch and a router and probably has built-in firewall technology; it just has to be enabled. Usually, the firewall on such a device is enabled by default, but perhaps someone inadvertently disabled this feature, and that's one of the reasons an attacker keeps trying to get into the network.

Incorrect answers: An intrusion detection system (IDS) is usually more elaborate and costs more money, but it would help to prevent network intrusion. (Some devices combine IDS and firewall technologies, but SOHO multifunction network devices usually do not.) Disabling the SSID helps to discourage the average user from accessing the wireless network, but any hacker worth his or her salt can get right past that; plus, the attacker could be trying to connect directly through the Internet connection. Antivirus software, regardless of where it is installed, does not repel attackers; it locates and quarantines malware. Disconnecting the Internet connection would work; the hacker wouldn't be able to get in, but none of the employees would be able to use the Internet. That's not a good compromise.

75. Answers: A and C

Explanation: The most likely reasons the users cannot connect are denied permissions and mapped drives. If the data was moved to another computer, the folders will inherit new permissions from the parent (by default). That will most likely eliminate the current user access. Also, the path to the share will change (again by default). Either the server name/IP address, the sharename, or both will be different when the data is moved to another server. So, to fix the problem, the user and group permissions will have to be modified for the new share, and new mapped drives will need to be configured.

Incorrect answers: There is no evidence that the time of day restrictions have been changed for any users. Administrative shares (such as C$) are for admins only; the users are not trying to access these shares in the scenario. Disabling proxy settings is done at the client computer. It *might* make sense that these settings have been disabled if this happened to one system, but because multiple users are affected, it is unlikely.

76. **Answer: C**

    Explanation: Use the FAT32 file system to format a drive that needs to be accessed by both Linux and Windows operating systems.

    Incorrect answers: exFAT works well for USB drive, and while a USB drive is external, these drives are not available in 8 TB sizes. The drive being worked with is most likely using some other technology, such as a NAS device or something similar. The Network File System (NFS) works well to store data on servers, and while both Windows and Linux systems can access NFS *over the network*, NFS is not the proper option for a drive that is being accessed directly. ext4 is used by Linux but is not compatible with Windows.

77. **Answers: A and D**

    Explanation: Use the **stop-computer** cmdlet or the **shutdown** command. Either of these can be used to turn off a local or remote computer. They can be used directly in PowerShell or within a script. For more information about stop-computer, see https://docs.microsoft.com/en-us/powershell/module/microsoft.powershell.management/stop-computer?view=powershell-7.2#parameters. For more information on shutdown, see https://docs.microsoft.com/en-us/windows-server/administration/windows-commands/shutdown.

    Incorrect answers: poweroff is used to turn off Linux systems. **kill** is used to terminate processes in Linux. **restart-computer** is a cmdlet in PowerShell that reboots the Windows system.

78. **Answer: C**

    Explanation: **/S** copies subdirectories but skips any empty ones.

    Incorrect answers: /E copies all subdirectories, including empty ones. **/B** copies files in backup mode. **/DCOPY:T** also copies timestamps of files and folders.

79. **Answers: A, C, and D**

    Explanation: When dealing with prohibited content, there will always be a first responder who is required to identify the issue, report through proper channels, and preserve data and possibly devices used. This person will be in charge of starting the documentation process, which includes maintaining a chain of custody, tracking evidence, and maintaining a chronological log of that evidence.

    Incorrect answers: You should always maintain a positive attitude and avoid distractions, but those concepts concern professional behavior, not first response and prohibited content.

80. Answers: C and D

Explanation: The HVAC system's primary responsibilities are to provide an appropriate ambient temperature for the equipment and to maintain appropriate humidity levels. This keeps the equipment from overheating and prevents electrostatic discharge (ESD).

Incorrect answers: HVAC equipment, by its very nature, is a producer of electromagnetic interference (EMI); it does not shield equipment from EMI—quite the reverse. HVAC equipment often needs to be shielded to reduce EMI after it is installed. Isolation can be provided by other methods, such as the material used in the perimeter of the room. A separate ventilation system can be installed to vent fumes away from the server room; however, there shouldn't be any fumes. Products that contain fumes should be stored in a separate and specially secured area. And if a fire were to occur, the sprinkler system or special hazards system should end that threat, eliminating any fumes that were a result of the fire.

That Was a Lot of Fun!

This is the end of Exam C, which is the last practice exam in the book. I hope you have enjoyed reading it as much as I enjoyed writing it.

If you scored 90% or higher on this 220-1102 practice exam, you are in pretty good shape. Now complete the book and access the companion website for more content.

CHAPTER TEN

Review of the Core 2 (220-1102)

Great work! You have completed all of the 220-1102 practice exams. That is a feat in and of itself. But the real test is yet to come. We discuss that in the next chapter.

Now that you have completed the practice exams, let's do a little review of the 220-1102 domains, talk about your next steps, and look at some test-taking tips.

Review of the Domains

Remember that the 220-1102 exam is divided into four domains, shown in Table 10.1.

TABLE 10.1   220-1102 Domains

Domain	Percentage of Exam
1.0 Operating Systems	31%
2.0 Security	25%
3.0 Software Troubleshooting	22%
4.0 Operational Procedures	22%
Total	100%

As you could see while taking the practice exams, Windows operating system questions are the bulk of what you will see on the real exam. Troubleshooting questions are generally more difficult than the questions from the other domains. You have to place yourself within the scenario and imagine that you are actually fixing software problems step by step. The way to succeed at troubleshooting is to (1) know the system and (2) use a logical troubleshooting process.

Even if you are a solid troubleshooter and really know your Windows operating systems, that still leaves half of the test unaccounted for. Security and Operational Procedures are also pivotal domains. Without knowledge of them, you could be in trouble; *with* knowledge of them, you will have all the tools you need to rule the exam.

Everyone who takes the exam gets a different group of questions. Because the exam is randomized, one person may see more questions on a particular topic than the next person. The exam differs from person to person. To reduce your risk of failing, be ready for any question from any domain and study all of the objectives.

Review What You Know

At this point, you should be pretty well versed in the topics covered on the 220-1102 exam. I still recommend going back through all of the questions and making sure there are no questions, answers, concepts, or explanations you are unclear about. If there are, additional study is probably necessary. If something really just doesn't make sense, is ambiguous or vague, or doesn't appear to be technically correct, feel free to contact me at my website, https://dprocomputer.com, and I will do my best to clarify. (Any errata is listed there as well.) Think through the issue carefully before you do so, though. Many questions are written in an ambiguous manner to replicate what you will see on the real exam.

Here are a few great ways to study further:

▶ **Take the exams in flash card mode:** Use a piece of paper to cover up the potential answers as you take the exams in this book. This approach helps make you think a bit harder and aids in committing everything to memory. There are also free flash card applications that you can download to your computer to help you organize your studies.

▶ **Download the A+ 220-1102 objectives**—You can get these from https://www.comptia.org/certifications/a. Go through the objectives one by one and check each item that you are confident in. If you are unsure about any items in the objectives, study them hard. That's where the test will trip you up. It's a big document, and going through them will take a while. But this approach really helps close any gaps in your knowledge and gives you an extra boost for the exam.

▶ **Check out my website for additional materials:** My A+ Study Page is designed to help you get ready for the exam. You never know what you might find there!

▶ **Consider my other A+ products:** For example, consider my *CompTIA A+ Core 1 (220-1101) and Core 2 (220-1102) Exam Cram* or my *CompTIA A+ 220-1102 Complete Video Course.* You can find more information about these resources at my website: https://dprocomputer.com.

More Test-Taking Tips

I've mentioned this point several times already, but it bears repeating: Take your time on the exam. The thing is, you either know the content or you don't. If you know it, you will probably end up with time left over when you take the exam, so there is no rush. Rushing can cause you to miss a key word, phrase, or other tidbit of information that could cost you the correct answer. Take it slow and read everything you see carefully.

While taking an exam, follow these recommendations:

▶ Use the process of elimination.

▶ Be logical in the face of adversity.

▶ Follow your gut instinct.

▶ Don't let one question beat you.

▶ If all else fails, guess.

I expand on these points in Chapter 11, "Wrap-up."

If you finish the exam early, use the time allotted to you to review all of your answers. Chances are you will have time left over at the end, and you want to use it wisely. Make sure that everything you have marked has a proper answer that makes sense to you. But try not to overthink! Give the exam your best shot and be confident in your answers.

Taking the Real Exam

Do not register for the actual exam until you are fully prepared. When you are ready, schedule the exam to commence within a day or two so that you don't forget what you have learned.

Registration can be done online. Register at Pearson VUE (https://home.pearsonvue.com). The site accepts payment by major credit card for the exam fee. First-timers need to create an account with Pearson VUE. Exams can be taken at a Pearson VUE testing site or from home.

Here are some good general practices for taking the real exam:

- Pick a good time for the exam.
- Don't overstudy the day before the exam.
- Get a good night's rest.
- Eat a decent breakfast.
- Show up early.
- Bring earplugs.
- Brainstorm before starting the exam.
- Take small breaks while taking the exam.
- Be confident.

I embellish on these concepts in Chapter 11.

Well, that's it for the 220-1102 portion of this book. Meet me at the final chapter for the wrap-up.

CHAPTER ELEVEN

Wrap-up

This chapter provides the following tools and information to help you be successful when preparing for and taking the CompTIA A+ Core 1 (220-1101) and Core 2 (220-1102) exams:

▶ Getting Ready and the Exam Preparation Checklist

▶ Tips for Taking the Real Exam

▶ Beyond the CompTIA A+ Certification

Getting Ready and the Exam Preparation Checklist

Anyone can take the CompTIA A+ certification exams; there are no prerequisites, but CompTIA recommends 12 months of experience in a help desk, desktop, or field service job role. If you don't have that experience, be sure to practice as many hands-on labs as you can on real computers or virtual systems.

For more information on the A+ certification, visit the A+ section of CompTIA's website, at https://www.comptia.org/certifications/a.

To acquire your A+ certification, you need to pass two exams: 220-1101 and 220-1102. These exams are administered by Pearson VUE (https://home.pearsonvue.com). You need to register with Pearson VUE to take the exams.

EXAM ALERT

I strongly suggest that you not take both exams on the same day. Instead, take them a week or so apart (at least). Trust me on this.

Each exam consists of two types of questions:

▸ **Multiple choice:** These pose a question to you and ask you to select the correct answer (or answers) from a group of four or more choices. They are quite similar to the questions you've seen throughout this book.

▸ **Performance based:** These ask you to answer a question, complete a configuration, or solve a problem in a hands-on fashion. The questions might ask you to drag and drop information to the correct location or complete a simulation in a virtual system.

To master both types of questions, you need to have a deep understanding of the theory, and you also need to know the hands-on steps. So, practice on your actual computers as much as possible. This is, of course, imperative for the exams, but it is even more important for the real world. The more you install, configure, and troubleshoot real systems, the more you will be prepared for job interviews as well as whatever comes your way after you have acquired a position within an organization.

EXAM ALERT

You've been warned! Practice as much as possible on the following:

▸ Real desktop/laptop computer hardware and software

▸ A SOHO router

▸ Smartphone and tablet

▸ Printers, displays, and other peripherals

▸ Windows, Linux, macOS, Android, and iOS

> **NOTE**
>
> This book does not offer the exact questions that are on the exam. There are two reasons for this:
>
> ▶ CompTIA reserves the right to change the questions at any time. Any changes, however, will still reflect the content within the current A+ objectives.
>
> ▶ The contents of the CompTIA A+ exams are protected by a nondisclosure agreement (NDA); anyone who sits an exam has to agree to the NDA before beginning the test. The NDA states that the questions within the exams are not to be discussed with anyone.
>
> Therefore, I cannot tell you exactly what is on the exams, but I do cover all of the objectives within this book to give you the best chance of passing the exams.

You must be fully prepared for the exams, so I created a checklist (see Table 11.1) that you can use to make sure you have covered all the bases. Go through the checklist twice—once for each exam. For each exam, place a check in the status column as you complete each item. Do this first with the 220-1101 exam and then again with the 220-1102 exam. I highly recommend completing each step in order and taking the 220-1101 exam first. Historically, my readers and students have benefited greatly from this type of checklist.

TABLE 11.1   Exam Preparation Checklist

Step	Item	Details	220-1101 Status	220-1102 Status
1.	Attend an A+ course.	(Optional) A hands-on A+ course can do *a lot* for you when it comes to installing, configuring, and especially troubleshooting. Especially if you don't have the CompTIA recommended experience (12 months), consider taking an A+ class.		
2.	Review your study guide.	Whatever main study guide or guides you used, be sure to review them carefully.		
3.	Complete the practice exams in this book.	Take the 220-1101 practice exams and review them carefully. On the second run-through of this checklist, take the 220-1102 practice exams and review them.		

Step	Item	Details	220-1101 Status	220-1102 Status
		If you score under 90% on any one practice exam, go back and study more.		
		If you have any trouble at this stage, consider getting my book *CompTIA A+ Core 1 (220-1101) and Core 2 (220-1102) Exam Cram* or another study guide of your choice and read it very carefully.		
4.	Create your own cheat sheet.	See Table 11.2 for an example. Writing down important details helps you commit them to memory. Keep in mind that you will not be allowed to take a cheat sheet into the actual testing room.		
5.	Register for the exam.	Do not register until you have completed the previous steps; you shouldn't register until you are fully prepared. When you are ready, schedule the exam to commence within a couple of days so that you don't forget what you have learned. Registration can be done online. Exams can be taken at a Pearson VUE test center or at home. Register at Pearson VUE (https://home.pearsonvue.com).		
		The site accepts payment by major credit card for the exam fee. (Keep in mind that you need to create an account to be able to sign up for exams.)		
6.	Review practice questions.	Keep reviewing practice questions until the day of the exam. Review your cheat sheet also if you created one.		
7.	Take the exam.	Check off each exam to the right as you pass it. Good luck!		

EXAM ALERT

Do not register for the exam until you are thoroughly prepared. Meticulously complete items 1 through 4 in Table 11.1 before you register to take an exam.

Table 11.2 provides a partial example of a cheat sheet that you can create to aid in your studies. Fill in the appropriate information in the right column. For example, the first step of the six-step troubleshooting methodology is "Identify the problem."

TABLE 11.2   Example Cheat Sheet

Concept	Fill in the Appropriate Information Here
The six-step A+ troubleshooting methodology	1.
	2.
	3.
	4.
	5.
	6.
Cloud-based services	
The laser imaging process	
The malware removal process	
Windows log files	
Commands and descriptions (For example: **ping** – tests to see if other systems on the network are live.)	
* Etc.	

* Continue Table 11.2 in this fashion on paper. The key is to write down various technologies, processes, step-by-step procedures, and so on and commit them to memory. Make separate cheat sheets for the 220-1101 and 220-1102 exams.

Tips for Taking the Real Exam

If you are new to exams, this section is for you. If you have taken exams before, feel free to skip this section or use it as a review.

The exam is conducted on a computer and is multiple choice and performance based. You have the option to skip questions. If you do so, be sure to mark them for review before moving on. Feel free to mark any other questions that you have answered but are not completely sure about. This approach is especially recommended for the performance-based questions. In fact, you might choose to leave all of the performance-based questions until the end. That, of course, is up to you.

When you get to the end of an exam, you will find an item review section that shows you any questions that you did not answer and any that you marked for review. Be sure to answer any questions that were not completed.

The following lists include tips and tricks that I have developed over the years. I've taken at least 20 certification exams over the past two decades, and the following points have served me well.

General Practices for Taking Exams

▶ **Pick a good time for the exam:** Keep in mind that you can take the exams at a testing center or from home. It appears that the fewest people are at test centers on Monday and Friday mornings. Consider scheduling during these times. Otherwise, schedule a time that works well for you, when you don't have to worry about anything else. Keep in mind that Saturdays can be busy. Oh, and don't schedule the exam until you are ready. I understand that sometimes deadlines have to be set, but in general, it's best not to register for an exam until you feel confident you can pass it. Things come up in life that can sometimes get in the way of your study time. Keep in mind that most exams can be canceled as long as you give 48 hours' notice. (To be sure, check that time frame when registering.)

▶ **Don't overstudy the day before the exam:** Some people like to study hard the day before; some don't. My recommendations are to study from your cheat sheet and maybe run through some quick Q&A, but in general, don't overdo it. It's not a good idea to go into overload mode the day before the exam.

▶ **Get a good night's rest:** A good night's sleep (seven to nine hours) before the day of the exam is probably the best way to get your mind ready for an exam.

▶ **Eat a decent breakfast:** Eating is good! Breakfast is number two when it comes to getting your mind ready for an exam, especially for a morning exam. Just watch out for the coffee and tea. Too much caffeine—especially if you are not used to it—can be detrimental to the thinking process.

▶ **Show up early:** The testing agency recommends that you be present 30 minutes prior to your scheduled exam time, regardless of whether you are taking the exam at a testing center or from home. This is important: Give yourself plenty of time. If you are taking the exam at a testing center, make sure you know where you are going. Know exactly how long it takes to get to the testing center and account for potential traffic and construction. You don't want to have to worry about getting lost or being late. Stress and fear are mind killers. Work on reducing any types of stress the day before and the day of the exam. By the way, you need extra time prior to the exam because you need to show ID, sign forms, get your personal belongings situated, and be escorted to your seat. Have two forms of (signed) ID ready for the administrator of the test center. Turn off your cell phone or smartphone; they'll check that, too.

▶ **Bring earplugs:** You never know when you will get a loud testing center or, worse yet, a loud test-taker next to you. Earplugs help block out any unwanted noise that might show up. This can help at home as well. Just be ready to show your earplugs to the test administrator. Also, if you do plan to use earplugs, consider doing a test run with them beforehand, so that you can become accustomed to them.

▶ **Brainstorm before starting the exam:** Write down as much as you can remember from your cheat sheet before starting the exam. The testing center is obligated to give you something to write on; make use of it! Getting all the memorization out of your head and on "paper" first clears the brain somewhat so that it can tackle the questions. (I put *paper* in quotation marks because it probably won't be paper; it could be a mini dry-erase board or something similar.)

▶ **Take small breaks while taking the exam:** Exams can be brutal. You have to answer a lot of questions (typically anywhere from 75 to 90 of them) while staring at a screen for an hour or more. Sometimes these screens are old and have seen better days; older flickering monitors can cause strain on your eyes. I recommend taking small breaks and using breathing techniques. For example, after going through every 25 questions or so, close your eyes and slowly take a few deep breaths, holding each one for five seconds and then releasing it slowly. Think about nothing while doing so. Remove the test from your mind during these breaks. This technique takes only about half a minute but can help get your brain refocused. It's almost a Zen type of thing; when I have applied this technique properly, I have gotten a few perfect scores. It's amazing how your mind-set can make or break you.

▶ **Be confident:** You've done everything you can to prep: You have studied hard, gone through the practice exams, and created your cheat sheet. These things alone should build confidence. But actually, you just have to be confident for no reason whatsoever. Think of it this way: You are great…I am great… (to quote Dr. Daystrom from *Star Trek*). But truly, there is no disputing this. That's the mentality you must have. You are not being pretentious about this if you think it to yourself. Acting that way to others...well, that's another matter. So build that inner confidence, and your mind-set should be complete.

Smart Methods for Difficult Questions

▶ **Use the process of elimination:** If you are not sure about an answer, first eliminate any answers that are definitely incorrect. You might be surprised how often this approach works. This is one of the reasons it is recommended that you not only know the correct answers to the practice exam questions but also know why the wrong answers are wrong. The testing center should give you something to write on; you can use it to write down the letters of the answers that are incorrect to keep track. Even if you aren't sure about the correct answer to a question, if you can logically eliminate anything that is incorrect, the answer will become apparent. The character Sherlock Holmes expressed this well: "When you have eliminated the impossible, whatever remains, however improbable, must be the truth." There's more to it, of course, but from a scientific standpoint, this method can be invaluable.

▶ **Be logical in the face of adversity:** The most difficult questions have two answers that appear to be correct, even though the test question requires you to select only one answer. Real exams do not rely on trick questions. Sometimes you need to slow down, think logically, and compare the two possible correct answers. Also, you must imagine the scenario that the question is a part of. Think through step by step what is happening in the scenario. Write out as much as you can. The more you can visualize the scenario, the more easily you can figure out which of the two answers is the best one.

▶ **Follow your gut instinct:** Sometimes a person taking a test just doesn't know the answer; it happens to everyone. If you have read through a question and all the answers and used the process of elimination, sometimes following your gut is all you have left. In some scenarios, you might read a question and instinctively know the answer, even if you can't explain why. Tap into this ability. Some test-takers write down their gut instinct answers before delving into the other answers and then compare their thoughtful answers with their gut instinct answers.

▶ **Don't let one question beat you!:** Don't let yourself get stuck on one question, especially a performance-based question. Skip it and return to it later. When you spend too much time on one question, your brain may get sluggish. The thing with these exams is that you either know the content or you don't. And don't worry too much about it; chances are you are not going to get a perfect score. Remember that the goal is to pass the exams; how many answers you get right beyond passing is irrelevant. If you have gone through this book thoroughly, you should be well prepared. You should have plenty of time to go through all the exam questions with time to spare to return to the ones you skipped and marked.

▸ **If all else fails, guess:** Remember that the exams might not be perfect. A question might seem confusing or appear not to make sense. Leave questions like this until the end. After you have gone through all the other techniques mentioned, make an educated, logical guess. Try to imagine what the test is after and why it would be bringing up this topic, as vague or as strange as it might appear.

Wrapping Up the Exam

Review all your answers. If you finish early, use the time allotted to you to review the answers. Chances are you will have time left over at the end, and you should use it wisely. Make sure that everything you have marked has a proper answer that makes sense to you. But try not to overthink. Give the exam your best shot and be confident in your answers. Don't second-guess yourself.

Beyond the CompTIA A+ Certification

A person who passes the CompTIA A+ exams will be certified for three years. To maintain the certification beyond that time, you must either pass the new version of the exams (before the three years is up), pass a higher-level CompTIA exam (such as the Security+ exam), or enroll in the CompTIA Continuing Education Program. This program has an annual fee and requires that you obtain Continuing Education Units (CEUs) that count toward recertification. There are a variety of ways to accumulate CEUs. See CompTIA's website for more information: https://www.comptia.org/continuing-education.

After you pass the exams, consider thinking about your technical future. It's important to keep up with new technology and keep your technical skills sharp, and technical growth is important as well. Consider expanding your technical horizons by learning different technologies.

Usually, companies wait at least six months before implementing new operating systems and other applications on a large scale, but you will have to deal with new technology sooner or later—most likely sooner. Windows, macOS, Linux, Android, and iOS are always coming out with new versions. Consider keeping up with the newest versions and obtaining access to the latest software and operating systems. Practice installing, configuring, testing, securing, maintaining, and troubleshooting them.

To keep on top of the various computer technologies, think about subscribing to technology websites, RSS feeds, and periodicals—and read them on a regular basis. Check out streaming video tech channels on the Internet. Join computer Internet forums and attend technology conventions. A technician's skills need to be constantly honed and kept up to date.

Information technology (IT) technicians need to keep learning to foster good growth in the field. Consider taking other certification exams after you complete the A+. The CompTIA A+ certification acts as a springboard to other certifications. For example, the CompTIA Security+ certification takes your skills to another level, evaluating your knowledge of how to secure networks, computers, their applications, and especially the *data*. Now that you know exactly how to go about passing a certification exam, consider earning more certifications to bolster your resume.

The best advice I can give is for you to do what you love. From an IT perspective, I usually break it down by technology, as opposed to by the vendor or certification. For example, you might want to learn more about email systems or securing internetworks or about systems administration or DevOps; or you might prefer to work on databases, build websites, develop apps—who knows! You are limited only by your desire.

I wish you the best of luck on your exams and in your IT career endeavors. Please let me know when you pass your exams. I would love to hear from you! Also, remember that I am available to answer any of your questions about this book via my website: https://dprocomputer.com.

Sincerely,

David L. Prowse

To receive your 10% off
Exam Voucher, register
your product at:

www.pearsonitcertification.com/register

and follow the instructions.